The best preparation for
LISTENING

Nexus Contents Development Team · Cedric S. Kim

3
Level

NEXUS Edu

How do we improve listening skills?

According to Asher (1974) and Hughes (1992), the four skills of language (speaking, listening, reading, and writing) are fundamentally intertwined. Then improving one language skill facilitates improvement in the other three language skills. In order to reflect this perspective during the development process of this new listening textbook, we designed tasks that give learners opportunities to relate their understanding of the sound-based messages to tasks that require speaking, reading and writing. There are several ways in which this listening series offers benefits to language learners.

Language learners need to be aware of variations in expression. We present listening information in different forms, such as in paraphrases and summaries, in order to help learners improve their awareness of how language structures are manipulated. Carefully chosen tasks encourage learners to compare, contrast, and analyze information received in different forms and to produce language appropriate to the different forms. Learners can notice the variety of language structures that reflect the way English is actually used. Sharing information in a real-life language interaction is not, after all, mostly contained in one structure.

Language learners need a variety of interesting contexts in order to make the learning experience memorable. The dialogs and passages in our listening series are in themselves interesting and offer a variety of information and ideas that add to the learner's store of general knowledge. As language learners work within these interesting contexts, they also gain awareness of differences in spoken and written discourse.

We encourage language learners to take advantage of the chances offered by this textbook to improve their listening skills in a more effective way, not only through sound-based comprehension drills, but also through our integrated skill-based tasks and structurally manipulated linguistic tasks such as summarizing and paraphrasing.

LISTENING

3
Level

The best preparation for Listening **Level 3**

Published by Nexus Co., Ltd.
24, Yanghwa-ro 8 gil, Mapo-gu, Seoul 121-893, Korea
www.nexusEDU.kr

Authors: Nexus Contents Development Team, Sedric S. Kim
Publisher: Yongbaeg Ahn
ISBN: 978-89-6790-704-4 54740 ㉓
        978-89-6790-701-3 (SET)

Printed in Korea

 Contents

Preface

Contents

Unit Preview

Answers

Unit Preview

Getting Ready

Students are introduced to the unit's topic.
Key expressions of the unit are presented
through simple exercises.

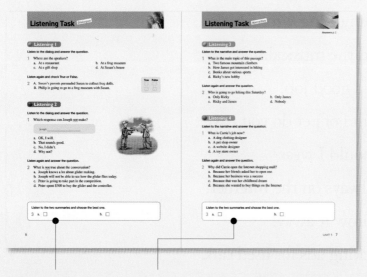

Listening Task

Students listen to four or five
short listening scripts commonly
used in everyday speech.
The exercises check general
comprehension of
the listening material.

In **Listening 2** and **Listening 4**, these simple exercises
require students to analyze and summarize the text-based
information.

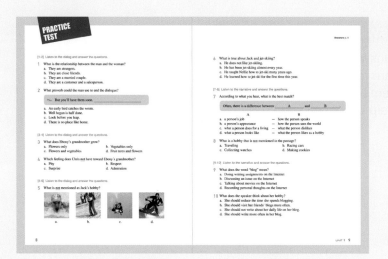

Practice Test

These multiple-choice exercises test students on material from the entire unit.

Dictation

Students can check their ability to write precisely what they hear.

Answers & Translations

The answers and translations for each unit are found in this section.
Students can match their answers with the help of the answer key.

Vocabulary Test

Available via download from **www.nexusEDU.kr,**
each unit's vocabulary test enables accurate assessment of student's retention of key vocabulary.

1

I'm into gardening.

GETTING READY

Answers p. 2

A   Read the conversation below and fill in the blanks.

- in common
- spend
- recipes
- interested in
- how often
- all my Sundays
- collect
- like
- collection
- post
- since when

Andrew   What is your hobby, Helen?

Helen   I _____ making cookies.

Andrew   _____ have you been doing that?

Helen   I have helped my mother make cookies since I was little.
I think that got me _____ it.

Andrew   _____ do you make cookies?

Helen   I _____ almost _____ making them.
What is your hobby, Andrew?

Andrew   I _____ miniature cars from all over the world.
I have been collecting them since I was four.

Helen   Really? What do you do with them?

Andrew   Every time I add a new car to my _____, I take a
picture of it and _____ the photo on my blog.

Helen   Me, too. I have posted a lot of pictures of cookies and their
_____ on my blog.

Andrew   Then, we have at least one hobby _____.

B   What is your hobby? Talk about it with your friends.

[A] taking pictures   scuba diving   hiking   gardening

[B] watching fish in the sea   taking pictures of my family
    growing flowers   taking walks in the woods

◁)))   My hobby is ^[A]hiking. I like spending my time ^[B]taking walks in the woods.

● Listening 1

Listen to the dialog and answer the question.

1   Where are the speakers?
   a. At a restaurant   b. At a frog museum
   c. At a gift shop   d. At Susan's house

Listen again and check True or False.

	True	False

2   A. Susan's parents persuaded Susan to collect frog dolls.
    B. Philip is going to go to a frog museum with Susan.

● Listening 2

Listen to the dialog and answer the question.

1   Which response can Joseph <u>not</u> make?

> Joseph _____

   a. OK, I will.
   b. That sounds good.
   c. No, I didn't.
   d. Why not?

Listen again and answer the question.

2   What is <u>not</u> true about the conversation?
   a. Joseph knows a lot about glider making.
   b. Joseph will not be able to see how the glider flies today.
   c. Peter is going to take part in the competition.
   d. Peter spent $300 to buy the glider and the controller.

Listen to the two summaries and choose the best one.

3   a. ☐   b. ☐

Listening Task

Listening 3

Listen to the narrative and answer the question.

1 What is the main topic of this passage?
  a. Two famous mountain climbers
  b. How James got interested in hiking
  c. Books about various sports
  d. Ricky's new hobby

Listen again and answer the question.

2 Who is going to go hiking this Saturday?
  a. Only Ricky   b. Only James
  c. Ricky and James   d. Nobody

Listening 4

Listen to the narrative and answer the question.

1 What is Carrie's job now?
  a. A dog clothing designer
  b. A pet shop owner
  c. A website designer
  d. A toy store owner

Listen again and answer the question.

2 Why did Carrie open the Internet shopping mall?
  a. Because her friends asked her to open one
  b. Because her business was a success
  c. Because that was her childhood dream
  d. Because she wanted to buy things on the Internet

Listen to the two summaries and choose the best one.

3   a. ☐   b. ☐

[1-2] Listen to the dialog and answer the questions.

1 What is the relationship between the man and the woman?
   a. They are strangers.
   b. They are close friends.
   c. They are a married couple.
   d. They are a customer and a salesperson.

2 What proverb could the man use to end the dialogue?

> Man But you'll have them soon. _____

   a. An early bird catches the worm.
   b. Well begun is half done.
   c. Look before you leap.
   d. There is no place like home.

[3-4] Listen to the dialog and answer the questions.

3 What does Ebony's grandmother grow?
   a. Flowers only   b. Vegetables only
   c. Flowers and vegetables   d. Fruit trees and flowers

4 Which feeling does Chris not have toward Ebony's grandmother?
   a. Pity   b. Respect
   c. Surprise   d. Admiration

[5-6] Listen to the dialog and answer the questions.

5 What is not mentioned as Jack's hobby?

    a.   b.   c.   d.

6 What is true about Jack and jet-skiing?
    a. He does not like jet-skiing.
    b. He has been jet-skiing almost every year.
    c. He taught Nellie how to jet-ski many years ago.
    d. He learned how to jet-ski for the first time this year.

[7-8] Listen to the narrative and answer the questions.

7 According to what you hear, what is the best match?

> Often, there is a difference between _____ A _____ and _____ B _____ .

A		B
a. a person's job	—	how the person speaks
b. a person's appearance	—	how the person sees the world
c. what a person does for a living	—	what the person dislikes
d. what a person looks like	—	what the person likes as a hobby

8 What is a hobby that is <u>not</u> mentioned in the passage?
    a. Traveling   b. Racing cars
    c. Collecting watches   d. Making cookies

[9-10] Listen to the narrative and answer the questions.

9 What does the word "blog" mean?
    a. Doing writing assignments on the Internet
    b. Discussing an issue on the Internet
    c. Talking about movies on the Internet
    d. Recording personal thoughts on the Internet

10 What does the speaker think about her hobby?
    a. She should reduce the time she spends blogging.
    b. She should visit her friends' blogs more often.
    c. She should not write about her daily life on her blog.
    d. She should write more often in her blog.

Listening Task

🎧 Listen and fill in the blanks.

Answers p. 6

Listening 1

Philip   Wow, look at _____. Why do you have _____, Susan?

Susan   I collect anything _____ frogs, Philip.

Philip   Why just frogs?

Susan   My parents _____ a little pink frog doll _____. Since then, I have been collecting frog dolls, ashtrays, pictures... _____.

Philip   Where _____?

Susan   I bought some, but _____ to me by others.

Philip   I think you could _____ with this collection.

Listening 2

Joseph   Did you make _____, Peter?

Peter   Actually, this is a glider, and I _____.

Joseph   I see. Where did you get it?

Peter   I got it from _____ our school.

Joseph   Was it expensive?

Peter   _____ for the glider and _____ for the radio controller.

Joseph   Wow, a _____ glider! Can you show me _____?

Peter   Not now, Joseph. I have a _____. Why don't you come to the competition tomorrow?

Listening 3

Ricky and James are _____, but they _____ very differently. While Ricky spends most of his free time _____, _____, and _____, James _____. But after reading an interesting book _____ _____, James is now interested in _____, and he has decided to go hiking _____ with Ricky. James is really excited about the trip because _____ to go to a mountain.

Listening 4

Although making _____ was Carrie's hobby during her childhood, she _____ that her hobby would later become _____. _____, she made clothes for her dog _____, and her friends liked them very much. They asked her to make _____, too. Because Carrie started getting _____, she decided to open a business. Her business _____ that she even opened an _____ this year.

PRACTICE TEST [1-2]

M   Hey, I often see you here _____ _____. Are you a _____ _____?

W   No, it's just my hobby.

M   _____ do you take?

W   I take pictures of _____.

M   Just clouds? _____ _____?

W   Well, all the clouds have _____ _____, so every picture is unique. Actually, I am _____ making a picture book of clouds. But I have not yet taken _____.

M   But you'll have them soon.

PRACTICE TEST [3-4]

Chris   What _____ you have, Ebony!

Ebony   Thanks, Chris. But we _____ our grandma. She spends _____ _____.

Chris   Are you into gardening, too?

Ebony   _____, but I help her from time to time when she needs to _____ _____.

Chris   Does she grow _____?

Ebony   If you go to the backyard, you will see _____. She grows _____, corn, peas, and other vegetables.

Chris   Wow, she is great. _____ a grandmother like her.

PRACTICE TEST [5-6]

Nellie   Hey, Jack. You _____.

Jack   Hi, Nellie. I have been spending a lot of time _____ this summer.

Nellie   What did you do there?

Jack   I went _____ and jet-skiing.

Nellie   How exciting! _____ _____?

Jack   I learned scuba diving many years ago, but I _____ jet-skiing _____.

Nellie   What do you do _____, then?

Jack   I swim _____. I love spending time in water.

Nellie   _____.

PRACTICE TEST [7-8]

It is very _____ a person's hobby just from _____. Ken Westwood, the famous rock star, loves to travel and _____ from all the restaurants _____. Sally Kim, the cute movie star, enjoys _____. She races almost every weekend, and she has already _____. Now, _____ what the 130kg boxer Sam Coleman likes to do? His hobby is _____! He especially loves to make _____.

PRACTICE TEST [9-10]

These days, I'm into _____. The word "blog" _____ the words " _____ " and "log." "Web" refers to the "Internet" and "log" means " _____." A blog is like a _____ on the web. In my blog, I write about _____ or movies I have seen. Every day, many of my friends visit my blog and leave _____ about _____. Blogging is fun, but I think I should probably cut down on the time I spend at the computer.

"Hope springs eternal (in the human breast)."

People will continue to hope even though they have evidence that things cannot possibly turn out the way they want.

UNIT 2

Are you coming to the party?

GETTING READY

A   Read the conversation below and fill in the blanks.

- enjoy
- be there
- anniversary
- make a reservation
- occasion
- to bring
- sent an invitation
- throw a surprise party
- ready
- have

Max   Julie, can you come home this Sunday? We're going to _____ for Mom and Dad.

Julie   What's the _____?

Max   This Sunday is their 20th wedding _____.

Julie   Oh, that's right.

Max   So, don't say anything to them about it.

Julie   I won't. Is there anything that you want me _____?

Max   No. I'll get everything _____. Do you think it would be nice for us all to watch their wedding video?

Julie   That's a great idea.

Max   I also _____ to our grandparents. They told me they will be here, too.

Julie   That's great. Did you _____ at a restaurant?

Max   No. We'll _____ a barbecue party at home. We'll _____ the fresh air in our backyard.

Julie   OK. I'll _____ at least by noon to help you.

Max   Thanks.

B   Match each party with what people do at the party.

(1) Surprise party •   • (a) People gather to share food that each person brings.

(2) Farewell party •   • (b) People celebrate with students who have successfully completed their studies.

(3) Barbecue party •   • (c) People enjoy music and dancing.

(4) Potluck party •   • (d) People enjoy grilled steaks or ribs outdoors.

(5) Graduation party •   • (e) People say good-bye and share the feeling of loss.

(6) Dance party •   • (f) People get to see the expression of astonishment on the face of the guest of honor.

Listening 1

Listen to the dialog and answer the question.

1 What is the main topic of this conversation?
   a. Looking for a dance partner
   b. Asking someone for a date
   c. Asking for a ride after the party
   d. Changing the meeting place

Listen again and check True or False.

		True	False
2	A. Tony knew that Jane would go to the party with victor.	☐	☐
	B. Tony asked if Jane wanted to be his dance partner at the school dance.	☐	☐

Listening 2

Listen to the dialog and answer the question.

1 Why are they throwing the party?
   a. To cheer Glen up
   b. To say good-bye to Glen
   c. To welcome a new student
   d. To celebrate Glen's birthday

Listen again and answer the question.

2 Which information is <u>not</u> given about the party?
   a. The time
   b. The place
   c. The people who will be invited
   d. The food they will have

Listen to the two summaries and choose the best one.

3 a. ☐   b. ☐

##

Listen to the narrative and answer the question.

1 Who can come to the graduation party?
- a. Anyone
- b. Seniors only
- c. Seniors and their partners
- d. Students and teachers

Listen again and answer the question.

2 How much is the cover charge per couple if you buy the ticket at the door?

a. $8   b. $10   c. $15   d. $20

##

Listen to the narrative and answer the question.

1 How did the speaker feel when he found his friends at home?
- a. Surprised and happy
- b. Scared and upset
- c. Happy but worried
- d. Surprised and worried

Listen again and answer the question.

2 Number the pictures in time order.   [   ] - [   ] - [   ]

a.

b.

c.

Listen to the two summaries and choose the best one.

3 a. ☐   b. ☐

[1-2] Listen to the dialog and answer the questions.

1 What is <u>not</u> true about the conversation?
   a. They are leaving for home.
   b. They didn't enjoy the party.
   c. They went to a dance party.
   d. They were at the party until 11 p.m.

2 You can infer from this conversation they are _____.
   a. freshmen   b. juniors
   c. seniors   d. teachers

[3-4] Listen to the dialog and answer the questions.

3 Where is the party going to take place?
   a. At a hotel
   b. At school
   c. In Susan's backyard
   d. In Susan's living room

4 What will they have at the party?

   a.   b.   c.   d.

[5-6] Listen to the dialog and answer the questions.

5 What does the man mean by his last response?
   a. He is interested in helping others.
   b. He wants to win a bicycle.
   c. He wants to see a concert.
   d. He is happy that he can go there by bike.

6 What is the purpose of the party?
   a. To help orphans
   b. To help earthquake victims
   c. To raise money for a new gym building
   d. To sell many bicycles

[7-8] Listen to the narrative and answer the questions.

7 What is the best title for this passage?
   a. The importance of having a party
   b. How to arrange a dance party
   c. Good ways to entertain people
   d. Things you need to know to have a great party

8 What is not mentioned in the passage?
   a. Good days for a party
   b. Tips for sending an invitation
   c. Entertainment people like
   d. How to cook for a party

[9-10] Listen to the dialog and answer the questions.

9 What are the speakers doing?

Man		Woman
a. Inviting	–	Accepting
b. Declining	–	Asking
c. Suggesting	–	Rejecting
d. Introducing	–	Introducing

10 What is true about the conversation?
   a. Maria is from Mexico.
   b. Maria is explaining what a potluck party is.
   c. The party will be this Saturday.
   d. Everyone should bring the same dish for the party.

Listening Task

🎧 Listen and fill in the blanks.

Answers p. 11

Listening 1

Jane   Hello.

Tony   Hi, Jane. _____, Tony.

Jane   Hey, Tony. How are you?

Tony   I'm fine. I was _____ you would like to _____ with me.

Jane   Oh, you _____ me sooner, Tony. Victor _____, and I told him that _____.

Tony   I see. Then, I guess I'll _____. Bye, Jane.

Jane   Bye, Tony.

Tony   (monolog) Oh well, _____ I won't be going with Jane _____.

Listening 2

Sunny   We need to _____ for Glen.

Allen   Is he _____?

Sunny   Didn't you know? He got admitted to the University of Chicago. He is _____ _____ two weeks.

Allen   Really? Good for him, but I _____. By the way, where do you want to throw the party?

Sunny   I _____ the pizzeria that _____ after school.

Allen   That's a good idea. They have great pizza. Then, why don't you _____ _____? I will _____.

Sunny   OK.

Listening 3

It's time _____, graduating seniors. There _____ on Friday, June 14th, at the Grand Imperial Hotel. _____ at 8:00 p.m. The party is for _____ only. There will be a _____ per couple _____. But, if you _____ the ticket _____, it is only _____.

Listening 4

Yesterday I had a _____ birthday, and this is _____. Yesterday my girlfriend called me and told me that she was going to be _____. At school, nobody would say "Happy birthday!" to me. I thought _____ _____ when my birthday is. _____ when I got home. But, when I _____, I heard "Surprise!" All my friends were there, _____ _____, holding _____. I was deeply moved.

18

PRACTICE TEST [1-2]

Jay   Bill, it's almost 11:00 p.m. Perhaps it's

     _____ .

Bill   Wow, already? Then, let's go home.

     _____ .

Jay   It was a great party. Did you _____

     _____ ?

Bill   Yes. it was _____ .

Jay   I guess this will be our last dance party

     _____ .

Bill   _____ .

Jay   You go get the girls. I'll _____ .

Bill   OK, Jay.

PRACTICE TEST [3-4]

Harry   Hello?

Susan   Harry? Hi. This is Susan.

Harry   Hi.

Susan   Hey, I am throwing _____

     _____ this Saturday, and

     I_____ . We will have

     some sausages and steaks.

Harry   _____ ?

Susan   No occasion. I just want us all to _____

     _____ before the summer is over.

Harry   Cool. I will _____ . But if I _____

     _____ , I'll _____ .

Susan   _____ 4:00 p.m.

Harry   I got it. _____ me.

PRACTICE TEST [5-6]

W   _____ the school's

     _____ this Friday?

M   Maybe not. Why?

W   _____ there would be bands,

     a lot of food, and a _____ , too.

M   By the way, _____

     this fundraising party?

W   To raise money for the earthquake

     _____ .

M   I see. What is the _____ ?

W   Five dollars, but you get a raffle ticket

     with which you can _____ .

M   A new bicycle? _____

     _____ . I think I will go to the party, just to

     have a chance to win that bicycle.

PRACTICE TEST [7-8]

_____ , there are
a few things you should _____ .
First, decide on the day of the party. Usually
Friday or Saturday is good. Then, decide
_____ and send the _____
early. On the invitation, you can ask _____
_____ and entertainment they _____
_____ . Usually good music will provide
enough entertainment. It's always a smart idea
to ask _____ great
parties for ideas.

PRACTICE TEST [9-10]

Ted   Maria, there will be _____

     this Sunday. Can you come?

Maria   What is a potluck party?

Ted   It is a party where everyone _____

     _____ , and everybody _____ .

     You can bring _____ .

Maria   _____ everyone brings the same

     food?

Ted   _____ . One time, everyone

     brought a pie.

Maria   Then, I will bring some Mexican food.

     Since I am the only Mexican _____

     _____ , probably no one else will bring

     Mexican food.

Ted   _____ .

Let's take a break!

"Laughter is the best medicine."

Something that you say which means that it is good for your physical and mental health to laugh

UNIT 3

Which class are you going to take?

Answers p. 12

GETTING READY

A Read the conversation below and fill in the blanks.

- attendance
- assignments
- gives a test
- semester
- taking
- fail the class
- experiments
- in the class
- chemistry
- signing up

Brad   Another new _____ is about to start.

Tim   That's right. Anyway, which classes are you going to take?

Brad   I'm thinking of _____ Mr. Brown's _____ class.

Tim   Don't you know that he is famous for giving a lot of _____? I even heard he _____ every class.

Brad   I know, but I also heard that we can do many interesting _____.

Tim   That may be true, but I don't think his class is meant for me. I'm thinking of _____ for Mr. Thomas's English class.

Brad   Oh, really? He is very harsh about _____. You're never on time. You could _____ because of that.

Tim   Well, I've changed a lot lately. On the positive side, there's a lot of reading _____, and I love reading.

B How is your class going? Talk about it with your friends.

< Subjects >

English	math	science	chemistry	physics	biology
history	music	art	geography	literature	sociology

Q1: What is your favorite subject?

Q2: Which subject are you good/bad at?

Q3: Which subject is difficult/easy for you?

Q4: Who is your favorite teacher?

Q5: What course does he/she teach?

A1: I like English the best.

A2: I'm good/bad at chemistry.

A3: Geography is difficult/easy for me.

A4: Mr./Ms. Brown.

A5: He/She teaches literature.

Listening Task  Dialogue

⬤ Listening 1

Listen to the dialog and answer the question.

1 What is Tony complaining about?
 a. Too much homework
 b. Too many exams
 c. Too many excuses
 d. Too many classes

Listen again and check True or False.

2 A. Tony has a lot of homework in other classes.
 B. Ms. Brown has finally decided not to give any homework to students.

True	False
☐	☐
☐	☐

⬤ Listening 2

Listen to the dialog and answer the question.

1 What are they talking about?
 a. On-line clubs
 b. Their favorite hobbies
 c. After-school classes
 d. A new trend in leisure

Listen again and answer the question.

2 Which class is Adam going to take?

 a.   b.   c.   d.

Listen to the two summaries and choose the best one.

3 a. ☐   b. ☐

Listening Task  Narrative

Listening 3

Listen to the narrative and answer the question.

1 Where is the speaker?
   a. In a laboratory
   b. In a library
   c. In a gym
   d. On a playground

Listen again and answer the question.

2 What should the students who have already finished the experiment do?
   a. Start another experiment right away
   b. Help others who are still working
   c. Turn in the results of the experiment
   d. Give a presentation

Listening 4

Listen to the narrative and answer the question.

1 What is Heather's complaint about Tim?
   a. He is always late for class.
   b. He doesn't work hard on the project.
   c. He talks too much in class.
   d. He spends too much time on the experiment.

Listen again and answer the question.

2 Where is Heather going after the experiment?
   a. Gym
   b. Singing rehearsal
   c. Library
   d. Chemistry lab

Listen to the two summaries and choose the best one.

3   a. ☐   b. ☐

[1-2] Listen to the dialog and answer the questions.

1 What kind of subject are they talking about?
   a. History and geometry
   b. History and geography
   c. Geometry and geography
   d. All of the above

2 What is the proverb that fits this situation?
   a. Rome wasn't built in a day.
   b. A bad workman always blames his tools.
   c. You scratch my back, I'll scratch yours.
   d. All is not gold that glitters.

[3-4] Listen to the dialog and answer the questions.

3 Which information is <u>not</u> given about the SAT?
   a. Why students need to take the SAT
   b. How to register for the SAT
   c. How to study for the SAT
   d. Where to get more information about the SAT

4 How often is the test offered?
   a. Twice a year
   b. Every month
   c. Only once a year
   d. Several times throughout the year

[5-6] Listen to the dialog and answer the questions.

5 What does the girl mean by her last response?
   a. We should listen to our parents.
   b. We should do what we really want.
   c. Parents sometimes don't understand their children.
   d. Engineering is a good job for a man.

6 Why does Brad want to be an engineer?
   a. Because he is very good at science
   b. Because he wants to make a lot of money
   c. Because his parents want him to be an engineer
   d. Because he is interested in making robots

[7-8] Listen to the narrative and answer the questions.

7 What is the main topic for this passage?
   a. How to give a lecture
   b. How to do homework well
   c. How not to fail a class
   d. How to review a class

8 Which advice is <u>not</u> mentioned in the passage?
   a. Prepare lessons before you go to the class.
   b. Ask teachers questions about the lectures.
   c. Do all the homework.
   d. Review all the lecture notes.

[9-10] Listen to the dialog and answer the questions.

9 How does Jonathan feel about Joan's volunteering?
   a. Disapproving
   b. Approving
   c. Content
   d. Good

10 What is Jonathan trying to say?
   a. We should change the volunteering system.
   b. It is important for everyone to help others.
   c. There's nothing you can gain without pain.
   d. One should volunteer only to help others, not for self-interest.

Listening Task

🎧 Listen and fill in the blanks.

Answers p. 16

Listening 1

Ms. Brown   Class, I'm going to _____ assignment.

Tony   Oh, Ms. Brown, _____. We have too much homework _____

_____.

Ms. Brown   Tony, you always _____. Do all the even numbered
problems on page 126.

Sandy   _____?

Ms. Brown   Since you have other homework, you can _____.

Tony   Can we have _____?

Ms. Brown   _____, Tony. The answer is "no."

Listening 2

Adam   _____ are you going to take, Ted?

Ted   I will take _____. How about you, Adam?

Adam   I've not decided yet. _____ auto-mechanics, but
_____. So, I'm _____ tennis or swimming.

Ted   _____, let's take the woodworking together. I heard that
_____ is making a canoe. We can make canoes together and
go canoeing.

Adam   That sounds great, Ted.

Listening 3

Students, _____ will be a continuation of the last experiment. _____
_____, you can _____ now. Then you may
_____ and start your homework. But those _____
the experiment must finish it today because we will begin a new experiment _____.
Do you have any questions? _____, you may start now.

Listening 4

Tim and Heather are _____. Although Tim loves _____
_____, Heather hates it. She always _____ as soon as possible
because she _____ her singing rehearsal. She thinks Tim
takes too much time _____ the experiment. But Tim thinks that Heather is
always _____, and that she is irresponsible.

26

DICTATION **Practice Test**

🎧 Listen and fill in the blanks.

PRACTICE TEST [1-2]

Andrew Hi, Lisa. _____ the geometry homework?

Lisa Yes, I have. But I am _____ _____ the history homework.

Andrew Then, why don't you _____ my geometry homework? Then I will help you _____.

Lisa That's a great idea. _____ _____ are you having?

Andrew I understood when the teacher explained this, but I _____ the problem solving.

Lisa _____ the problems.

Andrew Here are the _____.

PRACTICE TEST [3-4]

Andy What is an SAT?

Counselor _____ that many colleges use _____. So, if you _____, you should take the test.

Andy _____?

Counselor The test is offered several times throughout the year, so you can _____ _____.

Andy _____ for it?

Counselor You can _____, but why don't you visit the test administrator's website for more information? The URL is www.collegeboard.com.

PRACTICE TEST [5-6]

Sunny When you go to college, _____ _____, Brad?

Brad _____, but my parents want me to be a lawyer.

Sunny Why?

Brad They think lawyers _____.

Sunny Why do you want to be an engineer?

Brad I really love robots. _____ _____ when I first saw talking robots. Since then, _____ _____ myself.

Sunny If you like engineering that much, I think you need to _____ your parents _____ to become an engineer.

PRACTICE TEST [7-8]

Many students _____. If you are one of them, here is some advice for you. First, _____ to the lectures and take notes _____. If you have questions, _____ your teacher. At home, _____ _____ and do all the homework. Most test questions come from the materials _____ during lectures and _____.

PRACTICE TEST [9-10]

Betty _____ that Joan _____ _____ doing volunteer work.

Jonathan You didn't know? She does it just _____ _____, and to get _____ for a university application.

Betty I wondered a little why she was doing it. She really cares about grades.

Jonathan _____ with sincere motives, not for grades. Don't you think so?

Betty That's the best reason, Jonathan. But at least she is _____ _____.

Jonathan That is _____, but I still believe she is wrong.

Let's take a break!

"Knowledge is power."

The more you know, the more you can control.

UNIT 4

What's your plan for Mother's Day?

Answers p. 17

GETTING READY

A Read the conversation below and fill in the blanks.

• water
• of course
• celebrate
• New Year's resolutions
• get rid of
• lose
• gain weight
• a fresh start
• exchange
• accomplish

Linda   What are your favorite days of the year?

James   Christmas and Valentine's day, _____. I love to _____ gifts.

Linda   I like New Year's Day because I can get _____.

James   How do you _____ your New Year's Day?

Linda   Every year, I make _____. I write down the things that I want to do, along with the things I want to _____, like bad habits. Even if I don't _____ them all, I try hard.

James   What are your resolutions for this year?

Linda   One of them is to _____ ten pounds. Even though I've lost eight pounds so far, I may _____ again because Thanksgiving Day is next week.

James   Just speaking of Thanksgiving Day makes my mouth _____, to think of all the turkey I'll have.

B What do you do on these special days? Talk about them with your friends.

[A]
• New Year's Day (1.1)
• Valentine's Day (2.14)
• April Fool's Day (4.1)
• Mother's Day (Second Sunday of May)
• Halloween (10.31)
• Thanksgiving Day (Fourth Thursday of November)
• Christmas (12.25)

[B]
• tell people "Happy New Year"
• have a big dinner that includes turkey
• give chocolate to my boyfriend/ girlfriend
• decorate my Christmas tree
• fool people
• go trick-or-treating and get candies
• give my mother a nice present

◁))) [A]
New Year's Day is January first / the first of January.

[B]
On that day, I tell people "Happy New Year."

Listening Task `Dialogue`

● Listening 1

Listen to the dialog and answer the question.

1   What are they discussing?
  a. When to go for Christmas shopping
  b. Where to do Christmas shopping
  c. What to choose for Christmas gifts
  d. Whom to invite for Christmas dinner

Listen again and check True or False.

	True	False
	☐	☐
	☐	☐

2   A. The boy's father will get a Christmas tree and Christmas cards.
    B. Last year, they went Christmas shopping the day before Christmas Day.

● Listening 2

Listen to the dialog and answer the question.

1   What is Kevin doing?
  a. Asking Nina to lend him something
  b. Thanking Nina for her help
  c. Inviting Nina to join his barbecue on Independence Day
  d. Explaining what Independence Day is

Listen again and answer the question.

2   What will they do on Independence Day?

  a.   b.   c.   d.

Listen to the two summaries and choose the best one.

3   a. ☐   b. ☐

30

Listening Task  Narrative

Answers p. 17

Listening 3

Listen to the narrative and answer the question.

1　When does the New Year's Day celebration start?
   a.　On the evening of December 31st
   b.　In the early morning of January 1st
   c.　Midday of New Year's Day
   d.　On the evening of New Year's Day

Listen again and answer the question.

2　What are things that people <u>don't</u> do at a New Year's Day party?
   a.　Kissing and hugging   b.　Eating and dancing
   c.　Exchanging gifts   d.　Wishing others a happy new year

Listening 4

Listen to the narrative and answer the question.

1　How does the speaker feel about the Thanksgiving dinner?
   a.　Disappointed
   b.　Excited
   c.　Irritated
   d.　Worried

Listen again and answer the question.

2　What is <u>not</u> true about the passage?
   a.　The speaker is going to his relative's house for a Thanksgiving dinner.
   b.　Turkey is the main dish for Thanksgiving dinners.
   c.　Families and relatives have get-togethers on Thanksgiving Day.
   d.　The road is very crowded with cars on Thanksgiving Day.

Listen to the two summaries and choose the best one.

3　a.　☐   b.　☐

[1-2] Listen to the dialog and answer the questions.

1   What <u>cannot</u> be used in response to what Cherry said last?

Andy _____

   a. How dare you!   b. That's sweet!
   c. That's nice!   d. How romantic!

2   What gift(s) did Cherry give to Jake?

   a.   b.   c.   d.

[3-4] Listen to the dialog and answer the questions.

3   What are they talking about?
   a. Secret plans for Dave's mother's birthday
   b. Surprise gifts for Dave's brother
   c. Plans for Mother's Day
   d. Dave's long-time wishes

4   What will Dave's mother get?
   a. Nothing   b. Flowers
   c. Flowers and a pair of shoes   d. A cruise

[5-6] Listen to the dialog and answer the questions.

5   Why is the woman not going to the school Halloween party?
   a. Because she does not like to wear the Spider Man costume
   b. Because her parents told her not to go
   c. Because she is accompanying her brother when he goes trick-or-treating
   d. Because she is afraid of Halloween parties

6 What is true about the conversation?
   a. The man will go trick-or-treating with the woman together.
   b. The woman is the man's dance partner for the party.
   c. The woman suggests to the man that he wear a Spider Man costume.
   d. The woman's parents are not at home this week.

[7-8] Listen to the dialog and answer the questions.

7 What did Billy tell people last year?
   a. "I'm sick. I can't go to school today."
   b. "I won't fool anybody again."
   c. "Everybody is upset with you, Irene."
   d. "Tom was hit by a car this morning!"

8 Why will Billy not lie on April Fool's Day again?
   a. Because he is not a good liar
   b. Because he had a bad experience fooling people
   c. Because he doesn't want to be bothered to make plans
   d. Because he doesn't want to be fooled by his friends

[9-10] Listen to the narrative and answer the questions.

9 What day is Independence Day in the United States?

| (June 4th) | (April 17th) | (May 14th) | (July 4th) |
| a. | b. | c. | d. |

10 What do people <u>not</u> do on Independence Day?
   a. Post flags   b. Have a free dinner
   c. Go to the park   d. Watch fireworks

Listening Task

Listen and fill in the blanks.

Answers p. 21

Listening 1

Alex   When are we _____ Christmas shopping, Mom?

Mom   I think we will go this Saturday. Why? _____?

Alex   Last year we went to the mall _____ Christmas, and _____
_____. Don't you remember?

Mom   I know. _____ and parking was _____.

Alex   Let's not wait _____ this time. Also, _____
Christmas cards and a Christmas tree, too.

Mom   Don't worry. Your father _____ those things.

Listening 2

Nina   Hi, Kevin.

Kevin   Nina, do you have _____?

Nina   No, I don't have any plans.

Kevin   We will _____ and see _____. Do you want to come?

Nina   Sure, I love fireworks. _____?

Kevin   _____ 5:00 p.m.

Nina   Do you _____?

Kevin   No, we will have everything there.

Nina   OK, then. _____ at the park.

Kevin   See you, Nina.

Listening 3

In America, the New Year's Day celebration starts on _____.
On New Year's Eve, _____ and family members _____.
They eat, drink, and dance, _____. As it gets very_____,
cvcrybody _____. And when it is twelve o'clock, everybody _____
"Happy New Year!" Then they _____ people around them. The party continues
_____, sometimes until dawn.

Listening 4

For _____, Thanksgiving Day is a day _____, so it is
_____ travel days of the year. _____ for Thanksgiving
dinner is turkey, but _____ ham, salad, mashed potatoes, apple sauce, and
more. Tonight, there will be _____ at our home, and all our _____
_____ will join us for dinner. _____ Thanksgiving dinner.

DICTATION **Practice Test**

🎧 Listen and fill in the blanks.

PRACTICE TEST [1-2]

Andy   How was _____,
Cherry?

Cherry   It was great, Andy. Jake _____
_____ along with a CD _____
_____. Then, we had a
romantic dinner at a French restaurant.

Andy   _____ Jake?

Cherry   I gave him a card and _____
_____.

Andy   Did you make the chocolate _____?

Cherry   Yes. I found _____.
It was quite easy to make. I made one
big _____ chocolate with our
names written on it.

PRACTICE TEST [3-4]

Tanya   Dave, what's your plan _____
_____?

Dave   My brothers and I are _____
_____ with Dad.

Tanya   That is a great idea, but won't it _____
_____?

Dave   Yes, it will, but we _____
for her anyway because _____
_____. What is your plan,
Tanya?

Tanya   _____, I am just giving my mother
flowers and a pair of shoes, but _____
_____ something special for
_____.

PRACTICE TEST [5-6]

M   _____ the school Halloween
party?

W   _____.

M   Why not?

W   My parents are _____ this week, so

I have to put together my younger brother's
_____ and then _____
him when he goes trick-or-treating.

M   _____! We will miss you at the
party, though.

W   By the way, _____
to the party?

M   I'm wearing a Spider Man costume.

W   _____.

PRACTICE TEST [7-8]

Irene   Do you _____,
Billy? It's April Fool's Day.

Billy   No, Irene. I don't want to _____
on April Fool's Day any more.

Irene   _____?

Billy   On last April Fool's Day, I told my
friends that one of our classmates, Tom,
had been _____, and
everyone _____. But, once
they _____ it was a lie,
everybody _____.
Since then, I promised I _____
_____ again.

Irene   I see.

PRACTICE TEST [9-10]

_____ Independence Day,
the day their country _____
another country's rule. For the United States,
Independence Day is _____. Many people
_____ outside their homes and
in the streets. People _____
_____ to _____ or a barbecue in
the park. In the evening, the sky _____
fireworks while _____ the national
anthem and other patriotic songs.

UNIT 4   35

"Love covers a multitude of sins."

When you are in love with someone, you only see their good side.

I apologize to you.

GETTING READY

Answers p. 22

A   Read the conversation below and fill in the blanks.

• understanding	John	Hello?
• can't attend	Steve	John? This is Steve. I'm _____ you this, but I _____ the meeting today. I've got a problem.
• your fault	John	Oh, no. You _____ give a presentation. What do we do if you're _____?
• can't help it	Steve	I'm so sorry, but I _____. My brother has a high fever but there's no one to take care of him. I have to take him to the hospital.
• sorry to hear that	John	_____. When can you come then? We can postpone it a little bit.
• my apology	Steve	I don't think I can _____ at all. What if I give you the data? Then you could do the presentation for me.
• not coming	John	Okay. I will try.
• sorry to tell	Steve	Thank you for _____. please give _____ to all.
• are supposed to	John	Don't worry about that. It's not _____. Anyway, I hope your brother feels better soon.
• make it		

B   When you make mistakes like below, what would you say? Talk about it with your friends.

[A]
(1) stepped on someone's foot
(2) broke someone's computer
(3) were late for a meeting
(4) hurt someone's feelings

[B]
(a) Please forgive me. I'll pay for it.
(b) Sorry to have kept you waiting.
(c) I didn't mean that. I apologize.
(d) I'm so sorry. Are you OK?

◁)) When you ^[A] stepped on someone's foot, you can say "^[B]I'm so sorry. Are you OK?"

Listening 1

Listen to the dialog and answer the question.

1 How does the woman feel?
  a. Worried
  b. Upset
  c. Ashamed
  d. Discouraged

Listen again and check True or False.

	True	False
2 A. The man often forgets his appointments with the woman.	☐	☐
B. The woman will wait longer to have dinner with the man.	☐	☐

Listening 2

Listen to the dialog and answer the question.

1 What is the relation between the two people?
  a. They are neighbors.
  b. They are animal trainers.
  c. They are roommates.
  d. They are a married couple.

Listen again and answer the question.

2 What was the reason the dog barked?
  a. The dog barks every night.
  b. The dog was sick.
  c. A cat was walking by the window.
  d. The dog did not like the new house.

Listen to the two summaries and choose the best one.

3 a. ☐   b. ☐

Listening Task  Narrative

Answers p. 22

Listening 3

Listen to the narrative and answer the question.

1 What is Kate apologizing for?
   a. Her lateness
   b. Telling a lie
   c. Her rudeness
   d. Breaking an appointment

Listen again and answer the question.

2 What is not true about the passage?
   a. Daisy fought with her boyfriend.
   b. Kate and Daisy go to the same school.
   c. Kate wants Daisy to forgive her.
   d. Kate attached the file Daisy needed to the e-mail.

Listening 4

Listen to the narrative and answer the question.

1 What is the speaker apologizing for?
   a. Wrong bill
   b. A mistake of an employee
   c. Late delivery
   d. Items being out of stock

Listen again and answer the question.

2 What is the speaker offering to the customer?
   a. A $10 gift certificate
   b. A VIP card
   c. A list of products on sale
   d. A 10% discount on purchases

Listen to the two summaries and choose the best one.

3   a. ☐   b. ☐

[1-2] Listen to the dialog and answer the questions.

1 What can be inferred from this situation?
a. Mrs. Hopkins will cancel the order.
b. Mrs. Hopkins will eventually get the one she wanted.
c. Mrs. Hopkins will get another product.
d. Mrs. Hopkins will complain to the company.

2 What color refrigerator does Mrs. Hopkins want?
a. Red   b. White   c. Ivory   d. Gray

[3-4] Listen to the dialog and answer the questions.

3 Where are they talking?

  a.   b.   c.   d.

4 Why is Mr. Lopez making an apology to Stella?
a. Because he sold a broken product
b. Because he was too rude to the customers
c. Because he was too harsh with Stella
d. Because he didn't sell anything

[5-6] Listen to the dialog and answer the questions.

5 What is the proverb that fits this situation?
a. Nothing ventured, nothing gained.
b. As you sow, so shall you reap.
c. Never put off until tomorrow what may be done today.
d. The tongue is sharper than the sword.

6 What did Lisa say to Tony yesterday?
   a. That Tony is a liar.
   b. That Tony is stupid.
   c. That Tony never keeps his promise.
   d. That Tony is too talkative.

[7-8] Listen to the dialog and answer the questions.

7 What is the owner of the house like?
   a. Harsh   b. Careless   c. Selfish   d. Forgiving

8 What is true about the owner of the house?
   a. He will call the police.
   b. He will replace the window glass himself.
   c. He will make the boy buy him the window glass.
   d. He will punish the boy for his carelessness.

[9-10] Listen to the narrative and answer the questions.

9 What is the main idea of this passage?
   a. Accidents will happen.
   b. Everybody makes mistakes, so don't worry.
   c. It is important to apologize when you made mistakes.
   d. Bad apologies are worse than saying nothing.

10 Choose the right words to fill in the blanks.

> Even though you did something wrong, you don't need to ____A____ yourself so severely. Face the situation, and offer your sincere ____B____.

	A		B
a.	apologize to	–	help
b.	lie to	–	sympathy
c.	express	–	gratitude
d.	blame	–	apology

Listening Task

🎧 Listen and fill in the blanks.

Answers p. 26

Listening 1

M   Hello?

W   Where are you, John? I have been _____ now.

M   Oops, we _____ have dinner together tonight. I am so sorry. I was so busy, _____ .

W   How can you do that to me again? _____ . I hate you!

M   _____ . I will be there in twenty minutes.

W   _____ . I am going home.

M   I'm really sorry. _____?

W   No. I won't.

Listening 2

W   _____ my dog barking last night.

M   It's all right. _____ a dog, too.

W   I don't know _____ with him. He just kept barking.

M   I think I know _____ .

W   What was it?

M   My cat was _____ near your window last night.

W   Oh, _____ . My dog hates cats. Anyway, _____ all the barking.

M   _____ . It was my fault that _____ near your house.

Listening 3

Dear Daisy,

This is Kate. I am _____ last night. I was _____ when I told you I couldn't help you. I have been quite _____ since I _____ Josh last week. Anyway I am really sorry. I did find the information you wanted and I've emailed you and _____ . I hope it is _____ . Please _____ . I'll see you at school tomorrow. Bye.

Listening 4

This is _____ for the inconvenience you experienced in our store. We're really sorry for the trouble _____ you on your last visit here. We truly _____ . That employee is still _____ , and he did not understand our store policy completely. We hope you understand. _____ our regret, we want to present you with the enclosed certificate for _____ on any purchase you make _____ to our store.

PRACTICE TEST [1-2]

Tom   Mrs. Hopkins?

Mrs. Hopkins   _____.

Tom   This is Tom from Sam's Appliances. We _____ your refrigerator today, but we are _____ red refrigerators like the one you ordered. _____ _____ either white or ivory instead?

Mrs. Hopkins   No, _____ my kitchen. When will you have _____?

Tom   We will have one _____.

Mrs. Hopkins   I will _____.

Tom   I apologize, Mrs. Hopkins. _____ _____.

PRACTICE TEST [3-4]

Mr. Lopez   Stella, _____ with you?

Stella   Yes, Mr. Lopez.

Mr. Lopez   I think I was _____ yesterday. I don't think it was your fault that you _____ _____.

Stella   _____, Mr. Lopez. It may have been _____. Besides, _____ already.

Mr. Lopez   _____ my apology?

Stella   _____, Mr. Lopez.

PRACTICE TEST [5-6]

Lisa   Tony, I'm sorry about _____ _____.

Tony   You really _____ when you said I was stupid.

Lisa   I know. _____. I was very upset at that moment, so I didn't even realize what I was saying. I _____ _____. Please forgive me.

Tony   All right, but please _____ _____. You really _____.

Lisa   I'm so sorry. _____ that I will never say that again.

PRACTICE TEST [7-8]

Boy   _____, sir. Are you the owner of the house?

Man   Yes, why?

Boy   I broke your window glass _____ with my friends.

Man   _____ who broke it!

Boy   I am really sorry. I will _____ _____ as soon as possible.

Man   Hey, _____. I'll _____ myself. I broke a lot of windows _____ _____, too. So I understand.

Boy   Thank you for _____.

PRACTICE TEST [9-10]

People _____ and _____ _____. You can make a mistake and hurt someone knowingly or unknowingly. You _____ too much, but it is very _____ how to resolve _____. This means that you must learn _____. There are _____ _____ you can use to apologize: I am sorry, Will you accept my apology?, That was my fault, etc. They are simple, _____ _____.

"Better safe than sorry."

You should be cautious — if you are not, you may regret it.

How was your trip?

Answers p. 27

GETTING READY

A Read the conversation below and fill in the blanks.

- focus on
- planning to
- thoroughly
- looking for
- travel alone
- backpacking trip to
- get to
- travel information
- stay in
- how long

Gerry What are you _____ ?

Julio I'm searching for some _____ because I'm planning a _____ Europe next month.

Gerry Oh, really? With whom are you going?

Julio I'll _____ .

Gerry Wow, by yourself? _____ will you be gone?

Julio I will _____ Europe for a month.

Gerry Do you have any special countries in mind?

Julio I have not decided yet, but I am _____ go to about ten countries or more. I may not get another chance like this, so I will try to _____ as many countries as I can.

Gerry Well, if I were you, I would _____ just a few places so you can get to know them _____ .

Julio You have a point. I'll keep that in mind.

B What kind of trip have you taken? Talk about it with your friends.

[A]	[B]
backpacking trip	boring
vacation trip	terrible
group tour	great
overseas travel	wonderful
independent tour	lonely
city tour	awesome
school excursion	interesting
	impressive
	the greatest journey of my life

◁)) A: How was your [A]<u>backpacking trip</u>?   B: It was [B]<u>great</u>.

Listening Task **Dialogue**

⬤ Listening 1

Listen to the dialog and answer the question.

1   Where is Amy going?

a.　　　　　　　　b.　　　　　　　　c.　　　　　　　　d.

Listen again and check True or False.

2   A. The man thinks the travel package is a good deal.
    B. The package includes lodging and skiing for two people.

	True	False
A	☐	☐
B	☐	☐

⬤ Listening 2

Listen to the dialog and answer the question.

1   Why didn't Ted's family go to Florida?
   a. Because they did not want to go to Florida
   b. Because there was a big hurricane coming toward Florida
   c. Because they liked Louisiana better
   d. Because they wanted to go to a jazz concert

Listen again and answer the question.

2   How was Ted's trip?
   a. It was boring.　　　　　　b. It was unpleasant.
   c. It was great fun.　　　　　d. It was disappointing.

Listen to the two summaries and choose the best one.

3   a. ☐　　　　　　　　　　b. ☐

46

Listening 3

Listen to the narrative and answer the question.

1 Why can't the speaker fall asleep?
   a. Because he has a lot of things to do
   b. Because he is worried about his trip to Europe
   c. Because he does not want to go on the trip alone
   d. Because he does not have good friends

Listen again and answer the question.

2 How long will the speaker stay in Europe?
   a. A week
   b. A couple of weeks
   c. A month
   d. Two months

Listening 4

Listen to the narrative and answer the question.

1 How was the weather at Santa Monica Beach?
   a. Light showers
   b. Warm
   c. Cool and cloudy
   d. Windy

Listen again and answer the question.

2 Which picture is <u>not</u> related to the situation?

a.

b.

c.

d.

Listen to the two summaries and choose the best one.

3 a. ☐   b. ☐

[1-2] Listen to the dialog and answer the questions.

1 What is the woman's attitude toward traveling alone?
   a. Jealous   b. Interested
   c. Positive   d. Negative

2 According to Sam, what is good about traveling alone?
   a. He can save money.
   b. He can choose the places he wants to visit.
   c. He can make new friends.
   d. He can have many memorable moments.

[3-4] Listen to the dialog and answer the questions.

3 How will they get to Key West?

   a.   b.   c.   d.

4 What can be inferred from the conversation?
   a. They will stay in Key West for a month.
   b. They will stay at a hotel.
   c. They have been to Key West together before.
   d. This is their first trip together.

[5-6] Listen to the narrative and answer the questions.

5 The speaker is _____.
   a. asking for advice on visiting a new country
   b. making a list of places to visit
   c. giving advice about a trip abroad
   d. finding information about traveling alone

6 What advice did the speaker <u>not</u> give about traveling?
   a. Learn the foreign country's culture before you go there.
   b. Try to go to a market place to see how local people live.
   c. Try to cover as many areas as possible.
   d. Relax while traveling.

[7-8] Listen to the dialog and answer the questions.

7 What might the man reply to what the woman said last?

> Man _____

   a. Let's go to the museum, then.
   b. Sorry, but I'm not interested in sightseeing.
   c. Well, I think you'd better stay home.
   d. Good. I will call the tour company right away.

8 What is/are the difference(s) between the two packages?
   a. Price
   b. Time and price
   c. Time and places to visit
   d. Places to visit and price

[9-10] Listen to the narrative and answer the questions.

9 What place is the speaker talking about?
   a. The world's highest lake
   b. The world's most famous mountain
   c. The world's biggest country
   d. The world's largest desert

10 Why did the speaker get sick?
   a. Because the place was too far
   b. Because he ate bad food
   c. Because he flew on a plane for a long time
   d. Because the place was at a high altitude

Listening Task

🎧 Listen and fill in the blanks.

Answers p. 31

Listening 1

Dallas   What are you reading, Amy?

Amy   I am reading these _____.

Dallas   Are you _____?

Amy   No, just _____. Look at this ad. It says, "_____
Mammoth Ski Resort. _____ for just $99." What do
you think?

Dallas   _____. What time do they leave?

Amy   They leave Friday at 7:00 p.m.

Dallas   That _____. I think you should _____.

Amy   I agree.

Listening 2

Judith   _____ to Florida, Ted?

Ted   We never _____ Florida.

Judith   _____?

Ted   There was _____ Florida, so we _____.
We went to Louisiana _____.

Judith   Was it _____ Louisiana?

Ted   No. We went to a great jazz concert, and we _____, too.
_____, but Louisiana is _____.

Listening 3

I _____ because I'm excited and worried about my _____
_____ with my friends that starts tomorrow. This is my first _____
and one month is not a short time. Furthermore, we are _____
ten countries, and each country _____. But _____
is about my friends. Although we are good friends, we may have some _____
_____. Even now, we have not quite decided _____.

Listening 4

Yesterday, my family _____ Santa Monica Beach. Many people were there because it
was a long weekend and _____. Some people were _____
_____, but most of the people were just _____, and _____
_____ were swimming. I was wondering why _____.
I soon realized why _____; the water was _____.

PRACTICE TEST [1-2]

Jane Sam, _____ you are planning to travel alone.

Sam That is right.

Jane Why would you _____ ? You'll be lonely, and you'll have to do _____ _____ .

Sam You are probably right. But if you travel alone, you can go _____ at anytime you want.

Jane _____ , but you will have no one to _____ .

Sam You're right about that, too, but _____ _____ I like to travel.

PRACTICE TEST [3-4]

Eva Brad, let's _____ this summer.

Brad Good idea. We _____ the last time we took a vacation together.

Eva Do you want to go to Miami Beach again?

Brad Maybe _____ , we should try Key West.

Eva That sounds even better! _____ _____ . Why don't you check out _____ has the _____ ?

Brad OK. How many days are we _____ there?

Eva I can _____ .

Brad I have no problem with that.

PRACTICE TEST [5-6]

If you're _____ , keep the following advice in mind. First, learn the _____ , food, and climate _____ ____ . Secondly, don't try to visit too many places in one journey. _____ one area and _____ . Meet with

the natives. Try their traditional food, and see _____ . A market place would be _____ to start all that.

_____ .

PRACTICE TEST [7-8]

M Honey, let's _____ .

W _____ ?

M Well, there are two _____ . One will take about two hours, and the other one will take four hours.

W _____ ?

M The two-hour _____ Westminster Abbey and the London Tower. But the four-hour tour will also cover the Imperial War museum.

W _____ the first tour?

PRACTICE TEST [9-10]

It was not an easy task getting to _____ _____ , Lake Titicaca. Because it is _____ , I had difficulty breathing. I _____ to the lake. I thought I was going to die. But, once I arrived at the lake, I was _____ _____ . Even though I _____ while I was at the lake, it was _____ _____ .

Let's take a break!

"A journey of a thousand miles begins with a single step."

To progress at anything, just start!

We don't talk to each other.

GETTING READY

A Read the conversation below and fill in the blanks.

- asked me out
- closer
- constant
- open conversation
- in love
- getting along
- break up
- quarrel
- have made

Cathy   Angela, how are you doing at your new school?

Angela   So far, so good. I _____ some friends, and I'm _____ well with my roommate.

Cathy   Good for you. You know, my roommate and I used to _____ so often that we didn't talk for a long time.

Angela   Right, she was driving you crazy all the time.

Cathy   You know what? We had a chance to have an _____ last week, and we're trying to get _____ now.

Angela   That's nice!

Cathy   I have some other good news. Do you remember Tom, the guy I fell _____ with? He _____ yesterday.

Angela   Wasn't he dating Lisa? Did they _____ ?

Cathy   So I heard. I heard they had _____ problems.

B How are they getting along? Talk about it with your friends.

[A] love each other   are very close   are not getting along very well
    don't talk to each other any more

[B] had a big fight last month   are getting married this summer
    have difficulties sharing our opinions at work   have a lot in common

◁))) A: How are you getting along with your <u>boyfriend (new friend / boss / roommate)</u>?

B: We <u>love each other</u>. We <u>are getting married this summer</u>.
    [A]   [B]

Listening Task Dialogue

● Listening 1

Listen to the dialog and answer the question.

1 What kind of problem are Patrick and his roommate having this time?
a. Rent money
b. Grocery shopping
c. Making too much noise
d. House cleaning issues

Listen again and check True or False.

	True	False
2 A. Patrick and his roommate have been getting along very well.	☐	☐
B. Judy is suggesting to Patrick that he make up with his roommate.	☐	☐

● Listening 2

Listen to the dialog and answer the question.

1 Where did Nancy and her boyfriend first meet?

a.　　　　　　　b.　　　　　　　c.　　　　　　　d.

Listen again and answer the question.

2 What would be best for Nancy to say next?
a. Don't mention it.　　　　b. That's a shame.
c. No problem.　　　　　　d. Thank you.

Listen to the two summaries and choose the best one.

3 a. ☐　　　　　　　　　　b. ☐

Listening Task  Narrative

Answers p. 32

Listening 3

Listen to the narrative and answer the question.

1 What is the main topic of this passage?
   a. The reason why a fishing trip is boring
   b. How to prepare for a fishing trip
   c. How to have a good father-and-son talk
   d. Where to go fishing during the summer

Listen again and answer the question.

2 What is true about the trip?
   a. They caught a lot of fish.
   b. It was a short trip.
   c. It was a terrible trip.
   d. They went fishing last year.

Listening 4

Listen to the narrative and answer the question.

1 How does the speaker feel toward Matthew now?
   a. Apologetic   b. Upset
   c. Indifferent   d. Disappointed

Listen again and answer the question.

2 Why was the speaker upset with Matthew?
   a. Because Matthew did not talk to him
   b. Because Matthew did not help him with his test
   c. Because Matthew forgot to help him with his homework
   d. Because Matthew never asked for forgiveness

Listen to the two summaries and choose the best one.

3 a. ☐   b. ☐

UNIT 7   55

[1-2] Listen to the dialog and answer the questions.

1   Why is Barbara upset with Jane?
    a. Because Jane is always late
    b. Because Jane broke her promise to Barbara
    c. Because Jane says bad things about Barbara to others
    d. Because Jane is not talking to Barbara

2   What is <u>not</u> true about Jane?
    a. She is trying to change herself.
    b. She is nice to Barbara only when she is around.
    c. She is not getting along with others.
    d. She keeps saying bad things about people.

[3-4] Listen to the narrative and answer the questions.

3   How many tips were given in this passage?
    a. Two   b. Three
    c. Four   d. Five

4   What is <u>not</u> mentioned as a way to keep a good relationship?
    a. You must keep your friends' secrets to yourself.
    b. You must thank your friends when they help you.
    c. You must understand that you and your friends are different.
    d. You must help your friends when they need you.

[5-6] Listen to the narrative and answer the questions.

5   What is this passage about?
    a. How to find a good friend
    b. How to fix a broken relationship
    c. Ways to change a lifestyle
    d. What is important in a relationship of a couple

6   What is the main reason many couples break up?
    a. They don't love each other.
    b. They are different in personalities or lifestyles.
    c. They can't identify their problems.
    d. They don't make sacrifices for their partner.

[7-8] Listen to the dialog and answer the questions.

7   What is the relationship between the speakers?

Mr. Miller		Ted
a. A father	—	His son
b. A driver	—	A passenger
c. An employer	—	An employee
d. A principal	—	A student

8   Why does Mr. Miller want to have dinner with Ted?
    a. Because he wants to talk person to person with Ted
    b. Because Mr. Miller doesn't want to have dinner alone
    c. Because there is a problem with Ted
    d. Because Ted came to the office at seven

[9-10] Listen to the dialog and answer the questions.

9   Why did Len ask Brenda to introduce him to Cathy?
    a. Because he wants Cathy to help him with his project
    b. Because Cathy is an elementary school teacher
    c. Because Cathy knows a lot about Lisa
    d. Because he would like to go out with Cathy

10 Who will introduce Len to Cathy?
    a. Brenda   b. Lisa
    c. He will do it himself.   d. Nobody

Listening Task

🎧 Listen and fill in the blanks.
Answers p. 36

Listening 1

Judy   Patrick, _____? You look _____.

Patrick   It's my roommate again, Judy.

Judy   You guys have _____ these days. The last time it was _____ _____. What is it now?

Patrick   We agreed on _____ chores, but he did a bad job. For me, he is _____, but he thinks that I am _____.

Judy   If you have _____, I think you need to _____.

Patrick   I think so, too.

Listening 2

Toby   _____ been going out together, Nancy?

Nancy   We _____ for three years now.

Toby   That is a long time. How did you guys _____?

Nancy   He came to the café where I work to have coffee. I _____ the very first time I saw him, so I _____ first.

Toby   Are you guys going to _____?

Nancy   Yes. Actually, he _____ last week. We're getting married _____ _____.

Toby   Congratulations!

Listening 3

If you _____ a father-and-son talk, I strongly suggest _____ _____ together. Even though my father and I _____, we never had an opportunity to have an _____. But, everything changed after _____ with my father _____. The trip was long and we _____, so we started to talk. Eventually, we began to talk about some things we _____.

Listening 4

Matthew and I were _____ for a long time, but we are _____ these days. It _____ because he _____ to help me with my homework. I _____ in the library. He _____ several times, but I was _____ him. Now, he is not _____. I think I should call him and tell him how _____.

58

PRACTICE TEST [1-2]

Barbara Jane is _____, Alfred.

Alfred _____, Barbara?

Barbara She is nice _____ me, but
she says bad things about me _____
_____.

Alfred Does she _____, too? You
are not the only victim. She does that to
many people, so _____
with her any more.

Barbara Do you think I should _____
_____ that any more?

Alfred _____. I did that already,
but she _____.

PRACTICE TEST [3-4]

Even though everybody has friends, not too
many people know _____
_____ with them. Here are _____
_____ for keeping a good relationship with your
friends. First, don't _____
to others. A relationship _____
doesn't _____. Second, you must understand
that your friends may have _____
_____ than you and they may like different
things. Lastly, you should _____ for your
friends not only during good times but also
_____.

PRACTICE TEST [5-6]

Differences _____ or in lifestyle
preference are _____
why many married couples _____.
If two people have very different personalities
or lifestyles, _____ may not _____.
Often, one person must make sacrifices in order
for the other person _____. Therefore,
finding someone with whom _____
_____ over a long period of time is more
important than just finding someone _____.

PRACTICE TEST [7-8]

Mr. Miller Ted, _____ tonight?

Ted Yes, Mr. Miller. Is there _____?

Mr. Miller No, there is no problem at all. I just
want to _____.
Although you have been working for
me _____,
we've never had _____
together.

Ted I see, Mr. Miller. Where _____
_____?

Mr. Miller Come to my office at seven. I'll _____
_____ a restaurant
near the office.

Ted Yes, sir.

PRACTICE TEST [9-10]

Len Brenda, you are _____ Cathy,
right?

Brenda Well, I know her, but _____.
Why?

Len I would like to _____, and
I was hoping you _____
_____.

Brenda _____, Len, I think you need
to ask Lisa. They have been _____
_____. You know
Lisa well, right?

Len I didn't know _____.
Then, I will ask Lisa. Thank you for the
information, Brenda.

Brenda _____.

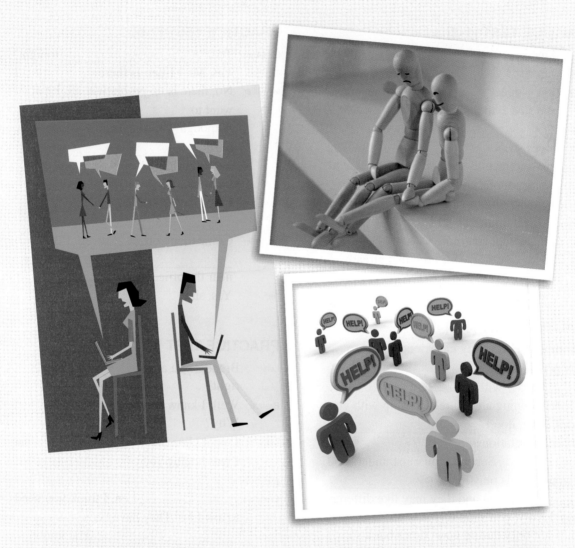

"Great talkers are little doers."

People who talk about how much work, they do usually work the least.

Answers p. 37

GETTING READY

A   Read the conversation below and fill in the blanks.

- didn't I tell you
- couldn't find
- take this
- you should have
- what's wrong
- worry
- why don't you
- need to
- terrible stomachache

Tracy   _____ with you, honey? You're sweating.

Bob   I have a _____ .

Tracy   I knew you would be sick. _____ not to eat too much? Have you taken any medicine?

Bob   No, I _____ anything in the first-aid kit.

Tracy   No way. There must be something here. Oh, I've found it. Here, _____ with a lot of water.

Bob   Thanks.

Tracy   _____ let me take you to the hospital? I think you _____ see a doctor.

Bob   No, I'll will be OK if I get some sleep. I couldn't sleep at all last night.

Tracy   _____ at least told me that you were sick.

Bob   Don't _____ . I feel like I'm getting better already.

Tracy   Then, go to bed and get some sleep.

B   Match the types of problem with the following situation.

<Types of Problems>

(1) Health   (2) Study   (3) Instrument / Tool   (4) Relationship   (5) Work   (6) Shopping

<Situation>

(a) I don't think I can handle this project. It's beyond my ability.   _____

(b) This copy machine is out of order.   _____

(c) I'm afraid that I will fail the exam.   _____

(d) This shirt has a rip in it. I'd like to get a refund.   _____

(e) I seem to have sprained my ankle. It really hurts.   _____

(f) I have quarreled with James. What should I do to make up with him?   _____

Listening Task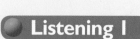

● Listening 1

Listen to the dialog and answer the question.

1   Which picture is related to this conversation?

a.   b.   c.   d.

Listen again and check True or False.

2   A. The traffic to the airport is usually not very bad on the weekend.
    B. They are scheduled to pick someone up from the airport at 12:30.

	True	False
A	☐	☐
B	☐	☐

● Listening 2

Listen to the dialog and answer the question.

1   Why is Cindy angry at James?
    a. Because James broke her watch
    b. Because James was late for dates
    c. Because James told a lie
    d. Because James didn't call her back

Listen again and answer the question.

2   What is Chris giving to James?
    a. Permission   b. Compliments
    c. Advice   d. An apology

Listen to the two summaries and choose the best one.

3   a. ☐   b. ☐

Listening Task

Answers p. 38

Listening 3

Listen to the narrative and answer the question.

1 What problem does the speaker have?
a. She quarreled with her friends.
b. She didn't finish her school project.
c. Two of her friends don't get along well with each other.
d. She has some problems with her partner over a school project.

Listen again and answer the question.

2 How does the speaker feel toward the situation?
a. Helpless   b. Satisfied
c. Thrilled   d. Indifferent

Listening 4

Listen to the narrative and answer the question.

1 What is the best title for this passage?
a. How to master English
b. Things to do for a successful life
c. Best ways to memorize things
d. How to improve school grades

Listen again and answer the question.

2 Which suggestion is not given in the passage?
a. Try to understand what you read.
b. Use your studying time wisely.
c. Study in a group.
d. Ask your teacher as many questions as possible.

Listen to the two summaries and choose the best one.

3 a. ☐   b. ☐

[1-2] Listen to the dialog and answer the questions.

1   What problem do the speakers have?
   a. They ran out of paint.
   b. The color does not match the furniture.
   c. The paint is too expensive.
   d. They can't get a refund on the paint.

2   When does the shop close?
   a. At 9 o'clock
   b. At 9:30
   c. At 10 o'clock
   d. It doesn't open on the weekend.

[3-4] Listen to the dialog and answer the questions.

3   What will Jeff do next?

   a.   b.   c.   d.

4   What is the proverb that fits to the situation?
   a. A sound mind in a sound body.
   b. A little knowledge is dangerous.
   c. Patience is a virtue.
   d. A stitch in time saves nine.

[5-6] Listen to the dialog and answer the questions.

5   How does Harrison feel about the problem?
   a. Relieved   b. Concerned
   c. Annoyed   d. Disappointed

6   What is Sally's suggestion?
    a. Tell the truth and apologize.
    b. Buy Harrison's brother a new digital camera.
    c. Have the camera repaired.
    d. Put the camera back first.

[7-8] Listen to the narrative and answer the questions.

7   What is the main idea of this passage?
    a. For a healthy life, you need to lose weight.
    b. Try to eat as little as possible when you are on a diet.
    c. If you feel weak, exercise regularly.
    d. Skipping meals is not a good way to lose weight.

8   What is the speaker's recommendation for losing weight?
    a. Drink a lot of water.
    b. Consult with an expert about a diet.
    c. Exercise and eat light.
    d. Do not eat junk food and become a vegetarian.

[9-10] Listen to the dialog and answer the questions.

9   Why is Joan panicked?
    a. Because a fire broke out in her apartment
    b. Because she can't enter her house
    c. Because there is a gas leak in her apartment
    d. Because a thief broke into her apartment last night

10 According to the conversation, Joan should not _____.
    a. call a technician
    b. turn off the gas stove
    c. open the windows
    d. light up a match

Listening 1

Veronica   Wow, _____ is really bad. Do you think we can _____
_____, Robert?

Robert   _____ that the traffic _____ the airport is
always bad.

Veronica   _____ be bad, but not this bad.

Robert   _____?

Veronica   It's at 12:30 p.m.

Robert   I think we can make it this time, but next time, _____.

Veronica   I agree.

Listening 2

Chris   Are you OK, James?

James   I _____ Cindy. She got upset because I have been _____
_____ a few times.

Chris   I knew something like that would _____. You are _____.

James   Chris, _____; you don't have to _____.

Chris   I am _____. Everybody says you are always late.

James   Really? Then, _____.

Chris   You really should. Now, go call Cindy and tell her that _____.

James   I think I should.

Listening 3

Dear Abby, I am _____. I have two close friends with whom
I _____, but they _____ with each other these
days. After they quarreled several times _____, they stopped
_____ even in class. I have tried to help them make up, but _____
_____. I _____ any morc. If you have _____,
please let me know.

Listening 4

If your _____ even though you study hard, then you should
_____. First, do not try to _____ you read
without _____. Secondly, you need to learn how to _____
_____ evenly among the subjects you study. Many students _____
only on the subjects they like. Thirdly, if studying alone is boring and difficult, _____
_____ is an excellent idea.

66

PRACTICE TEST [1-2]

Jessica   We are _____ .

Ben   I thought _____ .

Jessica   I didn't want to _____ . Don't worry. I will go to the paint shop now.

Ben   _____ the paint shop is open now.

Jessica   What time is it?

Ben   It's 9:30, and _____ 9:00.

Jessica   Well, we can _____ .

Ben   Next time, get a sufficient amount. They _____ on unused paint.

Jessica   _____ next time.

PRACTICE TEST [3-4]

Sarah   Jeff, _____ ?

Jeff   Yes, _____ . I took a pain reliever, but it is _____ .

Sarah   Why don't you _____ ?

Jeff   _____ seeing a dentist.

Sarah   If you don't, it will _____ .

Jeff   I can bear it. It may _____ _____ .

Sarah   I don't think so. If you don't see a doctor now, you may _____ .

Jeff   All right. I will.

PRACTICE TEST [5-6]

Harrison   Sally, can I _____ _____ ?

Sally   What is it, Harrison?

Harrison   I took my brother's new digital camera out _____ , and I dropped it. _____ ?

Sally   "Honesty is the best policy." I think you should _____ and _____ .

Harrison   Won't he get angry?

PRACTICE TEST

Sally   I am sure he will, but you _____ _____ for it anyway.

Harrison   Yes, you're right. Thank you _____ _____ .

PRACTICE TEST [7-8]

Have you tried to _____ ? I've tried several times. I drank only a cup of juice for breakfast, _____ , and skipped dinner entirely. It _____ in the beginning, but soon I _____ . I even had to be hospitalized. It was _____ _____ . So, if you _____ , don't just _____ . Eat light and exercise. That's _____ to lose weight.

PRACTICE TEST [9-10]

Joan   Hello?

David   Hello, Joan? Why do you _____ _____ ?

Joan   _____ my apartment.

David   Calm down and _____ _____ first. Then, open all the doors and windows.

Joan   OK. _____ ? I am so panicked that _____ _____ .

David   After you do what I have told you, _____ _____ and ask for a technician.

Joan   I see.

David   And, do not _____ or _____ .

Joan   OK. Thanks.

UNIT 8   67

"Great haste makes great waste."

If you try to hurry too much, you'll make mistakes and have to go back later to fix them.

I enjoyed the musical.

Answers p. 42

GETTING READY

A   Read the conversation below and fill in the blanks.

- main
  characters
- recommended
- the plot
- a love story
- what kind of
- favorite stars
- how about
  seeing
- romantic
  comedy
- action movies
- who's starring
- rented

Jane	Kathy, _____ a movie tonight? I have _____ a DVD of *Notting Hill*.
Kathy	_____ movie is it?
Jane	It's a _____. One of my friends _____ it to me because she really enjoyed it.
Kathy	Well, I don't like romantic comedies. I like _____ like *The Italian Job*.
Jane	Kathy, just try it. I know you won't regret it.
Kathy	Do you know _____?
Jane	I've heard it's just _____. That is all I know.
Kathy	_____ in it?
Jane	Hugh Grant and Julia Roberts are the _____.
Kathy	Hmm... Hugh Grant is one of my _____. What time should I come over?
Jane	Come about 6 p.m. We can either order something or go to a nearby restaurant. Then we can watch the movie.
Kathy	OK. I'll see you later.

B   What kind of entertainments do you like? Talk about it with your friends.

the movies   plays   pop concerts   classical concerts   musicals   magic shows

◁))   I enjoy going to musicals. I have seen *Beauty and the Beast* before.

C   What kind of movies do you like? Talk about it with your friends.

an action   a romantic comedy   a horror   a thriller   a comedy   a sci-fi

◁))   I like an action (movie) like *Die Hard*.

Listening Task *Dialogue*

● Listening 1

Listen to the dialog and answer the question.

1   What are they talking about?
   a. A sad love story they have seen before
   b. A sad love story Maria is going to see
   c. A romantic comedy they saw already
   d. A romantic comedy they are going to see

Listen again and check True or False.

	True	False

2   A. They are going to see a play together this weekend.
     B. Maria is telling her friend about the story of *Romeo and Juliet*.

● Listening 2

Listen to the dialog and answer the question.

1   What are they talking about?
   a. Their favorite hobby
   b. Their favorite singers
   c. Their favorite movie stars
   d. Their favorite movie genre

Listen again and answer the question.

2   What does the man's last response mean?
   a. He wants to see a horror movie.
   b. He also likes to scream during the movie.
   c. He doesn't need to get rid of stress.
   d. He didn't think screaming could be a way to release stress.

Listen to the two summaries and choose the best one.

3   a. ☐   b. ☐

Answers p. 43

Listening 3

Listen to the narrative and answer the question.

1   Why is Jessica so excited?
   a. Because she can go to the musical she wanted to see
   b. Because she bought a soundtrack of a famous musical
   c. Because a new musical is being made
   d. Because she can play in a successful musical

Listen again and and answer the question.

2   What does Jessica like most about the musical?
   a. The story
   b. The costume
   c. The soundtrack
   d. The main characters

Listening 4

Listen to the narrative and answer the question.

1   What is the speaker's attitude toward the concert?
   a. Thrilled   b. Expectant
   c. Discontented   d. Satisfied

Listen again and answer the question.

2   What is <u>not</u> true about the concert?
   a. It was a rock concert.
   b. The ticket didn't sell well.
   c. Some people could not hear the band performing.
   d. There was a problem with the lighting.

Listen to the two summaries and choose the best one.

3   a. ☐   b. ☐

[1-2] Listen to the dialog and answer the questions.

1 What kind of movie are they talking about?
   a. An SF movie   b. A romantic comedy
   c. A horror movie   d. A gangster movie

2 What is <u>not</u> mentioned about the movie?
   a. The main characters   b. The director
   c. The opening day   d. The story

[3-4] Listen to the narrative and answer the questions.

3 What is the main topic of this passage?
   a. Being a staff of *The Family*
   b. Attending the sit-com as part of the audience
   c. Dating the actor of *The Family*
   d. Playing an extra part in *The Family*

4 Which picture best describes what she did today?

   a.   b.   c.   d.

[5-6] Listen to the dialog and answer the questions.

5 Why is this concert different from other concerts?
   a. Because it is an outdoor concert.
   b. Because it is performed by a famous conductor.
   c. Because it has never been performed in this town before.
   d. Because it is the first concert that they have been to together.

6 According to the conversation, Helen _____.
   a. knows a lot about classical music
   b. loves classical music
   c. does not like classical music very much
   d. does not have much time for music

[7-8] Listen to the dialog and answer the questions.

7 What is the man's attitude toward the magic show?
   a. Satisfied
   b. Angry
   c. Dissatisfied
   d. Concerned

8 What was the problem at the magic show?
   a. The show started too late.
   b. The man bought the wrong tickets.
   c. The magician made too many mistakes.
   d. The rabbit disappeared.

[9-10] Listen to the dialog and answer the questions.

9 What does the woman's last response mean?
   a. She thinks that the performance is too modern.
   b. She agrees that the performance is awesome.
   c. She has no interest in the performance.
   d. She doesn't know why people like the performance.

10 What instrument is not used in the performance?
   a. Pencils
   b. Brooms
   c. Drums
   d. Cooking knives

Listening 1

Jackie   What are _____ , Maria?

Maria   These are _____ .

Jackie   A play? Which one?

Maria   *Romeo and Juliet* by William Shakespeare.

Jackie   Do you _____ ?

Maria   Well, I know it is a _____ where two young lovers from families who hate each other _____ at the end.

Jackie   How do they die?

Maria   Well, I don't know exactly how. I will _____ more _____ .

Listening 2

Jessica   Tom, _____ do you like?

Tom   I like _____ , and Ken Morris is my _____ .

Jessica   Really? I didn't know.

Tom   Well, what kind of movies do you like, Jessica?

Jessica   I like _____ .

Tom   Oh, really? I can see why boys like them, but I don't understand why girls like that kind of movie.

Jessica   Well, I think it's because we _____ during the movie. It is _____ .

Tom   Really? _____ .

Listening 3

The musical, *Yesterday Once More*, was _____ budgeted and the _____ _____ of recent musicals. Jessica _____ this musical ever since she first _____ . But she has not been able to go to the musical since the musical has _____ in her town. Finally, it will come to her town. It _____ the Washington Theater _____ next Friday. She is _____ .

Listening 4

_____ should be both _____ , but the last concert we went to was neither. It was my worst concert ever. Even though the concert _____ _____ a famous _____ , it was poorly organized. _____ , so we had to stand. Furthermore, we could barely _____ because the _____ was poorly _____ . Even _____ once in the middle of the concert.

74

PRACTICE TEST [1-2]

Halley   Did you see the movie *Friends and Enemies* _____?

Julio   Yes, I did. It is a _____, but it _____ and lots of _____.

Halley   What is the story about?

Julio   It is about _____ _____ later on in their lives.

Halley   Who are the _____?

Julio   John Anderson and Adam Williams.

Halley   They never _____ gangster movies before, did they?

Julio   No, you're right. _____ _____, too.

PRACTICE TEST [3-4]

Today, I had a great time _____ _____ for the sit-com *The Family*. It was so _____ see the _____.
They looked _____ on TV. Even though the show was only thirty minutes long, the actual filming _____ _____. I didn't know it would take that long. After the filming, I had _____ _____ with the actors. I even _____ _____ with them.

PRACTICE TEST [5-6]

Alex   Helen, _____ a classical music concert this Friday.

Helen   I am not _____ classical music, Alex. I don't think I would _____ _____.

Alex   You _____ this one because this is _____. I am sure you will enjoy it.

Helen   A _____ outdoors?

Alex   Yes. You will see the stars and feel the breeze during the concert.

Helen   Mmm, it really _____. I will try it, Alex.

Alex   _____, Helen.

PRACTICE TEST [7-8]

Tracy   How was the _____ last night?

Gerry   It was almost a _____.

Tracy   What happened?

Gerry   _____ because the _____ _____. One time, the rabbit stuck his head out when it was not supposed to. _____ the rabbit, but the magician didn't. Needless to say, _____.

Tracy   It _____ it was _____.

Gerry   Yes, I had a good time. If you love to laugh, _____.

PRACTICE TEST [9-10]

Kathy   How was *The Stomp*?

John   _____. Even though they didn't use any of the conventional _____ such as drums, they_____ _____ using only cooking knives, papers, brooms, and pencils. They _____ together.

Kathy   _____ with knives and papers? Wow!

John   That wasn't everything. They also had _____ that were _____. I think the _____ were dancers as well as musicians.

Kathy   No wonder that _____ _____ now.

"The darkest hour is just before the dawn."

Relief or victory comes just after the worst phase of a bad situation.

Answers p. 47

GETTING READY

A   Read the conversation below and fill in the blanks.

- encouraging
- good lab partner
- done with
- working on
- make me feel
- tried hard
- no problem
- capable of
- with enthusiasm
- clever

Joan	I'm _____ this math homework.
Tony	Oh, really? You're so _____. I'm still _____ it.
Joan	Not at all. I just _____.
Tony	I know that you were working on it _____. But I'm not. Anyway, would you look at this? I think I made some mistakes.
Joan	Let me see it. Well, there's _____. It will just take some time for you to complete it.
Tony	It's beyond me.
Joan	No! You are _____ accomplishing whatever you want to. Just believe in yourself.
Tony	Thank you, Joan. You're very _____. You _____ like I can do anything.
Joan	You're also a _____.

B   What compliments can you give in these situations? Talk about it with your friends.

[A]
(1) is dressed well
(2) helped an old man move heavy boxes
(3) won a prize at a singing contest
(4) solved a difficult math problem
(5) cooked a great pizza for you
(6) got rid of a computer virus

[B]
(a) How kind of you!
(b) You're so smart.
(c) You look so great today.
(d) Thanks. You're good with the computer.
(e) Congratulations! I'm so proud of you.
(f) It was so delicious. I really enjoyed it.

◁))) When your friend [A] is dressed well, you can say "[B] You look so great today."

Listening 1

Listen to the dialog and answer the question.

1 What happened to the woman yesterday?

     a.   b.   c.   d.

Listen again and check True or False.

	True	False

2 A. The woman called the man and asked him for help.
    B. The man is going to invite the woman to a dinner.

Listening 2

Listen to the dialog and answer the question.

1 Why is the woman satisfied?
  a. Because the man worked really hard
  b. Because the man finished the job quickly
  c. Because the man painted the room with the color she wanted
  d. Because the man chose a great color for the room

Listen again and answer the question.

2 What is the man's job?
  a. A carpenter   b. A painter
  c. An engineer   d. An electrician

Listen to the two summaries and choose the best one.

3 a. ☐   b. ☐

Listening Task

Answers p. 48

Listening 3

Listen to the narrative and answer the question.

1   Which is true about this passage?
a. It was their first game.
b. They cut down on the mistakes this time.
c. The speaker is complaining about the bad teamwork.
d. The team lost the game.

Listen again and answer the question.

2   What is the speaker's job?
a. A coach
b. A salesperson
c. A counselor
d. A pro-gamer

Listening 4

Listen to the narrative and answer the question.

1   Why was Len awarded "The Bravest Man of the City" award?
a. Because he can swim in the cold river
b. Because he is not afraid of water
c. Because he saved two people from drowning
d. Because he is a professional lifeguard

Listen again and answer the question.

2   Why did Len go to the Sacramento River?
a. To fish
b. To boat
c. To swim
d. To ice–skate

Listen to the two summaries and choose the best one.

3   a. ☐   b. ☐

[1-2] Listen to the dialog and answer the questions.

1 What is the woman talking about?
   a. The man's kindness
   b. The man's great job
   c. The man's clothing
   d. The man's good manners

2 What did the man first think about his shirt?
   a. It was too bright.
   b. It was too tight.
   c. It was too old.
   d. It was too expensive.

[3-4] Listen to the dialog and answer the questions.

3 What picture best describes the situation?

   a.   b.   c.   d.

4 What cannot be the feeling that Roy felt yesterday?
   a. Nervous   b. Uneasy   c. Tense   d. Cheerful

[5-6] Listen to the dialog and answer the questions.

5 This conversation is between a _____A_____ and a(n) _____B_____.

	A		B
a.	customer	–	clerk
b.	manager	–	salesperson
c.	professor	–	assistant
d.	librarian	–	student

6   What is the secret of Tony's success?
    a. He sold as much as possible to every customer.
    b. He sold expensive items whenever possible.
    c. He sold only what customers needed.
    d. He asked customers many questions.

[7-8] Listen to the dialog and answer the questions.

7   What can be the woman's response to what Bobby has said?

> Woman   _____ .

    a. Thanks for your help.
    b. Good luck to you.
    c. Don't say that again.
    d. I envy you.

8   What is the main topic for this conversation?
    a. Giving proper compliments
    b. Responding properly to a compliment
    c. Several ways to make people feel great
    d. Advantages and disadvantages of compliments

[9-10] Listen to the narrative and answer the questions.

9   What is true about this passage?
    a. Compliments make people feel good.
    b. Giving compliments is worthy but complicated.
    c. People usually feel shy when given a compliment.
    d. It's better to compliment people in front of others.

10 What is <u>not</u> mentioned as an example of compliments?
    a. Compliment people's nice behavior.
    b. Compliment people's clothing.
    c. Compliment people's achievement at work.
    d. Compliment people's intelligence.

 **Listening Task**

🎧 Listen and fill in the blanks.
Answers p. 51

Listening 1

Clair Kurt, thank you very much for _____ for me last night, especially since _____.

Kurt _____. What are friends for? I'm glad you called me.

Clair Well, I _____. Why don't you come to my house tomorrow? I'd like to _____ a nice dinner. We can go to a movie _____.

Kurt You don't have to do that. But _____, I'd love to.

Listening 2

W _____?

M It is done. Why don't you _____?

W Wow, it really _____. How did you know the room would _____ _____ with gray rather than white?

M I once painted a similar room with gray, and it came out really nice, too.

W I think _____. I'm glad that I listened to you. _____.

M I am _____.

Listening 3

Even though we made mistakes, it was a good game. Most of you guys were _____ _____, and I know you _____. First of all, John, you _____ _____ out there. And Sam, you made _____ in the second inning. If we just _____ and try a little harder, I think we can _____. You guys have the _____.

Listening 4

Today, Len was awarded " _____ " award at City Hall for saving _____ in the Sacramento River. Last Saturday, Len _____ _____ and saw a boy _____. Then, the boy's father _____ _____ to save the boy, but because the water was too cold to swim in, _____ _____. Len went into the river _____ and _____.

82

PRACTICE TEST [1-2]

Linda Hi, Steve. _____ that shirt?

Steve Why, Linda? Is there _____ _____?

Linda No, no. That shirt would not look good on most people, but it _____ _____.

Steve Thanks, Linda. From now on, _____ _____ when I wear this shirt. Honestly, I _____ enough to wear this shirt before today. I thought _____.

Linda Don't worry, Steve. You look great in it.

Steve _____, Linda. _____ _____ from embarrassment.

PRACTICE TEST [3-4]

Ben Roy, that was _____ that you made yesterday.

Roy You really think so? I felt very nervous _____.

Ben You didn't _____.
You sounded fine.

Roy It's nice to hear that, but _____ _____. They say public speaking is _____. I realized exactly what they meant when I stood _____.

Ben I've never _____, but I think I can understand what you mean.

PRACTICE TEST [5-6]

W Tony, you did a great job. _____ _____ by 200% compared to the same time last year. You are _____ _____ I have ever had. _____ _____?

M There is no secret. I _____ to help customers. I don't _____ _____ things. The customers know that I try to _____ _____. Therefore, _____ _____, they know who to ask.

W That is a great secret.

PRACTICE TEST [7-8]

W Bobby, _____?

M Sure. What is it?

W I don't know _____ when people give me compliments. _____ _____ "You are smart?" If I say "Thank you," _____ _____ that I am smart.

M I think "Thanks" is fine. But if you ____ _____, what about "That's very nice of you?" _____ _____ than saying nothing.

PRACTICE TEST [9-10]

_____ to a person is a very good thing. You can _____ many things, and it makes the person _____ _____. You can, for example, compliment a person about _____ _____, how nice he acted, and how well he _____. So, go ahead and compliment _____. You'll also feel great _____.

"The truth hurts."

Relief or victory comes just after the worst phase of a bad situation.

What kind of pet do you have?

Answers p. 52

GETTING READY

A   Read the conversation below and fill in the blanks.

- attacked
- imitate
- endangered
- speaking of
- raise
- a pet
- what do you feed
- a pet shop
- habitats
- cut down

Julie   You have a monkey as _____ ! I'm surprised. Where did you get it?

Dan   I got him from _____ last year. It's really fun to _____ a monkey because a monkey is like a little kid. My monkey loves to _____ me.

Julie   Isn't it difficult to raise a monkey? _____ it?

Dan   Well, monkeys can eat almost anything. My monkey doesn't care whether it's for him or not. He once _____ my neighbor's dog to take away his food.

Julie   _____ monkeys, I heard that some wild monkeys are an _____ species because they have lost their _____ .

Dan   Really?

Julie   Yeah, some monkeys in the Philippines are almost extinct because too many trees are _____ in their habitats.

Dan   That's so sad.

B   What do you have as a pet? Talk about it with your friends.

[A] lizards
hamsters
parrots
fish

[B] They are the only animal that can say something.
It is very relaxing to see them swimming.
They are so little and cute like squirrels.
I want something unusual for a pet.

◁))) I'm interested in having ^[A] fish as a pet. ^[B] It is very relaxing to see them swimming.

Listening 1

Listen to the dialog and answer the question.

1   What is Don scared of?
    a. Snakes   b. Bugs
    c. Birds   d. Nothing

Listen again and check True or False.

	True	False
2 A. Don has a history of being attacked by bugs when he was little.	☐	☐
B. Sally has never seen a person afraid of swans.	☐	☐

Listening 2

Listen to the dialog and answer the question.

1   Where is the girl?

       a.   b.   c.   d.

Listen again and answer the question.

2   What are the things hamsters can eat?
    a. Vegetables and nuts
    b. Cookies and chocolates
    c. Garlic and onion
    d. All of the above

Listen to the two summaries and choose the best one.

3   a. ☐   b. ☐

Listening Task

Answers p. 52

Listening 3

Listen to the narrative and answer the question.

1 What is the main topic of this passage?
   a. Animals that should not be pets
   b. Various types of pets
   c. Pets in the past and in the future
   d. Why people don't keep pets

Listen again and and answer the question.

2 According to the passage, what is the least common kind of pets?
   a. Dogs and cats   b. Birds and fish
   c. Snakes and lizards   d. Spiders and ants

Listening 4

Listen to the narrative and answer the question.

1 What is this passage mainly about?
   a. Reasons why we should protect wild animals
   b. Places where wild animals live
   c. Endangerment of wild animals
   d. Important tips for hunting

Listen again and and answer the question.

2 According to the passage, why do people kill wild animals?
   a. Because people are scared of wild animals
   b. Because people want their furs
   c. Because wild animals often invade people's homes
   d. Because wild animals destroy forests

Listen to the two summaries and choose the best one.

3 a. ☐   b. ☐

[1-2] Listen to the dialog and answer the questions.

1 What does Paul's last response mean?
   a. He agrees with Diane's opinion.
   b. He disagrees with Diane's opinion.
   c. He doesn't understand what Diane has said.
   d. He wants to change the subject.

2 According to Paul, wild animals _____.
   a. should be held in a bigger cages
   b. are very dangerous
   c. should live in the wild
   d. are safer in the zoo than in the wild

[3-4] Listen to the dialog and answer the questions.

3 What does the woman feel about birds as pets?
   a. They're fascinating.   b. They're amusing.
   c. They're boring.   d. They're annoying.

4 What is <u>not</u> true about the man and his parrots?
   a. He has three parrots.
   b. His parrots say, "Have a nice day" every day.
   c. He agrees that parrots create a lot of mess.
   d. He thinks parrots are fun as a pet.

[5-6] Listen to the dialog and answer the questions.

5 What sound is <u>not</u> mentioned in the conversation?

a.   b.   c.   d.

6 How do the guide dogs for the deaf help their owners?
   a. By barking when there is no sound
   b. By informing the owners about important sounds
   c. By stopping at dangerous spots
   d. By taking the owners to a quiet place

[7-8] Listen to the dialog and answer the questions.

7 How did Tina get her dog?
   a. She had the dog already.
   b. Someone gave the dog to her.
   c. She adopted the dog.
   d. She bought the dog from a pet shop.

8 How much does one have to pay to adopt an animal?
   a. Nothing
   b. Actual price for the animal
   c. A small fee for its cage
   d. A small amount of money for vaccination

[9-10] Listen to the narrative and answer the questions.

9 What sense do sharks use when they are far away from the prey?
   a. Only hearing
   b. Only vision
   c. Smell and vision
   d. Hearing and smell

10 According to the passage, what is true about sharks?
    a. They use mainly their eyes to find food.
    b. They can find the prey even when they cannot see it.
    c. They use different senses depending on the size of the prey.
    d. They can't hear well when the prey is far away.

Listening 1

Sally Look at those swans, Don. _____?

Don Wait, Sally, let's not _____ them.

Sally What? Don't tell me that _____.

Don Actually, I am. I was _____ a goose _____.
Since then, _____.

Sally I have seen people scared of _____ or _____, but not birds.

Don Well, _____, but I don't _____ snakes or bugs.

Listening 2

Man Did you find _____?

Girl I think I like hamsters, but I wonder _____?

Man It is not _____.

Girl What do they eat?

Man You can _____ fresh _____ and nuts.

Girl How about cookies and chocolates?

Man _____ for hamsters, and you _____ garlic or onion either.

Girl I think I will take _____ and _____.

Man OK.

Listening 3

Pets are animals _____ or for companionship. _____, animals like dogs and cats were _____, but nowadays many other animals are also considered pets. Although traditional pets, such as dogs, cats, birds, or fish are _____ _____, some people have _____. _____ pets, such as _____, are gaining _____ fast. Even though _____ are rare pets, there are some people who keep them as pets.

Listening 4

Today, _____ many wild animals face is _____.
Every day, a large number of trees are _____, and others _____ for natural resources, such as wood or minerals. _____ _____ is another big reason for the endangerment of wild animals. Many animals are hunted _____ or for their _____.

DICTATION Practice Test

Listen and fill in the blanks.

Answers p. 56

PRACTICE TEST [1-2]

Diane Paul, what did you do ____________ __________?

Paul I went to the zoo.

Diane ______________________________.

Paul No, ______________.

Diane Why?

Paul I felt sorry for the ________________ _____. I believe wild animals ________ ____________. It was really sad to see the polar bear __________________ _____.

Diane I agree. But ______________________, people can realize _________________ ______________.

Paul ____________________ there, Diane.

PRACTICE TEST [3-4]

M ____________ you have there! I didn't know ______________.

W I love fish because _______________ _________. Do you have any pets?

M I have ______________________.

W I don't like birds because they are _____ _____ and create ______________.

M That is true. But parrots are fun because ___________.

W They don't talk. They just __________ ___________.

M I know. But, I feel good when they say, "____________" to me every morning.

PRACTICE TEST [5-6]

Juan Yesterday, I saw a TV show about ____ ____________________. It was amazing.

Sunny I saw it, too. They were very smart.

Juan They do so well because they _______ _______ a very ________________.

Sunny Do you know there are dogs ________ _________, too?

Juan Really? How do they _____________ _________?

Sunny When they hear __________, doorbells, or ___________, they let their owners know _______________________.

Juan That's wonderful.

PRACTICE TEST [7-8]

Rich Is that your new dog, Tina? ________.

Tina Yes, it is.

Rich How much ________________?

Tina I didn't pay anything because I got it ___________________.

Rich What is an adoption center?

Tina It's a place where ________________ ____________ are kept and cared for. All of the animals there ___________ ___________.

Rich So, they didn't _________________?

Tina No. All you have to do is pay _______ ________ their vaccination.

PRACTICE TEST [9-10]

Sharks use _______________ to find food, _____________________ of their prey. When the prey is very far away, sharks _____ _____ hearing and ______. They can hear their prey ___________________ and can smell small traces of ______ in the water. Sharks rely on their _________ only when they are very ___________ the prey.

"Love me, love my dog."

If you love someone, you should accept everything and everyone

that the person loves.

What should I wear?

GETTING READY

Answers p. 57

A   Read the conversation below and fill in the blanks.

- in a bigger size
- go well with
- what size
- tight on
- take
- latest
- looking for
- out of style
- try it on
- how about
- out of

Salesperson   How can I help you?

Woman   I'm _____ a leather jacket to go with my white jeans.

Salesperson   _____ this one?

Woman   Well... it looks kind of _____. It's something my grandmother would wear.

Salesperson   I see... Oh, you'll love this one. This beige jacket will _____ your white jeans. It's the _____ fashion.

Woman   I like that. Can I _____ ?

Salesperson   Sure, _____ do you wear?

Woman   Size 6.

Salesperson   This one is size 6. Here you are.

Woman   Hmm... It's a little _____ me. Do you have this jacket _____ ?

Salesperson   Sorry, we're all _____ the next size up.

Woman   Well, I'll just _____ the size six, then.

B   What are they wearing? Talk about it with your friends.

a gray polo shirt   a white skirt   a dark brown dress shirt   jeans
a tan suit   a white dress shirt with pink stripes   a black leather jacket

◁))   The person in the picture is wearing a gray polo shirt.

Listening Task

Listening 1

Listen to the dialog and answer the question.

1   Where is the woman?
    a. At a men's clothing store   b. At a shoe store
    c. At a baby's clothing store   d. At a shoe repair shop

Listen again and check True or False.

		True	False
2	A. She wears a size seven, but she is trying a size six-and-a-half now.	☐	☐
	B. Her usual size is a six-and-a-half, but she will buy a size seven this time.	☐	☐

Listening 2

Listen to the dialog and answer the question.

1   What is this conversation about?
    a. Choosing clothes for a job interview
    b. Shopping for clothes to go on a date
    c. Complaining about having nothing to wear
    d. Talking about clothes on a TV interview

Listen again and answer the question.

2   What will the boy wear for his job interview?

     a.   b.   c.   d.

Listen to the two summaries and choose the best one.

3   a. ☐   b. ☐

Listening 3

Listen to the narrative and answer the question.

1 What is this passage about?
   a. School uniforms that a store sells
   b. Advice from a TV show about teenagers' clothing
   c. School rules for students' clothes
   d. Students' favorite fashions

Listen again and answer the question.

2 Which of the following clothing is <u>not</u> acceptable for girls?
   a. Brown pants   b. Black skirts
   c. White polo shirts   d. Dark blue pants

Listening 4

Listen to the narrative and answer the question.

1 What is the best topic for this passage?
   a. Popularity of jeans worldwide
   b. How to choose a tie
   c. Changes in fashion trends
   d. Fashion during the 70s

Listen again and answer the question.

2 According to the passage, when were/are jeans popular?
   a. During the 70s
   b. During the 90s
   c. Today
   d. All the time

Listen to the two summaries and choose the best one.

3   a. ☐   b. ☐

[1-2] Listen to the dialog and answer the questions.

1 Why is Sabrina worried?
   a. Because she is not quite sure if she likes the pants
   b. Because the pants may be out of her size
   c. Because the pants have too many pockets and zippers
   d. Because she doesn't like to wear the same things that Mary wears

2 What is <u>not</u> mentioned in the conversation?
   a. Size   b. Color
   c. Price   d. Style

[3-4] Listen to the dialog and answer the questions.

3 What is wrong with the shirt?
   a. It's too long.
   b. It's too small.
   c. It's too expensive.
   d. It's too big.

4 What will the man do?
   a. He will start exercising.
   b. He will exchange the shirt.
   c. He will buy another shirt.
   d. He will get a refund.

[5-6] Listen to the dialog and answer the questions.

5 What would be the best response to follow the conversation?

Man	_____

   a. I'll show you the way.
   b. I'll do it myself.
   c. I'll be right back.
   d. I'll come again tomorrow then.

6   What is true about the conversation?
   a. The man has to wait for two days to have his pants altered.
   b. One of the man's pants will be altered by this afternoon.
   c. Both of the man's pants will be altered by this afternoon.
   d. The man will not be able to have any alterations done.

[7-8] Listen to the dialog and answer the questions.

7   Why do the women dislike the bag?
   a. Because it is out of style
   b. Because it is worn out
   c. Because its buckle is too big
   d. All of the above

8   Where will the women go next?
   a. A shopping center   b. A library
   c. A restaurant   d. A hair shop

[9-10] Listen to the narrative and answer the questions.

9   What is the main topic of this passage?
   a. How to find a good bag
   b. The origin of bags
   c. New bags for men
   d. The difference between men's and women's fashions

10 Based on what you hear, what is the best matching choice?

> When buying a bag, women think more about _____A_____ , but men consider _____B_____ first.

	A		B
a.	how it looks	—	its function
b.	how much it is	—	where it is made
c.	what it is made of	—	how well it is selling
d.	when it was made	—	how it looks

Listening 1

Man   Can I help you?

Kate   Yes. I saw _____ I liked last week. _____ them. Umm...
Oh, these are the ones.

Man   Would you like to _____? What size do you wear?

Kate   My size is _____, but let me try both the _____ and the
_____, just in case the six-and-a-half _____.

Man   Why don't you try _____? That pair is size seven.

Kate   Let me try them... Well, _____. I will take them.

Man   These are beautiful shoes. You have great taste.

Listening 2

Jay   Mom, _____ for today's _____? I am
considering either my black suit or this blue shirt.

Mom   I don't think you should _____ to an interview for _____
_____ at an ice cream shop. Why don't you wear _____ with
_____ that I bought you last month?

Jay   OK. _____ the pants?

Mom   I think _____, and try that brown belt _____.

Jay   Thanks, Mom.

Listening 3

This is the dress code of our school. Boys should wear a _____ or _____
_____, and _____ pants. The belt can be _____, such as
black, brown, or dark blue, but the shoes _____. Girls must follow _____
_____ as the boys, with the _____ being that girls can wear
_____. A _____ is optional for both the boys and the girls.

Listening 4

Even though new fashions _____ every day, many of them _____
_____ at all. They _____ before. For example,
wide ties _____ during the 70s, and narrow ties _____. Today, more
people are _____ again. Similarly, the popularity of _____
has gone _____. But fortunately for the jeans makers, jeans have never
been _____.

PRACTICE TEST [1-2]

Mary   _____ these pants, Sabrina? This is the new _____.

Sabrina   I like them, Mary. They look kind of funky. Look at all those _____

_____.

Mary   I think they will _____ my T-shirts.

Sabrina   Do they have them _____

_____?

Mary   Yes, they do, but they _____

_____ in certain colors because _____

_____.

Sabrina   Maybe they are _____ because it's a very popular size.

Mary   _____. Why don't you find out?

Sabrina   I think I will.

PRACTICE TEST [3-4]

W   Is that your new shirt?

M   Yes, I bought this shirt two days ago, but I think it is _____ for me. _____?

W   I am sorry to say this, but it is small. I noticed that from _____ of the street. Why did you get one so small?

M   I don't know. This is _____, fifty-two. But I think I've _____ _____ lately.

W   Maybe you should either _____ _____ or _____.

M   I cannot exchange this because they don't have it _____.

W   Then, you have _____, right?

PRACTICE TEST [5-6]

W   Hi, do you need alterations?

M   Yes. I need to have these _____

_____ at the bottom. Can you do it by this afternoon?

W   _____. We have a lot of work today. I can _____ by tomorrow, though.

M   I have a date tonight, and _____

_____. Could you do _____, then?

W   Well, then. I'll do just one pair. _____

_____ so that I can _____?

M   Thanks, where is the _____?

W   Go _____.

PRACTICE TEST [7-8]

Kim   _____ her bag?

Sally   Ugh, that is totally _____. _____ I saw one of those?

Kim   The leather is all _____. I think she's had that bag _____.

Sally   And, look at the buckle. It is so huge. I think _____ a new one.

Kim   Speaking of bags, I need a new purse.

Sally   OK, let's _____. But why don't we _____?

Kim   _____.

PRACTICE TEST [9-10]

Even _____ buying bags, the difference between _____ shows. Even though men consider bags as something you carry _____ in, women consider them as an _____ _____ just like _____, _____, or shoes. That is why women sometimes buy bags _____ or too expensive just _____.

"Clothes make the man."

The way you dress tells people something about you, and can influence

their opinion of you.

UNIT 13 You're always on the Internet!

GETTING READY

A   Read the conversation below and fill in the blanks.

- email you
- usually
- Internet addiction
- homepage
- surf the net
- post
- address
- searches
- email
- chat

Sam   It seems like you're always using the Internet.

Amy   I use the Internet a lot because it's fun and useful.

Sam   What do you _____ do on the Internet? I only use it for _____ and to check _____.

Amy   Well, I _____, read the latest news, and do Internet shopping. But, I also like to _____ with my friends.

Sam   What about blogging? Do you have a _____?

Amy   Yes. I have a nice blog. Almost every day, I _____ the poems I like. I'll _____ my homepage _____ so you can visit it later.

Sam   Amy, I hate to say this, but I think you're spending too much time on the Internet.

Amy   Hmm... Maybe you're right. I should go online and find out what the symptoms of _____ are.

Sam   Oh, no! There you go again!

B   Match the words on the left with the definitions on the right.

(1) Bookmark   •   • (a) An unwanted advertisement letter that is sent to many people

(2) Server   •   • (b) A place where you can have a conversation online through text messaging

(3) Chat room   •   • (c) A service that enables you to pay your bills over the Internet.

(4) Internet banking •   • (d) A list of the addresses of Internet pages that you can click on to find the addresses more easily in the future.

(5) Junk mail   •   • (e) The main computer that controls all the others on a network

Listening Task

Listening 1

Listen to the dialog and answer the question.

1 What is this conversation about?
   a. Problems with the Internet connection
   b. The history of the Internet
   c. A tip for an effective Internet search
   d. How to get information from a friend

Listen again and check True or False.

	True	False
2 A. Cindy doesn't know how to use the Internet at all.	☐	☐
B. Ted is suggesting to Cindy that she type in more specific keywords.	☐	☐

Listening 2

Listen to the dialog and answer the question.

1 What is the advantage of buying things over the Internet?
   a. The ease
   b. Lower price
   c. Fast delivery
   d. Better products

Listen again and answer the question.

2 When did the man order the Star wars Series DVDs?
   a. Yesterday
   b. Two days ago
   c. Three days ago
   d. A week ago

Listen to the two summaries and choose the best one.

3 a. ☐   b. ☐

Listening Task  Narrative

Answers p. 62

Listening 3

Listen to the narrative and answer the question.

1　What recommendations does the speaker make about using email?
　　a. You should not spend a lot of money.
　　b. You should use the email service more often.
　　c. You should not use email service.
　　d. You should be careful when using email.

Listen again and answer the question.

2　According to the passage, what is the disadvantage of email service?
　　a. It is very costly.
　　b. Messages cannot be sent instantly.
　　c. You can get junk mail or viruses.
　　d. Attaching files is not easy.

Listening 4

Listen to the narrative and answer the question.

1　How many symptoms of Internet addiction were discussed in this passage?
　　a. Three　　　　　　　　　　b. Four
　　c. Five　　　　　　　　　　 d. Six

Listen again and answer the question.

2　What is <u>not</u> a symptom of Internet addiction?
　　a. You spend too much money on your computer.
　　b. You often eat in front of your computer.
　　c. You spend less time outdoors.
　　d. You use the Internet too much.

Listen to the two summaries and choose the best one.

3　a. ☐　　　　　　　　　　b. ☐

[1-2] Listen to the dialog and answer the questions.

1   What are they talking about?
   a. Exchanging email
   b. Blind dating on the Internet
   c. Internet chatting
   d. Their best friend's homepage

2   What is true about Lindsey's friend?
   a. She chats with Lindsey once a week.
   b. She stayed in the United States for about six months.
   c. She lived by herself when she was in the United States.
   d. She is living in Austria now.

[3-4] Listen to the dialog and answer the questions.

3   What is the main topic of this conversation?
   a. Misuse of the Internet
   b. New ways to download songs and pictures
   c. Sandy Hilton's secret marriage
   d. How to see pictures on the Internet

4   What did Gina find on the Internet?
   a. Sally Hilton's wedding photos
   b. Songs written by Sally Hilton
   c. Sally Hilton's past movies
   d. Sally Hilton's kids' photos

[5-6] Listen to the dialog and answer the questions.

5   Why couldn't Michael log onto the Internet at first?
   a. Because his computer was too old
   b. Because the server was down
   c. Because too many people were logged onto the Internet
   d. Because the school shut down its server

6 What will Michael do next?
   a. He will ask Kate to figure out the problem.
   b. He will try another site.
   c. He and Kate will fix his computer.
   d. He will wait for the school server to be up again.

[7-8] Listen to the dialog and answer the questions.

7 What is <u>not</u> a proper response to the last thing that the man said?

> Woman _____

   a. No way!   b. No problem.
   c. My pleasure.   d. You're welcome.

8 What is the man's problem?
   a. He doesn't know how to bookmark his favorite websites.
   b. He can't quickly find what he wants from his bookmark list.
   c. He doesn't know which dictionary to use.
   d. He is not good at typing on the keyboard.

[9-10] Listen to the narrative and answer the questions.

9 What is the speaker's attitude toward the Internet?
   a. Approving   b. Indifferent
   c. Negative   d. Disappointed

10 What is <u>not</u> one of the advantages of the Internet?
   a. File exchange is easy.
   b. Bank accounts can be checked from home.
   c. You can order without seeing the merchandise.
   d. Information gathering is easy.

Listening 1

Ted Do you _____, Cindy?

Cindy Yes, Ted. Whenever I _____, I get _____.

Ted I think you need to learn _____ your search with _____

_____.

Cindy How do you do that?

Ted For example, if you want to know _____, instead of _____ just "Internet," try "Internet history." In that way, you will get the information _____ the history of the Internet only.

Cindy _____.

Listening 2

M I wonder _____.

W What are you talking about?

M I _____ Star Wars Series DVDs through the Internet _____ _____, but they're _____.

W Why didn't you get them _____?

M Because they're _____ from an _____. But they're 60 dollars at local stores.

W That is a big difference, but I wouldn't _____.

M That's why you should _____.

W   I see.

Listening 3

_____ the Internet can provide, email service may be _____ _____. It saves _____ for many people. But, email service can give you _____ or a _____. If you get _____ _____, it is very difficult to find your important mail. If you get a virus, your _____ or the contents in it may _____. So enjoy using email, but _____ at the same time.

Listening 4

These are the symptoms of _____. First, you must use the Internet every day, otherwise you _____. Second, you _____ when you use the Internet. Third, you don't _____. Fourth, you _____ _____ too many times a day. _____, you frequently eat _____ _____. The more symptoms you have, _____ you might be.

PRACTICE TEST [1-2]

Morris   What are you doing, Lindsey?

Lindsey   I am _____ a friend in
_____. She came to the United
States three years ago as _____
_____ and she lived with us _____
_____.

Morris   _____ do you guys chat?

Lindsey   Almost every day. I think I chat _____
_____ than _____
_____ here.

Morris   I chat with my brother in New York, but
we only chat _____.

PRACTICE TEST [3-4]

John   Gina, _____ the movie
actress, Sandy Hilton? She _____
and has two kids.

Gina   I know. I even saw _____
on the Internet.

John   Really? How could anyone _____
such _____ on the
Internet?

Gina   I know! The Internet is great, but so
many people are _____.

John   You're right. _____ copyrighted
materials illegally is _____
_____ with the Internet.

Gina   You mean, _____ songs or
pictures?

PRACTICE TEST [5-6]

Michael   Ugh, _____.

Kate   What is the problem, Michael?

Michael   I cannot _____.
I think it's because too many people
_____. Wait, I can log
in now.

Kate   _____.

Michael   Ugh! What is it now? I can't _____
_____.

Kate   It looks like _____
_____.

Michael   Yeah. The school server is too small, so
it _____ too often
these days.

Kate   I think you _____.

PRACTICE TEST [7-8]

M   Do you remember _____
_____ the online dictionary?

W   Yes, it is www.nexdictionary.com.

M   That's right. _____.

W   Why don't you _____?

M   Because I have so many things in my
bookmarks already, _____
_____ anything _____.
It is faster _____.

W   That is _____
how to _____ your bookmarks. Let
me show you _____.

M   Thanks.

PRACTICE TEST [9-10]

These are _____ of how the Internet
has changed _____. People can easily
_____ from their
computers. You can _____
information, the latest news, and the _____
_____ from anywhere at anytime. Any
hard-to-find merchandise _____
from any store _____. Almost any
information you can think of is _____
_____.

"Experience is the mother of wisdom."

You become wiser as you gain more experience in life.

GETTING READY

Answers p. 67

A   Read the conversation below and fill in the blanks.

• mass
  transportation
• turn off
• reusing
• garage sale
• recycling
• other products
• pull out
• energy saving
• the
  environment
• gas
  consumption

Teacher   Today, let's talk about the environment. Is there anything you can do to protect _____ ?

Julia   We can sort cans, paper, and bottles.

Teacher   All right. They will be turned into _____ . We call it _____ . Anyone else?

Tony   My mom always says, "_____ the lights, turn off the water, and _____ the plugs from all electrical products when you're not using them."

Teacher   _____ is a good way of protecting the environment. Another way of protecting the environment is to use more _____ . It causes less _____ and less air pollution. Anything else?

John   What about _____ , sir?

Teacher   Like what for example?

John   Like a _____ – My brother and I sold clothes, toys, and books that we used when we were young.

Teacher   Great. They can be very good items for other kids, too.

B   What can you do to protect the environment? Talk about it with your friends.

[A] (1) unplug any electrical appliance when it's not in use
    (2) use fans instead of air-conditioners
    (3) throw food waste into the flower garden
    (4) recycle newspapers, aluminum cans, and bottles
    (5) avoid using hair spray
    (6) walk or bike to school instead of driving
    (7) turn water off while brushing my teeth

[B] (a) to avoid too much waste
    (b) to make less pollution
    (c) to save energy

◁))   I <u>[A]
unplug any electrical appliance when it's not in use</u> <u>[B]
to save energy.</u>

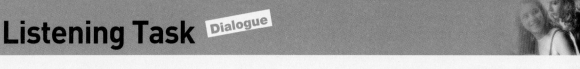

Listening Task `Dialogue`

Listening 1

Listen to the dialog and answer the question.

1   What is the main topic of this conversation?
    a. Traffic jam
    b. Air pollution
    c. Noise pollution
    d. Energy shortage

Listen again and check True or False.

2   A. Fiona won't jog today because of the smog.
    B. Using mass transportation increases air pollution such as smog.

	True	False
A	☐	☐
B	☐	☐

Listening 2

Listen to the dialog and answer the question.

1   Where is this conversation taking place?
    a. In a classroom
    b. In a market place
    c. In a hardware store
    d. In a recycling center

Listen again and answer the question.

2   What is the total poundage of the cans and bottles the girl brought?
    a. 2 pounds   b. 4 pounds
    c. 5 pounds   d. 6 pounds

Listen to the two summaries and choose the best one.

3   a. ☐   b. ☐

Listening Task ^{Narrative}

Answers p. 67

Listening 3

Listen to the narrative and answer the question.

1 What is the main purpose of this passage?
  a. To get members for a study group
  b. To raise money for the environment
  c. To advertise an environmental club
  d. To campaign for collecting things

Listen again and answer the question.

2 How often will they meet?
  a. Once a week   b. Once a month
  c. Every day after school   d. Unknown

Listening 4

Listen to the narrative and answer the question.

1 What is this passage about?
  a. Importance of energy   b. Concerns about waste
  c. Tips for protecting the environment   d. Environmental issues worldwide

Listen again and answer the question.

2 What is <u>not</u> mentioned as a way of helping the environment?

     a.   b.   c.   d.

Listen to the two summaries and choose the best one.

3   a. ☐   b. ☐

[1-2] Listen to the dialog and answer the questions.

1 What is the main idea of this conversation?
   a. We must learn how to throw away paper properly.
   b. Some energy comes from trees.
   c. It is the law that you must use both sides of paper.
   d. Less use of paper is a way to save energy and protect the environment.

2 What is the proverb that fits the situation?
   a. Experience is the best teacher.
   b. As you sow, so shall you reap.
   c. Many drops make a shower.
   d. Where there is a will, there is a way.

[3-4] Listen to the narrative and answer the questions.

3 What is the main idea of this passage?
   a. Protecting the environment must start from the government.
   b. Protecting the environment is an easy task.
   c. We must not pollute the environment for the future's sake.
   d. We should take action to protect the environment.

4 Which of the following words should go in the blank?

   The speaker feels _____ about people's attitude toward the environment.

   a. content   b. critical
   c. indifferent   d. positive

[5-6] Listen to the dialog and answer the questions.

5 What is the main idea of this conversation?
   a. We need to save electricity.
   b. We need to reduce air pollution.
   c. We need to find new sources of energy.
   d. We must not use oil because it causes pollution.

6 What <u>cannot</u> be considered as a future source of energy?
   a. Oil
   b. The sun's energy
   c. Wind
   d. Sea waves

[7-8] Listen to the dialog and answer the questions.

7 What is the picture that best describes the situation?

 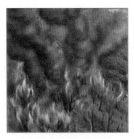  

     a.   b.   c.   d.

8 how long will it take for the environment to recover from the disaster?
   a. Several years
   b. 3,000 years
   c. Several decades
   d. 30,000 years

[9-10] Listen to the narrative and answer the questions.

9 What is the main topic of this passage?
   a. The importance of conserving water
   b. The importance of flood control
   c. Ways to conserve water
   d. The seriousness of sea pollution

10 What percent of the earth's water is usable freshwater?
   a. 70%
   b. 97%
   c. 2%
   d. Less than 1%

🎧 Listen and fill in the blanks.

Answers p. 71

Listening 1

Victor   Look, Fiona. _____.

Fiona   _____. I don't think I want to jog today.

Victor   Good thinking. _____ on a day like this is _____.

Fiona   There should be _____, and cars should be smaller in size. Smaller cars _____.

Victor   I believe that _____ is an even better way to reduce smog.

Fiona   I think you're right. It will also help solve some of _____ _____.

Listening 2

Daisy   _____ some aluminum cans _____.

Man   You have four pounds of aluminum cans and two pounds of plastic bottles. I _____.

Daisy   Thanks. By the way, _____?

Man   _____ to other companies. They will _____ new cans and bottles.

Daisy   Great.

Man   _____ the environment. So tell your friends _____ empty cans and bottles. They can _____ at the same time, right?

Listening 3

Our school will be _____. The purpose of our club is to _____ and _____. We will collect recyclable materials and _____ environmental protection. We will also _____ for the club and _____ environmental _____. The club will meet every Monday _____ in the auditorium. Anyone who is _____ is welcome.

Listening 4

There are _____ to help the environment. One thing you can do is _____ by turning off lights and unplugging _____ when _____. You can save water _____ or _____ _____ while brushing your teeth. You can try to _____ by using mass transportation such as buses or subways. Finally, _____. Newspaper, cans and bottles are good _____.

114

PRACTICE TEST [1-2]

Jack   Stop! Are you _____ that piece of paper?

Ken   Yes. It has _____ on the front.

Jack   You can use _____.

Ken   Well, I _____ the back of paper.

Jack   You are _____ _____ by writing on the back of paper and you are protecting the environment, too.

Ken   One sheet of paper will not _____ _____.

Jack   Yes, it will. _____.

PRACTICE TEST [3-4]

_____ for the environment is more important than just _____ doing something. Everyone wants _____, but the streets are littered with cigarette butts, _____ _____, and _____. Even though people know that mass transportation _____, most people _____ _____ their own cars. Furthermore, _____ the importance of recycling? Nonetheless, how many people actually recycle? So, if you really care about the environment, _____.

PRACTICE TEST [5-6]

Teacher   One of these days, we will _____. Then, we will _____ use cars or gas burning heaters. Therefore, let's talk about _____ _____.

PRACTICE TEST

John   I think we should _____ _____. We can _____ _____ into electricity and _____ _____ for later use.

Teacher   That is very good, John. We can also consider _____ as other sources of energy in the future.

PRACTICE TEST [7-8]

Andrea   Did you see _____ _____?

Bryan   Yes. I heard that it was caused _____ _____. The _____ of the forest.

Andrea   One big fire like this will _____ _____ of an area for a long time. Imagine how long it will take for the _____ and the animals _____. It will _____ _____.

Bryan   I think one of the ways to conserve the environment is to _____ _____.

PRACTICE TEST [9-10]

_____ of the earth _____. But, more than 97% of _____ is saltwater and _____ is frozen ice. Of all the water on earth, _____ is usable freshwater. However, even this little amount _____. Therefore, we must learn to _____ it properly. Otherwise, we will have _____ _____.

"Habit is second nature."

The things you do regularly reveal who you are.

UNIT 15

I'm checking ads for used cars.

Answers p. 72

GETTING READY

A Read the conversation below and fill in the blanks.

- apply
- check out
- a clearance sale
- part-time
- big help
- house-for-rent
- bulletin board
- can't afford
- next semester
- contact number

John   Hey, Meg. What are you reading?

Meg   Actually, I'm checking the _____ ads in the newspaper. I need a place to stay during _____ _____.

John   Have you found any place nice?

Meg   Yes, but I'm afraid I _____ it.

John   How about having a _____ job at the school cafeteria for the summer? I saw an advertisement for a part-time server on the _____.

Meg   Oh, really? That's great! How do I _____?

John   Here's the _____. Why don't you ask them directly? By the way, if you need any furniture, _____ this flyer. A furniture store near our school is holding _____.

Meg   Thank you, John. You're a _____.

B What is the woman doing? Talk about it with your friends.

[A] a TV commercial
   a flyer
   an advertising poster
   a newspaper advertisement

[B] a new car
   a new movie
   a flea market
   a new shopping center

◁)) The woman is looking at <u>a TV commercial</u> [A]. It is advertising <u>a new car</u> [B].

Listening 1

Listen to the dialog and answer the question.

1 What are they doing?
    a. They are discussing how to make a for-sale ad for a used bike.
    b. They are trying to buy a used bike.
    c. They are shopping for a new bike at a bike shop.
    d. They are reading an ad for a used bike on a bulletin board.

Listen again and check True or False.

		True	False
2	A. Daisy is trying to get a new bicycle for Peter.	☐	☐
	B. Daisy will post an ad which will have a photo of the bike.	☐	☐

Listening 2

Listen to the dialog and answer the question.

1 Where did they find out about the sale?

    a.   b.   c.   d.

Listen again and answer the question.

2 What is true about the sale?
    a. Books – 10% off   b. CDs – 5% off
    c. Magazines – 15 % off   d. With a membership card – always 5 % off

---

Listen to the two summaries and choose the best one.

3 a. ☐   b. ☐

Listening Task

Answers p. 72

Listening 3

Listen to the narrative and answer the question.

1 What is this advertisement for?
a. A summer camp is looking for applicants.
b. A hospital is looking for experienced doctors.
c. A university in Chicago is looking for medical students.
d. A hospital is looking for applicants for summer internship positions.

Listen again and answer the question.

2 What is a requirement for the applicants?
a. Experience in the medical field   b. Age of applicant at least 18
c. Grade point average of B or better   d. A recommendation letter

Listening 4

Listen to the narrative and answer the question.

1 How often do they have the bike tour?
a. Once a year
b. Twice a year
c. Every other month
d. Once a month

Listen again and answer the question.

2 What is not true about the trip?
a. It is a bicycle tour.
b. The entire trip will cover about 500 miles.
c. The trip will start in San Diego.
d. The trip will cover 50 miles a day.

Listen to the two summaries and choose the best one.

3 a. ☐   b. ☐

[1-2] Listen to the dialog and answer the questions.

1 Why did Dorothy buy the exercise machines?
   a. Because she collects exercise machines.
   b. Because the machines were on sale.
   c. Because she thought a new machine would help her exercise more.
   d. Because she exercises a lot.

2 What did Edward advise Dorothy to do when buying things?
   a. Dorothy should think carefully before buying things.
   b. Dorothy should ask Edward first.
   c. Dorothy should order an exercise machine on the Internet.
   d. Dorothy should stop ordering things on TV.

[3-4] Listen to the dialog and answer the questions.

3 What will they do first?
   a. They will buy a different newspaper to check for more ads.
   b. They will use the rental agency.
   c. They will put an ad in the rental agency.
   d. They will check the ads they found in the newspaper and on the Internet.

4 What is a source not mentioned in the conversation?
   a. Newspapers
   b. Flyers
   c. The Internet
   d. A rental agency

[5-6] Listen to the narrative and answer the questions.

5 What is the main topic of this passage?
   a. The most effective way to advertise
   b. Different opinions regarding the use of celebrities in advertisements
   c. Advantages and disadvantages of advertisements
   d. Different types of advertisement

6   According to the passage, advertisements with celebrities will _____.
    a. make the price of the products more expensive
    b. help people to buy the right product
    c. Create best-selling products because people like celebrities
    d. have no information about products at all

[7-8] Listen to the dialog and answer the questions.

7   Why did the man say "Indeed?"
    a. Because he has a different opinion from Sunny's
    b. Because he doesn't understand what Sunny has said
    c. Because he doesn't want to tell his opinion
    d. Because he agrees with what Sunny has said

8   What are they talking about?
    a. Why smoking is harmful
    b. Anti-smoking campaigns' effectiveness
    c. How non-smokers start smoking
    d. Smoking areas in public places

[9-10] Listen to the narrative and answer the questions.

9   According to the passage, what is the best way to advertise?
    a. TV ads
    b. Newspaper ads
    c. Word-of-mouth
    d. Advertising signs

10 What is not needed for a good word-of-mouth advertisement?
    a. Good quality products
    b. Money
    c. Satisfied customers
    d. Good service

Listening Task

🎧 Listen and fill in the blanks.

Answers p. 76

Listening 1

Daisy   Peter, _____ my old bicycle. Do you have any ideas _____?

Peter   Why don't you _____ on the school's _____?

Daisy   Why didn't I think of that? But what kind of information _____?

Peter   You should tell _____, _____, and the price.

Daisy   OK. Anything else?

Peter   Oh, Daisy, don't forget to _____.

Daisy   Right. Should I _____?

Peter   That's a good idea.

Listening 2

Jessica   _____, Calvin?

Calvin   Look at this flyer. The new bookstore is holding _____.

Jessica   Is there _____?

Calvin   All the magazines are 10% off, and _____. If you have a _____, you can always _____.

Jessica   That's great. Anything else?

Calvin   Oh, CDs are 30% off, too.

Jessica   _____?

Calvin   It ends this Sunday.

Jessica   _____ go to the sale this Saturday?

Calvin   That's a great idea.

Listening 3

The Chicago Hospital is offering _____ to students who are interested in the _____. The applicants must be _____. Although _____, applicants must have achieved _____ _____ of B or better. Pay is six dollars to eight dollars an hour. Several different positions are _____. Anyone who is interested must email an _____ by _____.

Listening 4

Summer is _____. Do you want to make this summer _____ _____ of your life? If so, _____ California Coast Bike Tour. This _____ will last 2 weeks. _____ San Diego and _____ San Francisco. During the trip, you will be biking about _____, and viewing the coastal cities along _____ of California. _____, call us.

122

PRACTICE TEST [1-2]

Edward Dorothy, you have a lot of exercise machines. I didn't know _____ _____.

Dorothy Actually, Edward, I _____ any of the machines for a long time.

Edward Then, why _____?

Dorothy Because whenever I see a new exercise machine _____, I feel that the new machine will _____ _____ than I do now. But, _____ _____, I don't use it.

Edward You should _____ before you buy things.

Dorothy I think you're right.

PRACTICE TEST [3-4]

Leslie Rachel, _____ yet?

Rachel I found this room in the newspaper, and on the Internet, I found two places _____. _____?

Leslie I found a rental agency which has hundreds of _____.

Rachel Did you check any of their ads?

Leslie No, there was a fee _____ _____. Let's check _____ first, and if we don't like them, then we can use _____.

Rachel Good.

PRACTICE TEST [5-6]

Advertisements provide _____ _____ products, but they also can _____ _____ of products. A good example may be advertisements _____ _____. When people buy a product because _____ in the advertisements, they are just buying the image of the celebrity, not _____. Also, the cost of the advertisements increases _____ _____.

PRACTICE TEST [7-8]

Henry Sunny, did you see the _____ _____ on TV?

Sunny Yes, I saw them. Smoking is really a _____.

Henry _____ people are campaigning _____, such as on cigarette boxes.

Sunny _____?

Henry Yes. According to _____, anti-smoking advertisements are very effective in _____ from starting to smoke.

Sunny Then, _____ more advertisements about not smoking.

Henry _____.

PRACTICE TEST [9-10]

Even though TV and newspaper ads are _____ _____ way to advertise, they are very _____. That is why many people believe _____ is the best way to advertise. This cost-free advertisement relies on _____ _____ about their products or _____. Therefore, for a successful _____ advertisement, it is important to give _____ _____ and services to _____. Otherwise, people will advertise _____ the product or the service is.

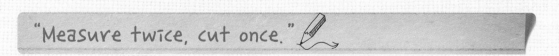

"Measure twice, cut once."

Consider your options carefully in order to make a good decision.

16 I've bought an MP3 player!

GETTING READY

Answers p. 77

A   Read the conversation below and fill in the blanks.

- replacing
- medical field
- MP3 players
- will change
- without
- for example
- impossible
- has been invented
- interested in
- equipment

Julia   What are you doing, Matthew?

Matthew   I am reading an article about a new technology in the _____. _____ which will help doctors during difficult surgeries _____.

Julia   I always see you reading science magazines. You must be _____ science.

Matthew   Yeah, I like anything that is related to new technology. Technology has made many things that seemed _____ in the past possible. Take a microwave oven _____. Isn't it amazing that we can cook _____ using fire?

Julia   How about digital cameras and _____? They don't need films or CDs at all! They are quickly _____ analog cameras and CD players.

Matthew   At the rate new technologies are emerging, I can't imagine how our lives _____ in the next 30 years.

B   What do you have? Talk about it with your friends.

[A] LCD monitor   MP3 player   laser printer   digital camera

[B] it takes less time printing out   I can check the photos I took right away
     it doesn't take much space on my desk   I don't have to carry around any CDs

◁))   I got a new MP3 player [A] as a gift.

I like it because I don't have to carry around any CDs. [B]

 Listening 1

Listen to the dialog and answer the question.

1 Which product was used twenty years ago?

a.   b.   c.    d.

Listen again and check True or False.

	True	False

2 A. The microwave oven has been used for more than 30 years.
  B. They are talking about things that will be available in 20 years.

 Listening 2

Listen to the dialog and answer the question.

1 What does wendy mean by her last response?
  a. She still can't understand why digital cameras are good.
  b. She prefers analog cameras.
  c. She doesn't understand what Bob is talking about.
  d. She understands why people like digital cameras.

Listen again and answer the question.

2 What is true about the conversation?
  a. Bob has a digital camera.
  b. Bob is going to buy a digital camera.
  c. Wendy is recommending a digital camera to Bob.
  d. Wendy is showing Bob her digital camera.

Listen to the two summaries and choose the best one.

3 a. ☐   b. ☐

Listening Task Narrative

● Listening 3

Listen to the narrative and answer the question.

1 What is the main topic of this passage?
   a. Things Edison invented
   b. Advantages of MP3 players
   c. Development of sound storing technology
   d. Comparison of CDs and MP3 players

Listen again and answer the question.

2 What did Edison use first to save sound?
   a. LPs
   b. Cylinders
   c. Cassette tapes
   d. CDs

● Listening 4

Listen to the narrative and answer the question.

1 What is the speaker talking about?
   a. Machines that will appear in the future
   b. How advancements in technology affect people at work
   c. An increase in jobs because of technology
   d. Machines that help people's work

Listen again and answer the question.

2 What is the speaker's attitude toward advancements in technology?
   a. Positive
   b. Negative
   c. Indifferent
   d. Concerned

Listen to the two summaries and choose the best one.

3 a. ☐   b. ☐

[1-2] Listen to the dialog and answer the questions.

1 What is this conversation about?
   a. Things they will buy soon.
   b. Things they read from a news article.
   c. Things they wish they had.
   d. None of the above

2 Where are the speakers?
   a. In a car
   b. In a classroom
   c. At a restaurant
   d. In a bank

[3-4] Listen to the narrative and answer the questions.

3 Where did Frank find out about the history of airplanes?
   a. From a book about airplanes
   b. From a TV program he saw last night
   c. From a history class
   d. From an article he read

4 What is <u>not</u> mentioned in the conversation?

   a.   b.   c.   d.

[5-6] Listen to the dialog and answer the questions.

5 What is the man's attitude regarding so many computer graphics being in the movie?
   a. Not satisfied
   b. Angry
   c. Disappointed
   d. Surprised

6 What part of the movie was <u>not</u> a computer graphic?
   a. Battle scenes   b. Castles
   c. Actors   d. Boats

[7-8] Listen to the dialog and answer the questions.

7 What is the relationship between the speakers?
   a. A salesperson and a customer
   b. A father and his daughter
   c. A teacher and his student
   d. An engineer and his co-worker

8 What is <u>not</u> true about the conversation?
   a. By the 50s, lasers were used in many places.
   b. Albert Einstein first theorized laser.
   c. Some hospital equipment use laser technology.
   d. Laser is used in many areas these days.

[9-10] Listen to the narrative and answer the questions.

9 What is the speaker talking about?
   a. Robots in science fiction movies
   b. Patients who need difficult surgeries
   c. Machines used in the hospital
   d. New technologies in the medical field

10 According to the passage, what is <u>not</u> the thing possible in the future?
   a. Patients will be able to have mechanical body parts.
   b. Robots will be used in surgeries.
   c. More diseases will be cured by new drugs.
   d. People will not have to take drugs at all.

Listening 1

Teacher   Today let's talk about things _____ used _____ _____.

Student   Back then, I don't think we had _____ and _____.

Teacher   That is right. _____?

Student   How about LCD monitors and _____?

Teacher   Well, we did not have LCD monitors twenty years ago, but microwave ovens _____ for more than _____.

Student   Really? I didn't know that.

Listening 2

Bob   Wendy, take a look at my _____.

Wendy   _____ these days. What is the big deal about digital cameras, Bob?

Bob   Well, they _____ that analog cameras don't. They don't need film, and you can _____.

Wendy   Oh yeah, I always have to wait until the film is _____.

Bob   Furthermore, you can _____ to your computer and _____ _____ to others by email easily.

Wendy   _____ everybody _____ one.

Listening 3

_____, Edison invented _____ on a cylinder. Since then, _____ _____ have been invented, _____ LPs, cassette tapes, CDs, and MP3 files. The CD, which stands for _____, is an important milestone in sound storing methods because _____ to store sound _____. Now, with MP3 players, _____ can be stored and played with a device _____ a cigarette box.

Listening 4

Because _____ have rapidly been replacing _____, some people worry that there will be _____ for people in the future. However, others believe that technology will provide us _____. Although nobody knows how the future will _____, people's _____ has gone up as a result of _____. Therefore, it seems unnecessary to worry too much about _____.

PRACTICE TEST [1-2]

Jake The traffic is very bad. _____ _____ if we had cars that could fly? Then, we wouldn't have to _____ _____.

Celina That would be nice, but _____ a machine that could _____ _____. Then, I wouldn't have to worry about my French homework.

Jake Do you know what would be really nice — a _____ that could cook _____ _____.

Celina That is another great idea. Do you really think _____ all these things?

Jake Someday, I hope.

PRACTICE TEST [3-4]

Bessie What are you reading, Frank?

Frank Hey, Bessie. I am _____ _____ the history of airplanes. According to the article, people _____ _____ and gliders more than a hundred years before the _____ _____ was invented.

Bessie When was the first airplane _____?

Frank In _____, but it could only fly for a very _____. Yet, by 1947, people could fly faster than _____ _____, and today's space shuttles can fly _____ than the speed of sound.

Bessie That is _____!

PRACTICE TEST [5-6]

W Did you see the movie *Troy*?

M Yes, I did. It was a great movie.

W But, did you know that _____ _____ in the movie were _____?

M _____! They looked so real.

W And most of the boats and the _____ _____ were _____, too.

M Wow, that is amazing. That means, one of these days, _____ can be made with out _____.

W I am sure those days are not too _____ _____.

PRACTICE TEST [7-8]

Teacher Class, do you know who first theorized the laser?

Student _____, sir.

Teacher It was Albert Einstein in 1917, but the first laser was _____.

Student What happened?

Teacher Well, technology that is worth having takes time _____ something useful. Now, you see _____ _____ everywhere. Can you _____ that use the laser?

Student I heard that CD players, _____, and some _____ use laser technology.

PRACTICE TEST [9-10]

Of all the different fields, the _____ has been affected the most by _____ _____. Newly invented medical equipment has made _____ less difficult, while new drugs _____ _____. In the near future, small robots will _____ and fix medical problems just like _____ _____. People will also _____ _____ with mechanical parts, so that they can live _____.

"Practice makes perfect!"

The more you practice, the better you become at anything.

7단계로 필수 어휘를 정복한다!

예비 중학생부터 각종 시험을 준비하는 수험생에 이르기까지
단계별 학습이 가능한 체계적인 어휘 교재

- 기본 필수 어휘와 더불어 단계마다 테마별, Phrasal verb, 숙어, 다의어, 어근 등의 다양한 어휘 클러스터링 제공

- 각 단어마다 유용한 Collocation 또는 Sentence를 붙여 단어를 효율적으로 외울 수 있도록 구성

- 연계 학습을 통해 각 단어와 관련된 파생어 학습

- Exercise → Review Test → Accumulative Test로 이어지는 단계적 테스트를 통해 효과적인 어휘 학습 유도

- 학습한 단어를 음성으로 복습할 수 있도록 MP3 파일 무료 다운로드 제공(www.nexusEDU.kr)

- 온라인(www.nexusEDU.kr) 리뷰 테스트 제공

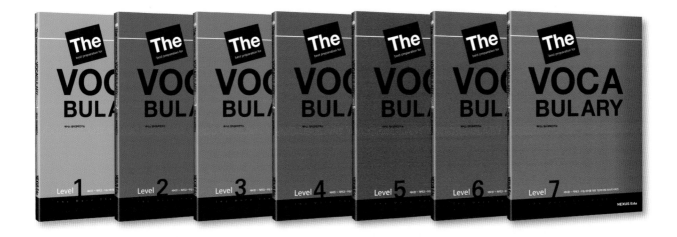

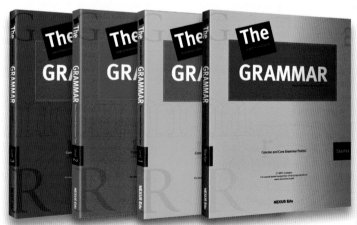
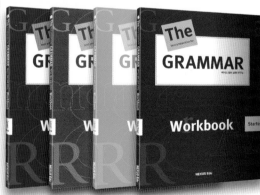

The More The Better

The
best preparation for

LISTENING

Answers

Nexus Contents Development Team · Cedric S. Kim

Integrated Approach to Listening Comprehension

The more language structures are presented,
the better language awareness is improved.

www.nexusbook.com / www.nexusEDU.kr
MP3 Free Download

3
Level

NEXUS Edu

The best preparation for
LISTENING

Answers

Nexus Contents Development Team · Cedric S. Kim

3
Level

NEXUS Edu

UNIT 1
I'm into gardening.

Listening Task   p. 6~7

Listening 1   1. d   2. A. F   B. F
Listening 2   1. c   2. a   3. a
Listening 3   1. b   2. c
Listening 4   1. a   2. b   3. b

Getting Ready   p. 5

A

like, Since when, interested in, How often, spend, all my Sundays, collect, collection, post, recipes, in common

B

• My hobby is gardening. I like spending my time growing flowers.
• My hobby is taking pictures. I like spending my time taking pictures of my family.
• My hobby is scuba diving. I like spending my time watching fish in the sea.

A 아래 대화를 읽고 빈칸을 완성하시오.

공통으로, (시간을) 쓰다, 요리법, ~에 흥미를 갖는, 얼마나 자주, 모든 일요일, 수집하다, 좋아하다, 수집(물), 올리다(게시하다), 언제부터

Andrew 네 취미는 뭐야, Helen?

Helen 나는 쿠키를 만드는 것을 좋아해.

Andrew 언제부터 해 왔는데?

Helen 어릴 때부터 엄마가 쿠키 만드는 것을 도왔어. 그렇게 해서 (쿠키 만드는 데에) 관심을 갖게 된 것 같아.

Andrew 얼마나 자주 쿠키를 만들어?

Helen 거의 매 일요일마다 쿠키를 만들어. 그런데 네 취미는 뭐니, Andrew?

Andrew 나는 전 세계의 자동차 미니어처를 모아. 네 살 때부터 모아 왔어.

Helen 정말? 그 미니어처로 뭘 하는데?

Andrew 새로운 차를 내 수집품에 추가할 때마다 그 사진을 찍어서 내 블로그에 올려.

Helen 나도. 나는 내 블로그에 쿠키 사진과 요리법을 많이 올려 놓았어.

Andrew 그럼 우린 적어도 한 가지 취미를 공통으로 가진 셈이네.

B 당신의 취미는 무엇인가? 친구들과 이야기해 보시오.

[A] 사진 찍기, 스쿠버 다이빙, 등산, 정원 가꾸기
[B] 바다에서 물고기를 보며, 가족들의 사진을 찍으며, 꽃을 키우며, 숲 속을 산책하며

◁))) 내 취미는 [A]등산이다. 나는 [B]숲 속을 산책하며 시간을 보내는 것을 좋아한다.

Listening 1   p. 6

다음 대화를 듣고 질문에 답하시오.

스크립트

Philip Wow, look at all these frogs. Why do you have so many frogs, Susan?

Susan I collect anything that has to do with frogs, Philip.

Philip Why just frogs?

Susan My parents got me a little pink frog doll when I was ten. Since then, I have been collecting frog dolls, ashtrays, pictures... You name it.

Philip Where did you get all these?

Susan I bought some, but many were given to me by others.

Philip I think you could open a museum with this collection.

해석

Philip 와, 이 개구리들 좀 봐. 왜 이렇게 개구리를 많이 가지고 있어, Susan?

Susan 난 개구리와 관련된 것은 무엇이나 다 수집해, Philip.

Philip 왜 개구리만 모으는데?

Susan 내가 열 살 때 부모님이 나에게 작은 분홍색 개구리 인형을 주셨는데, 그때부터 개구리 인형, 재떨이, 사진 등을 모으고 있어. 무엇이든 말이야.

Philip 이것들 다 어디서 구한 건데?

Susan 일부는 내가 산 것이고, 다른 사람들에게서도 많이 받았어.

Philip 너 이 수집품으로 박물관 하나 열어도 되겠다.

1. 두 사람은 어디에 있는가?
   a. 식당   b. 개구리 박물관
   c. 선물 가게   ★d. Susan의 집

다시 듣고 True(참) 또는 False(거짓)에 표시하시오.

2. A. Susan의 부모님은 Susan에게 개구리 인형을 모으라고 설득했다. (F)
   B. Philip은 Susan과 함께 개구리 박물관에 갈 것이다. (F)

Listening 2

p. 6

다음 대화를 듣고 질문에 답하시오.

스크립트

Joseph Did you make this nice plane, Peter?

Peter Actually, this is a glider, and I made it using a kit.

Joseph I see. Where did you get it?

Peter I got it from the hobby shop next to our school.

Joseph Was it expensive?

Peter I spent about 100 dollars for the glider and another 200 dollars for the radio controller.

Joseph Wow, a radio-controlled glider! Can you show me how to fly it?

Peter Not now, Joseph. I have a competition coming up. Why don't you come to the competition tomorrow?

해석

Joseph 이 멋진 비행기 네가 만든 거야, Peter?

Peter 사실, 이건 글라이더야. 키트(조립식 모형)로 만들었어.

Joseph 그렇구나. 어디에서 샀는데?

Peter 학교 옆에 있는 취미용품 가게에서 샀어.

Joseph 비싸니?

Peter 글라이더에 100달러가 들었고, 무선 조종 장치에 또 200달러 들었어.

Joseph 와, 무선 조종으로 움직이는 글라이더네! 어떻게 나는지 보여줄 수 있어?

Peter 지금은 안 돼, Joseph. 곧 대회가 있거든. 내일 대회에 오지 그러니?

1. Joseph이 할 수 없는 대답은 무엇인가?
   a. 그래, 그렇게.   b. 좋아.
   ★c. 아니, 나는 그러지 않았어. d. 안될 것 없지(=좋아).

다시 듣고 질문에 답하시오.

2. 이 대화에 관해 사실이 아닌 것은 무엇인가?
   ★a. Joseph은 글라이더 만들기에 대해 많이 알고 있다.
   b. Joseph은 오늘 글라이더가 어떻게 나는지 볼 수 없을 것이다.
   c. Peter는 경기에 참가할 것이다.
   d. Peter는 글라이더와 조종기를 사는 데 300달러를 썼다.

두 개의 요약을 듣고 올바른 것을 고르시오.

3.

스크립트

a. Peter and Joseph are talking about Peter's hobby, making radio-controlled gliders, and Joseph is interested in seeing how the glider flies.

b. Joseph has made a radio-controlled glider, and he is going to participate in the glider competition with his friend Peter.

해석

a. ★ Peter와 Joseph은 Peter의 취미인 무선 조종 글라이더 만들기에 대해 이야기하고 있으며, Joseph은 글라이더가 어떻게 나는지 보고 싶어한다.

b. □ Joseph은 무선 조종 글라이더를 만들었고, 친구 Peter와 함께 글라이더 대회에 참가할 것이다.

Listening 3

p. 7

다음 이야기를 듣고 질문에 답하시오.

스크립트

Ricky and James are good friends, but they spend their free time very differently. While Ricky spends most of his free time swimming, running, and hiking, James likes reading. But after reading an interesting book about mountain climbers, James is now interested in hiking, and he has decided to go hiking this Saturday with Ricky. James is really excited about the trip because this is his first time to go to a mountain.

해석

Ricky와 James는 친한 친구 사이지만 그들은 여가 시간을 매우 다르게 보낸다. Ricky가 그의 여가 시간 대부분을 수영, 달리기, 등산을 하며 보내는 반면, James는 독서를 좋아한다. 그러나 산악인에 관한 흥미로운 책을 읽은 후, James는 이제 등산에 관심을 가지게 되었고 이번 주 토요일에 Ricky와 등산을 가기로 결심했다. James는 이 여행에 매우 들떠 있는데, 이번이 그가 처음으로 산에 가 보는 것이기 때문이다.

1. 이 단락의 주요 화제는 무엇인가?
   a. 두 명의 유명한 산악인
   ★b. James가 어떻게 등산에 관심이 생겼는가
   c. 다양한 스포츠에 관한 책
   d. Ricky의 새 취미

다시 듣고 질문에 답하시오.

2. 누가 이번 주 토요일에 등산을 갈 것인가?
   a. Ricky만   b. James만
   ★c. Ricky와 James   d. 아무도 가지 않는다.

Listening 4

p. 7

다음 이야기를 듣고 질문에 답하시오.

스크립트

Although making clothing for dolls was Carrie's hobby during her childhood, she never dreamed that her hobby would later become her career. A few years ago, she made clothes for her dog with her old sweaters, and her friends liked them very much. They asked her to make some for their dogs, too. Because carrie started getting more and more orders, she decided to open a business. Her business began doing so well that she even opened an Internet shopping mall this year.

해석

어렸을 때 인형 옷을 만드는 것이 Carrie의 취미였지만, 그녀는 자신의 취미가 후에 자신의 직업이 될 것이라고는 꿈도 꾸지 못했다. 몇 년 전, 그녀는 자신의 낡은 스웨터로 개에게 입힐 옷을 만들었는데, 그녀의 친구들이 그 옷을 매우 좋아했다. 친구들은 그녀에게 자신들의 개에게 입힐 옷도 만들어 달라고 부탁했다. Carrie는 점점 더 많은 주문을 받게 되었고, 그래서 그녀는 가게를 열기로 결심했다. 그녀의 사업이 아주 번창하였기 때문에, 그녀는 심지어 올해는 인터넷 쇼핑몰도 열게 되었다.

1. Carrie의 현재 직업은 무엇인가?
★a. 애완견 옷 디자이너   b. 애완동물 가게 주인
c. 웹 사이트 디자이너   d. 장난감 가게 주인

다시 듣고 질문에 답하시오.

2. Carrie는 왜 인터넷 쇼핑몰을 열었는가?
a. 친구들이 그녀에게 쇼핑몰을 열도록 요청했기 때문에
★b. 그녀의 사업이 성공적이었기 때문에
c. 그것이 그녀의 어릴 적 꿈이었기 때문에
d. 인터넷에서 물건을 사고 싶었기 때문에

두 개의 요약을 듣고 올바른 것을 고르시오.

3.

스크립트

a. Carrie has wanted to be a pet clothing designer ever since she was little, and these days she is selling her products on her friend's Internet shopping site.

b. Carrie makes money doing what she likes – designing and making clothing for dogs. These days, she also sells her products on her own Internet shopping site.

해석
a. ☐ Carrie는 어릴 적부터 항상 애완동물 옷 디자이너가 되기를 원했고, 요즘은 친구의 인터넷 쇼핑몰에서 그녀의 상품을 팔고 있다.
b. ★ Carrie는 그녀가 좋아하는 것, 즉 애완견 옷을 디자인하고 만들어서 돈을 번다. 요즘 그녀는 자신의 인터넷 쇼핑몰에서 상품을 판매하고 있다.

Practice Test
p. 8~9

1. a	2. b	3. c	4. a	5. b	6. d
7. d	8. c	9. d	10. a		

[1~2] 다음 대화를 듣고 질문에 답하시오.

스크립트

M Hey, I often see you here with a camera. Are you a professional photographer?
W No, it's just my hobby.
M What kind of pictures do you take?
W I take pictures of clouds.
M Just clouds? What do you do with them?
W Well, all the clouds have different shapes, so every picture is unique. Actually, I am thinking of making a picture book of clouds. But I have not yet taken enough good pictures.
M But you'll have them soon.

해석
남 저기요, 카메라를 들고 여기에 계신 걸 자주 보는데, 전문 사진작가세요?
여 아니에요, 그냥 취미예요.
남 어떤 종류의 사진을 찍으세요?
여 구름 사진을 찍어요.
남 그냥 구름만요? 그걸로 뭘 하시는데요?
여 음, 구름은 모두 다른 모양을 가졌어요. 그래서 각 사진들이 독특하죠. 사실, 저는 구름 사진책을 만들까 생각 중이에요. 하지만 아직 좋은 사진을 충분히 찍질 못했어요.
남 하지만 곧 (좋은 사진을 많이) 찍게 될 거예요.

1. 남자와 여자는 무슨 관계인가?
★a. 그들은 서로 모르는 사람이다. b. 그들은 친한 친구이다.
c. 그들은 결혼한 부부이다.   d. 그들은 손님과 판매원이다.

2. 이 대화를 마치면서 남자는 어떤 속담을 쓸 수 있는가?

> 남자 하지만 곧 (좋은 사진을 많이) 찍게 될 거예요.
> _____.

a. 일찍 일어나는 새가 벌레를 잡아요.
★b. 시작이 반이에요.
c. 뛰기 전에 살펴보세요(=유비무환).
d. 내 집 만한 곳은 없어요.

4

[3–4] 다음 대화를 듣고 질문에 답하시오.

스크립트

Chris   What a nice garden you have, Ebony!

Ebony   Thanks, Chris. But we owe it to our grandma. She spends most of her time gardening.

Chris   Are you into gardening, too?

Ebony   Not really, but I help her from time to time when she needs to move something heavy.

Chris   Does she grow only flowers?

Ebony   If you go to the backyard, you will see her vegetable garden. She grows tomatoes, corn, peas, and other vegetables.

Chris   Wow, she is great. I wish I had a grandmother like her.

해석

Chris   멋진 정원을 가졌구나, Ebony!

Ebony   고마워, Chris. 하지만 다 우리 할머니 덕분이야. 할머니는 대부분의 시간을 정원 가꾸는 데 보내셔.

Chris   너도 정원 가꾸기를 좋아하니?

Ebony   그렇진 않아. 하지만 할머니가 무거운 물건을 옮기셔야 할 때 내가 가끔씩 도와드려.

Chris   할머니는 꽃만 기르시니?

Ebony   뒤뜰에 가 보면 우리 할머니의 채소밭도 볼 수 있을 거야. 할머니는 토마토, 옥수수, 콩, 그리고 다른 채소들도 기르셔.

Chris   와아, 대단하다. 나도 네 할머니 같은 할머니가 있었으면 좋겠어.

3. Ebony의 할머니가 기르는 것은 무엇인가?

  a. 꽃만   b. 채소만

★c. 꽃과 채소   d. 과일 나무와 꽃

4. 다음 중 Chris가 Ebony의 할머니에게 느끼는 감정이 <u>아닌</u> 것은 무엇인가?

★a. 동정   b. 존경   c. 놀라움   d. 감탄

[5–6] 다음 대화를 듣고 질문에 답하시오.

스크립트

Nellie   Hey, Jack. You look tanned.

Jack   Hi, Nellie. I have been spending a lot of time at the beach this summer.

Nellie   What did you do there?

Jack   I went scuba diving and jet-skiing.

Nellie   How exciting! When did you learn to do those things?

Jack   I learned scuba diving many years ago, but I picked up jet-skiing this year.

Nellie   What do you do in the winter, then?

Jack   I swim at an indoor pool. I love spending time in water.

Nellie   You certainly do.

해석

Nellie   안녕, Jack. 너 햇볕에 좀 탄 것 같아 보인다.

Jack   안녕, Nellie. 이번 여름에 해변에서 시간을 많이 보냈거든.

Nellie   거기서 뭘 했는데?

Jack   스쿠버 다이빙도 하고 제트스키도 탔어.

Nellie   정말 재밌었겠다! 언제 그것들을 배웠니?

Jack   스쿠버 다이빙은 몇 년 전에 배웠는데, 제트스키는 올해 배웠어.

Nellie   그럼 넌 겨울에는 뭘 해?

Jack   실내 수영장에서 수영해. 난 물에서 시간 보내는 걸 좋아하거든.

Nellie   정말 그런 것 같네.

5. Jack의 취미로 언급되지 <u>않은</u> 것은 무엇인가?

  a.   ★b.   c.   d.

6. Jack과 제트스키에 관해 사실인 것은 무엇인가?

  a. 그는 제트스키를 좋아하지 않는다.

  b. 그는 거의 매년 제트스키를 탔다.

  c. 그는 몇 년 전에 Nellie에게 제트스키 타는 법을 가르쳐 주었다.

★d. 그는 올해 제트스키 타는 법을 처음 배웠다.

[7–8] 다음 이야기를 듣고 질문에 답하시오.

스크립트

It is very hard to tell a person's hobby just from his appearance. Ken Westwood, the famous rock star, loves to travel and collect napkins from all the restaurants he has visited. Sally Kim, the cute movie star, enjoys car racing. She races almost every weekend, and she has already won a few races. Now, can you guess what the 130kg boxer Sam Coleman likes to do? His hobby is cookie making! He especially loves to make chocolate chip cookies.

해석

어떤 사람의 취미를 그 사람의 외모만으로 판단하기는 정말 어렵다. 유명한 록 스타인 Ken Westwood는 여행하는 것을 좋아해서 그가 갔던 모든 식당의 냅킨을 모은다. 귀여운 영화 스타인 Sally Kim은 자동차 경주를 즐긴다. 그녀는 거의 매 주말마다 경주를 하며, 벌써 몇몇 경기에서 우승을 했다.

그럼, 130킬로그램이나 나가는 권투 선수 Sam Coleman은 무엇을 좋아할지 짐작할 수 있겠는가? 그의 취미는 쿠키 만들기이다! 그는 특히 초콜릿 칩 쿠키 만드는 것을 좋아한다.

7. 들은 내용을 토대로, 가장 어울리는 보기는 무엇인가?

> 종종 ___A___ 와(과) ___B___ 에는 차이가 있다.

	A	B
a.	어떤 사람의 직업	그 사람이 말하는 방식
b.	어떤 사람의 외모	그 사람이 세상을 보는 방식
c.	어떤 사람이 생계를 위해 하는 일	그 사람이 싫어하는 것
★d.	어떤 사람이 어떻게 생겼나	그 사람이 취미로 좋아하는 것

8. 이 단락에서 언급되지 않은 취미는 무엇인가?
   a. 여행   b. 자동차 경주
★c. 시계 수집   d. 쿠키 만들기

[9–10] 다음 이야기를 듣고 질문에 답하시오.

스크립트
These days, I'm into blogging. The word "blog" comes from the words "web" and "log." "Web" refers to the "Internet" and "log" means "record." A blog is like a personal diary on the web. In my blog, I write about the places I have visited or movies I have seen. Every day, many of my friends visit my blog and leave their opinions about what I have written. Blogging is fun, but I think I should probably cut down on the time I spend at the computer.

해석
요즘 나는 블로그에 빠져 있다. blog라는 말은 web과 log에서 유래한다. 'web'은 '인터넷'을 의미하고 'log'는 '기록'이라는 의미이다. 블로그는 웹 상의 개인 일기와 같은 것이다. 나는 블로그에 내가 가봤던 장소들이나 내가 봤던 영화들에 대해 쓴다. 날마다 많은 친구들이 내 블로그를 방문해서 내가 쓴 글들에 대해 자신들의 의견을 남겨놓는다. 블로그를 하는 게 재미있긴 하지만 컴퓨터 앞에 있는 시간은 좀 줄여야 할 것 같다.

9. "blog"의 의미는 무엇인가?
   a. 인터넷에서 작문 숙제를 하는 것
   b. 인터넷에서 어떤 문제에 관해 토론하는 것
   c. 인터넷에서 영화에 관해 이야기하는 것
★d. 인터넷에 개인 생각을 기록하는 것

10. 말하는 사람은 자신의 취미에 관해 어떻게 생각하는가?
★a. 블로그를 하는 데 쓰는 시간을 줄여야 한다.
   b. 친구들의 블로그를 더 자주 방문해야 한다.
   c. 자신의 블로그에 일상생활에 대해 쓰지 말아야 한다.
   d. 블로그에 더 자주 글을 써야 한다.

Dictation (Listening Task)   p. 10

LISTENING 1
all these frogs, so many frogs, that has to do with, got me, when I was ten, You name it, did you get all these, many were given, open a museum

LISTENING 2
this nice plane, made it using a kit, the hobby shop next to, I spent about 100 dollars, another 200 dollars, radio-controlled, how to fly it, competition coming up

LISTENING 3
good friends, spend their free time, swimming, running, hiking, likes reading, about mountain climbers, hiking, this Saturday, this is his first time

LISTENING 4
clothing for dolls, never dreamed, her career, A few years ago, with her old sweaters, some for their dogs, more and more orders, began doing so well, Internet shopping mall

Dictation (Practice Test)   p. 11

PRACTICE TEST [1-2]
with a camera, professional photographer, What kind of pictures, clouds, What do you do with them, different shapes, thinking of, enough good pictures

PRACTICE TEST [3-4]
a nice garden, owe it to, most of her time gardening, Not really, move something heavy, only flowers, her vegetable garden, tomatoes, I wish I had

PRACTICE TEST [5-6]
look tanned, at the beach, scuba diving, When did you learn to do those things, picked up, this year, in the winter, at an indoor pool, You certainly do

PRACTICE TEST [7-8]
hard to tell, his appearance, collect napkins, he has visited, car racing, won a few races, can you guess, cookie making, chocolate chip cookies

PRACTICE TEST [9-10]
blogging, comes from, web, record, personal diary, the places I have visited, their opinions, what I have written

UNIT 2
Are you coming to the party?

Listening Task   p. 14~15

Listening 1	**1.** a	**2.** A. F	**B.** T
Listening 2	**1.** b	**2.** a	**3.** a
Listening 3	**1.** c	**2.** d	
Listening 4	**1.** a	**2.** c-a-b	**3.** b

Getting Ready   p. 13

A

throw a surprise party, occasion, anniversary, to bring, ready, sent an invitation, make a reservation, have, enjoy, be there

B

(1)-(f)   (2)-(e)   (3)-(d)   (4)-(a)   (5)-(b)   (6)-(c)

A 아래 대화를 읽고 빈칸을 완성하시오.

> 즐기다, 거기에 가다, 기념일, 예약하다, 특별한 일, 가져오다, 초대장을 보내다, 깜짝 파티를 열다, 준비된, 하다(열다)

Max Julie, 이번 주 일요일에 집에 올 수 있어? 엄마 아빠를 위해 깜짝 파티를 열려고 하는데.

Julie 무슨 특별한 일이라도 있어?

Max 이번 주 일요일이 엄마 아빠의 스무 번째 결혼기념일이야.

Julie 아, 맞다.

Max 그러니까 엄마 아빠께 아무것도 말씀드리면 안 돼.

Julie 알겠어. 내가 가져와야 할 거라도 있어?

Max 아니. 내가 다 준비해 둘 거야. 그리고 함께 엄마 아빠의 결혼식 비디오를 보면 어떨까?

Julie 좋은 생각이네.

Max 할아버지 할머니께 초대장도 보냈어. 두 분도 오신다고 하셨어.

Julie 잘됐다. 식당에 예약은 했어?

Max 아니. 집에서 바비큐 파티를 할 거야. 뒤뜰에서 신선한 공기도 즐기게 말이야.

Julie 알겠어. 내가 적어도 낮 12시까지는 가서 도와줄게.

Max 고마워.

B 각각의 파티와 그 파티에서 사람들이 하는 것을 연결하시오.

(1) 깜짝 파티 - (f) 사람들이 주인공 얼굴에서 놀라는 표정을 보게 된다.

(2) 송별 파티 - (e) 사람들이 작별 인사를 하고 떠나보내는 마음을 나눈다.

(3) 바비큐 파티 - (d) 사람들이 야외에서 석쇠에 구운 스테이크와 갈비를 즐긴다.

(4) Potluck 파티 (각자 음식을 마련해 오는 파티) - (a) 사람들이 모여 각자가 가져온 음식을 함께 먹는다.

(5) 졸업 파티 - (b) 사람들이 학업을 성공적으로 마친 학생들과 함께 축하한다.

(6) 댄스 파티 - (c) 사람들이 음악과 춤을 즐긴다.

Listening 1   p. 14

다음 대화를 듣고 질문에 답하시오.

스크립트

Jane Hello.

Tony Hi, Jane. It's me, Tony.

Jane Hey, Tony. How are you?

Tony I'm fine. I was wondering if you would like to go to the school dance with me.

Jane Oh, you should have called me sooner, Tony. Victor called me earlier, and I told him that I would go with him.

Tony I see. Then, I guess I'll see you at the party. Bye, Jane.

Jane Bye, Tony.

Tony (monolog) Oh well, I guess I won't be going with Jane after all.

해석

Jane 여보세요.

Tony 안녕, 제인. 나야, Tony.

Jane 안녕, Tony. 어떻게 지내?

Tony 잘 지내지. 네가 나랑 같이 학교 댄스 파티에 갈 생각이 있는지 알고 싶은데.

Jane 이런, 좀 더 일찍 전화하지. Victor가 먼저 전화해서 걔랑 같이 가겠다고 했는데.

Tony 알겠어. 그러면 파티에서 보겠구나. 안녕, Jane.

Jane 안녕, Tony.

Tony (혼잣말) 음, 결국 Jane하고는 갈 수 없겠네.

1. 이 대화의 주요 화제는 무엇인가?

  ★a. 댄스 파트너 구하기

  b. 데이트 신청하기

  c. 파티 후에 차를 태워달라고 부탁하기

  d. 약속 장소 바꾸기

다시 듣고 True(참) 또는 False(거짓)에 표시하시오.

2. A. Tony는 Jane이 Victor와 파티에 갈 것을 알고 있었다. (F)

  B. Tony는 Jane에게 학교 댄스 파티에서 그의 댄스 파트너가 되어줄 수 있는지 물어봤다. (T)

Listening 2
p. 14

다음 대화를 듣고 질문에 답하시오.

스크립트

Sunny We need to throw a farewell party for Glen.

Allen Is he going somewhere?

Sunny Didn't you know? He got admitted to the University of Chicago. He is leaving in two weeks.

Allen Really? Good for him, but I will miss him. By the way, where do you want to throw the party?

Sunny I am considering the pizzeria that we used to go to after school.

Allen That's a good idea. They have great pizza. Then, why don't you make a reservation? I will let our classmates know.

Sunny OK.

해석

Sunny Glen을 위한 작별 파티를 해야겠는데.

Allen Glen이 어디라도 가?

Sunny 몰랐어? 시카고 대학에 입학 허가를 받았잖아. 2주 후에 떠날 거야.

Allen 정말? 잘됐네. 하지만 걔가 보고 싶을 것 같아. 그런데 파티는 어디서 열 생각이야?

Sunny 우리가 방과 후에 가곤 했던 피자 가게를 생각 중이야.

Allen 좋은 생각이야. 거기 피자가 맛있지. 그럼 네가 예약을 하는 게 어때? 내가 반 애들에게 알릴게.

Sunny 그래.

1. 두 사람이 파티를 여는 이유는 무엇인가?
   a. Glen을 격려해 주기 위해
   ★b. Glen에게 작별 인사를 하기 위해
   c. 새로 온 학생을 환영하기 위해
   d. Glen의 생일을 축하하기 위해

다시 듣고 질문에 답하시오.

2. 파티에 관해서 주어진 정보가 아닌 것은 무엇인가?
   ★a. 시간   b. 장소
   c. 초대할 사람들   d. 먹게 될 음식

두 개의 요약을 듣고 올바른 것을 고르시오.

3.

스크립트

a. They will have a farewell party for Glen at the pizzeria.

b. They will celebrate Glen's birthday with classmates at the pizzeria.

해석

a. ★ 그들은 피자 가게에서 Glen을 위한 작별 파티를 할 것이다.

b. □ 그들은 피자 가게에서 반 친구들과 Glen의 생일을 축하할 것이다.

Listening 3
p. 15

다음 이야기를 듣고 질문에 답하시오.

스크립트

It's time for some fun, graduating seniors. There will be a graduation dance party on Friday, June 14th, at the Grand Imperial Hotel. The party will start at 8:00 p.m. The party is for seniors and their partners only. There will be a cover charge of $20 per couple at the door. But, if you purchase the ticket in advance, it is only $15.

해석

졸업하는 3학년 학생 여러분, 즐거움을 만끽할 시간입니다. 6월 14일 금요일, 그랜드 임페리얼 호텔에서 졸업 댄스 파티가 있습니다. 파티는 저녁 8시에 시작하며 3학년생과 그들의 파트너만을 위한 파티입니다. 입구에서 커플 당 20달러의 입장료를 받습니다. 하지만 사전에 표를 구매할 경우 입장료는 15달러입니다.

1. 졸업 파티에 올 수 있는 사람은 누구인가?
   a. 누구나   b. 3학년 학생들만
   ★c. 3학년 학생들과 파트너   d. 학생들과 교사들

다시 듣고 질문에 답하시오.

2. 입구에서 표를 살 경우, 커플 당 입장료는 얼마인가?
   a. 8달러   b. 10달러   c. 15달러   ★d. 20달러

Listening 4
p. 15

다음 이야기를 듣고 질문에 답하시오.

스크립트

Yesterday I had a memorable birthday, and this is how it went. Yesterday my girlfriend called me and told me that she was going to be out of town for a few days. At school, nobody would say "happy birthday!" to me. I thought all of them had forgotten when my birthday is. I was very upset when I got home. But, when I opened the door, I heard "Surprise!" All my friends were there, including my girlfriend, holding a cake. I was deeply moved.

어제 나는 기억에 남을 만한 생일을 보냈다. 얘기는 이렇다. 어제 여자친구가 전화를 해서 며칠 동안 다른 곳에 가 있을 거라고 말했다. 학교에서는 아무도 내게 "생일 축하해!"라며 인사하지도 않았다. 모두들 내 생일을 잊은 줄 알았다. 너무 화가 난 채로 집에 왔다. 그런데 문을 열자 "놀랐지!"하는 소리가 들렸다. 그곳엔 케이크를 들고 있는 여자친구를 포함해, 내 친구들 모두가 있었다. 나는 무척 감동받았다.

1. 말하는 사람은 집에서 친구들을 발견했을 때 기분이 어떠했는가?
   ★a. 놀랍고도 행복했다.
   b. 무섭고 화가 났다.
   c. 행복하지만 걱정스러웠다.
   d. 놀랐고 걱정스러웠다.

다시 듣고 질문에 답하시오.

2. 시간 순서대로 그림을 배열하시오.
   [c] - [a] - [b]

두 개의 요약을 듣고 올바른 것을 고르시오.

3.

   a. The speaker was very disappointed because his family forgot his birthday.
   b. The speaker's girlfriend and classmates acted as if they had forgotten all about his birthday so that they could throw a surprise party for him.

   a. □ 말하는 사람은 가족이 그의 생일을 잊어버려서 매우 실망했다.
   b. ★ 말하는 사람의 여자친구와 반 친구들은 그를 위한 깜짝 파티를 열기 위해 그의 생일을 잊어버린 척 했다.

Practice Test
p. 16~17

| 1. b | 2. c | 3. c | 4. d | 5. b | 6. b |
| 7. d | 8. d | 9. a | 10. a | | |

[1-2] 다음 대화를 듣고 질문에 답하시오.

   Jay   Bill, it's almost 11:00 p.m. Perhaps it's time to head home.
   Bill Wow, already? Then, let's go home. How time flies.
   Jay   It was a great party. Did you have a good time?

   Bill Yes, it was a great party.
   Jay   I guess this will be our last dance party before graduation.
   Bill I guess you're right.
   Jay   You go get the girls. I'll get the car.
   Bill Ok. Jay.

   Jay   Bill, 거의 11시야. 집에 가야할 시간인 것 같아.
   Bill 와, 벌써? 그럼 집에 가자. 시간 정말 빠르네.
   Jay   굉장한 파티였어. 너도 재밌었어?
   Bill 응, 정말 멋진 파티였어.
   Jay   아마 이것이 졸업 전 우리의 마지막 댄스 파티겠지.
   Bill 내 생각도 그래.
   Jay   여자애들 데리고 와. 나는 차를 가지고 올게.
   Bill 알았어, Jay.

1. 이 대화에 관해 사실이 아닌 것은 무엇인가?
   a. 그들은 집으로 갈 것이다.
   ★b. 그들은 파티가 즐겁지 않았다.
   c. 그들은 댄스 파티에 갔다.
   d. 그들은 11시까지 파티에 있었다.

2. 이 대화로부터 두 사람은 _____이라고 추론할 수 있다.
   a. 신입생들   b. 2학년 학생들
   ★c. 3학년 학생들   d. 교사들

[3-4] 다음 대화를 듣고 질문에 답하시오.

   Harry Hello?
   Susan Harry? Hi. this is Susan.
   Harry Hi.
   Susan Hey, I am throwing a barbecue party in our backyard this Saturday, and I want you to come. We will have some sausages and steaks.
   Harry What's the occasion?
   Susan No occasion. I just want us all to get together before the summer is over.
   Harry Cool. I will be there. But if I can't make it, I'll give you a call.
   Susan Come by 4:00 p.m.
   Harry I got it. Thanks for inviting me.

   Harry 여보세요?
   Susan Harry? 안녕, 나 Susan이야.
   Harry 안녕.
   Susan 있잖아, 이번 주 토요일에 우리집 뒤뜰에서 바비큐 파티를 하려고 하는데, 너도 왔으면 해서. 소시지와 스테이크를 먹을 거야.

Harry	무슨 특별한 날이야?
Susan	아니. 그냥 여름이 끝나기 전에 다 같이 한번 모이고 싶어서.
Harry	좋아. 갈게. 그런데 만약 못 가게 되면 전화할게.
Susan	오후 4시까지 와.
Harry	알았어. 초대해줘서 고마워.

3. 파티는 어디에서 열릴 것인가?
   a. 호텔   b. 학교   ★c. Susan네 뒤뜰   d. Susan네 거실

4. 그들은 파티에서 무엇을 먹을 것인가?
   a.   b.   c.   ★d.

[5–6] 다음 대화를 듣고 질문에 답하시오.

스크립트

W Are you coming to the school's fundraising party this Friday?

M Maybe not. Why?

W I heard that there would be bands, a lot of food, and a bazaar, too.

M By the way, what is the reason for this fundraising party?

W To raise money for the earthquake victims.

M I see. What is the admission fee?

W Five dollars, but you get a raffle ticket with which you can win a bicycle.

M A new bicycle? I've changed my mind. I think I will go to the party, just to have a chance to win that bicycle.

해석

여 이번 주 금요일 학교 자선기금 모금 파티에 갈 거니?

남 아마도 안 갈 것 같아, 왜?

여 밴드들도 올 거고, 음식도 많고, 바자회도 있을 거래.

남 그나저나, 이 기금 모금 파티는 뭐를 위한 거야?

여 지진 피해자를 위해 모금을 하는 거야.

남 그렇구나. 참가비는 얼마야?

여 5달러인데, 그 돈으로 자전거에 당첨될 수도 있는 추첨권도 받는 거야.

남 새 자전거란 말이지? 생각 바뀌었어. 아무래도 자전거에 당첨될 기회를 잡으려면 파티에 가야겠다.

5. 남자의 마지막 대답은 무슨 의미인가?
   a. 그는 다른 이들을 돕는 데 관심이 있다.
   ★b. 그는 자전거에 당첨되기를 원한다.
   c. 그는 콘서트를 보고싶어 한다.
   d. 그는 자전거로 그 곳에 갈 수 있어서 기쁘다.

6. 파티의 목적은 무엇인가?
   a. 고아들을 돕기 위해
   ★b. 지진 피해자들을 돕기 위해
   c. 새 체육관 건설을 위한 돈을 모으기 위해
   d. 자전거를 많이 팔기 위해

[7–8] 다음 이야기를 듣고 질문에 답하시오.

스크립트

In order to throw a great party, there are a few things you should consider carefully. First, decide on the day of the party. Usually Friday or Saturday is good. Then, decide whom to invite and send the invitation early. On the invitation, you can ask what kind of food and entertainment they would like to have. Usually good music will provide enough entertainment. It's always a smart idea to ask those who have thrown great parties for ideas.

해석

멋진 파티를 열려면 몇 가지 사항을 신중하게 고려해야 한다. 첫째, 파티의 날짜를 정한다. 일반적으로 금요일이나 토요일이 좋다. 그리고 누구를 초대할지 결정해서 일찍 초대장을 보낸다. 초대장에는 어떤 음식이나 어떤 오락거리가 있었으면 좋겠는지를 물어볼 수 있다. 대개는 좋은 음악이면 충분히 좋은 여흥거리가 된다. 그리고 멋진 파티들을 열어본 사람들에게 (파티) 아이디어를 물어보는 것도 현명한 생각이다.

7. 이 단락의 제목으로 가장 알맞은 것은 무엇인가?
   a. 파티를 여는 것의 중요성
   b. 댄스 파티를 준비하는 법
   c. 사람들을 즐겁게 하는 좋은 방법들
   ★d. 멋진 파티를 열기 위해 알아야 할 것들

8. 이 단락에서 언급되지 않은 것은 무엇인가?
   a. 파티를 위해 좋은 요일
   b. 초대장을 보내는 것에 관한 조언
   c. 사람들이 좋아하는 오락거리
   ★d. 파티를 위한 요리를 하는 법

[9–10] 다음 대화를 듣고 질문에 답하시오.

스크립트

Ted	Maria, there will be a potluck party this Sunday. Can you come?
Maria	What is a potluck party?
Ted	It is a party where everyone brings a dish, and everybody shares the food. You can bring whatever you want.
Maria	What if everyone brings the same food?

Ted	That's a possibility. One time, everyone brought a pie.
Maria	Then, I will bring some Mexican food. Since I am the only Mexican in the group, probably no one else will bring Mexican food.
Ted	That's an excellent idea.

해석

Ted	Maria, 이번 주 일요일에 potluck 파티가 있을 거야. 올 수 있어?
Maria	potluck 파티가 뭔데?
Ted	모두가 음식을 한 가지씩 가지고 와서 다 함께 그 음식을 나누어 먹는 파티야. 넌 네가 원하는 것 아무거나 가지고 오면 돼.
Maria	만약 다들 똑같은 음식을 가져오면 어떡해?
Ted	그럴 수도 있어. 한 번은 모두가 다 파이만 가지고 왔었거든.
Maria	그럼, 난 멕시코 음식을 가져갈게. 우리 중에 멕시코 사람은 나 뿐이니까 아마 나 말고 멕시코 음식을 가져오는 사람은 없을 거야.
Ted	좋은 생각이야.

9. 두 사람은 무엇을 하고 있는가?

남자		여자
★a. 초대	—	수락
b. 거절	—	부탁
c. 제안	—	거절
d. 소개	—	소개

10. 이 대화에 관해 사실인 것은 무엇인가?

★a. Maria는 멕시코 사람이다.
  b. Maria는 potluck 파티가 무엇인지 설명하고 있다.
  c. 파티는 이번 주 토요일에 있을 것이다.
  d. 사람들은 모두 파티에 같은 음식을 가져와야 한다.

Dictation (Listening Task)　　p. 18

LISTENING 1

It's me, wondering if, go to the school dance, should have called, called me earlier, I would go with him, see you at the party, I guess, after all

LISTENING 2

throw a farewell party, going somewhere, leaving in, will miss him, am considering, we used to go to, make a reservation, let our classmates know

LISTENING 3

for some fun, will be a graduation dance party, The party will start, seniors and their partners, cover charge of $20, at the door, purchase, in advance, $15

LISTENING 4

memorable, how it went, out of town for a few days, all of them had forgotten, I was very upset, opened the door, including my girlfriend, a cake

Dictation (Practice Test)　　p. 19

PRACTICE TEST [1-2]

time to head home, How time flies, have a good time, a great party, before graduation, I guess you're right, get the car

PRACTICE TEST [3-4]

a barbecue party in our backyard, want you to come, What's the occasion, get together, be there, can't make it, give you a call, Come by, Thanks for inviting

PRACTICE TEST [5-6]

Are you coming to, fundraising party, I heard that, bazaar, what is the reason for, victims, admission fee, win a bicycle, I've changed my mind

PRACTICE TEST [7-8]

In order to throw a great party, consider carefully, whom to invite, invitation, what kind of food, would like to have, those who have thrown

PRACTICE TEST [9-10]

a potluck party, brings a dish, shares the food, whatever you want, What if, That's a possibility, in the group, That's an excellent idea

UNIT 3
Which class are you going to take?

Getting Ready
p. 21

A

semester, taking, chemistry, assignments,
gives a test, experiments, signing up,
attendance, fail the class, in the class

B

박스 안의 과목을 골라서 자유롭게 응답

A 아래 대화를 읽고 빈칸을 완성하시오.

> 출석, 숙제, 시험을 내다, 학기, 택하는(수강하는), 낙제하다,
> 실험, 수업에, 화학, 등록하는

Brad 새 학기가 이제 곧 시작이야.

Tim 그래. 그런데 넌 어느 수업을 수강할 거야?

Brad Brown 선생님의 화학 수업을 들을 생각이야.

Tim 그 선생님은 숙제를 많이 내는 것으로 유명한 거 모르니?
그리고 매 수업마다 시험을 낸다고 들었어.

Brad 알아. 그렇지만 재미있는 실험도 많이 할 수 있다고 하더라고.

Tim 그럴지도 모르지. 하지만 그 수업은 나한테는 안 맞는 거
같아. 난 Thomas 선생님의 영어 수업에 등록할까 고려 중
이야.

Brad 오, 정말? 그 분은 출석에 무척 엄격하셔. 넌 제시간에 오는
법이 없잖아. 그것 때문에 그 과목 낙제할 수도 있어.

Tim 왜 이래, 나 요새 많이 변했어. 좋은 쪽을 보면, 수업 시간에
책 읽는 것이 많은데 난 책 읽는 게 좋거든.

B 당신의 수업은 어떠한가? 친구들과 이야기해 보시오.

〈과목〉

영어	수학	과학	화학	물리학	생물학
역사	음악	미술	지리	문학	사회학

Q1: 당신이 가장 좋아하는 과목은 무엇인가?
A1: 나는 영어를 제일 좋아한다.

Q2: 당신이 잘하는/못하는 과목은 무엇인가?
A2: 나는 화학을 잘한다/못한다.

Q3: 당신에게 어려운/쉬운 과목은 무엇인가?
A3: 지리가 어렵다/쉽다.

Q4: 당신이 가장 좋아하는 선생님은 누구인가?
A4: Brown 선생님이다.

Q5: 그/그녀는 무슨 과목을 가르치는가?
A5: 그/그녀는 문학을 가르친다.

Listening Task
p. 22~23

Listening 1	1. a	2. A. T	B. F
Listening 2	1. c	2. d	3. a
Listening 3	1. a	2. c	
Listening 4	1. d	2. b	3. b

Listening 1
p. 22

다음 대화를 듣고 질문에 답하시오.

스크립트

Ms. Brown	Class, I'm going to give you a homework assignment.
Tony	Oh, Ms. Brown, give us a break. We have too much homework in other classes.
Ms. Brown	Tony, you always have the same excuse. Do all the even numbered problems on page 126.
Sandy	When is it due?
Ms. Brown	Since you have other homework, you can turn it in the day after tomorrow.
Tony	Can we have one more extra day?
Ms. Brown	There you go again, Tony. The answer is "no."

해석

Brown 선생님	여러분, 여러분께 숙제를 내주겠어요.
Tony	오, Brown 선생님, 좀 봐주세요. 다른 수업에서 내준 숙제도 너무 많다고요.
Brown 선생님	Tony, 넌 항상 같은 핑계를 대는구나. 126 페이지의 짝수 번호 문제들을 모두 해 오세요.
Sandy	언제까지 해야 되죠?
Brown 선생님	다른 숙제들도 있다고 하니까, 모레까지 제출하세요.
Tony	하루 더 주실 수 없나요?
Brown 선생님	또 그러는구나, Tony. 대답은 "안 돼"예요.

1. Tony는 무엇에 대해 불평하고 있는가?
★a. 너무 많은 숙제   b. 너무 많은 시험
   c. 너무 많은 변명   d. 너무 많은 수업

다시 듣고 True(참) 또는 False(거짓)에 표시하시오.

2. A. Tony는 다른 수업들도 숙제가 많다. (T)
   B. Brown 선생님은 결국 학생들에게 숙제를 내주지 않기로 결정했다. (F)

Listening 2

다음 대화를 듣고 질문에 답하시오.

Adam   Which after-school class are you going to take, Ted?

Ted   I will take a woodworking class. How about you, Adam?

Adam   I've not decided yet. I was going to take auto-mechanics, but the class is full. So, I'm thinking of taking tennis or swimming.

Ted   If you've not decided yet, let's take the woodworking together. I heard that this year's class project is making a canoe. We can make canoes together and go canoeing.

Adam   That sounds great, Ted.

해석

Adam   Ted, 넌 방과 후 수업으로 어떤 것을 들을 거니?

Ted   목공 수업을 들을 거야. Adam, 너는 어떻게 할 건데?

Adam   아직 결정 못했어. 자동차 정비 수업을 들으려고 했는데, 정원이 꽉 차서 말이야. 그래서 테니스나 수영을 해볼까 생각 중이야.

Ted   아직 결정하지 못했다면 목공 수업을 같이 듣자. 올해 수업 계획이 카누를 만드는 거야. 우리 같이 카누를 만들어서 카누 타러 가자.

Adam   그거 괜찮은데, Ted.

1. 두 사람은 무엇에 대해 말하고 있는가?
   a. 온라인 클럽들
   b. 두 사람이 좋아하는 취미들
   ★c. 방과 후 수업들
   d. 레저의 새로운 경향

다시 듣고 질문에 답하시오.

2. Adam은 어떤 수업을 들을 것인가?
   a.   b.   c.   ★d.

두 개의 요약을 듣고 올바른 것을 고르시오.

3.

스크립트

a. Because the after-school class that Adam wanted to take originally was full, he will take the woodworking class with Ted.

b. Because Adam doesn't want to do any kind of after-school activity, Ted will take the woodworking class alone.

해석

a. ★ Adam이 처음에 들으려고 했던 방과 후 수업은 정원이 꽉 찼기 때문에, 그는 Ted와 함께 목공 수업을 들을 것이다.

b. ☐ Adam은 방과 후 활동을 하고 싶어하지 않기 때문에, Ted는 혼자서 목공 수업을 들을 것이다.

Listening 3

다음 이야기를 듣고 질문에 답하시오.

스크립트

Students, today's experiment will be a continuation of the last experiment. If you have already finished it, you can turn in the results now. Then you may go to the library and start your homework. But those who have not yet completed the experiment must finish it today because we will begin a new experiment next week. Do you have any questions? If there are no questions, you may start now.

해석

여러분, 오늘 실험은 지난 실험을 계속 이어서 하게 됩니다. 만약 이미 실험을 마쳤다면, 지금 결과를 제출하면 됩니다. 그러고 나면 도서관에 가서 숙제를 시작하세요. 하지만 아직 실험을 끝내지 못한 사람들은 반드시 오늘까지 실험을 마쳐야 합니다. 다음 주에는 새로운 실험을 시작할 테니까요. 질문 있나요? 질문 없으면, 이제 시작해도 좋습니다.

1. 말하는 사람은 지금 어디에 있는가?
   ★a. 실험실   b. 도서관   c. 체육관   d. 운동장

다시 듣고 질문에 답하시오.

2. 이미 실험을 끝낸 학생들은 무엇을 해야 하는가?
   a. 곧바로 다른 실험을 시작한다.
   b. 아직 실험 중인 다른 사람을 돕는다.
   ★c. 실험 결과를 제출한다.
   d. 발표를 한다.

Listening 4

다음 이야기를 듣고 질문에 답하시오.

스크립트

Tim and Heather are chemistry lab partners. Although Tim loves every moment in the lab, Heather hates it. She always tries to get out of the lab as soon as possible because she does not want to be late for her singing rehearsal.

She thinks Tim takes too much time on every step of the experiment. But Tim thinks that Heather is always in a hurry, and that she is irresponsible.

해석
Tim과 Heather는 화학 실험 파트너이다. Tim은 실험실에서의 매 순간순간을 좋아하는 반면, Heather는 실험을 싫어한다. 그녀는 노래 연습에 늦지 않으려고 항상 가능하면 빨리 실험실을 빠져나가려 애쓴다. 그녀는 Tim이 매 실험 단계마다 너무 많은 시간을 소요한다고 생각한다. 그러나 Tim은 Heather가 항상 서두르는데다, 무책임하다고 생각한다.

1. Heather는 Tim의 어떤 점에 대해 불평하는가?
   a. 그는 수업에 항상 지각한다.
   b. 그는 프로젝트를 열심히 하지 않는다.
   c. 그는 수업 중에 너무 떠든다.
   ★d. 그는 실험에 너무 많은 시간을 보낸다.

다시 듣고 질문에 답하시오.

2. Heather는 실험 후에 어디에 가는가?
   a. 체육관 ★b. 노래 연습 c. 도서관 d. 화학 실험실

두 개의 요약을 듣고 올바른 것을 고르시오.

3.

스크립트

a. Tim and Heather are very similar in character. After they finish their classes, they go to their singing rehearsal together.

b. Tim and Heather are different. Tim likes to do experiments, but Heather is not interested in doing them at all.

해석
a. ☐ Tim과 Heather는 성격이 아주 비슷하다. 그들은 수업을 마치면 함께 노래 연습을 하러 간다.

b. ★ Tim과 Heather는 (성격이) 다르다. Tim은 실험을 좋아하지만 Heather는 실험에는 전혀 관심이 없다.

Practice Test
p. 24~25

| 1. a | 2. c | 3. c | 4. d | 5. b |
| 6. d | 7. c | 8. a | 9. a | 10. d |

[1–2] 다음 대화를 듣고 질문에 답하시오.

스크립트

Andrew Hi, Lisa. Have you done the geometry homework?

Lisa Yes, I have. But I am having difficulties with the history homework.

Andrew Then, why don't you help me with my geometry homework? Then I will help you with history.

Lisa That's a great idea. What kind of problem are you having?

Andrew I understood when the teacher explained this, but I cannot apply it to the problem solving.

Lisa Let me take a look at the problems.

Andrew Here are the ones I couldn't solve.

해석

Andrew 안녕, Lisa. 기하학 숙제는 다 했어?

Lisa 응, 다 했어. 그런데 역사 숙제 때문에 골치가 아퍼.

Andrew 그러면, 내 기하학 숙제를 도와주지 않을래? 난 네 역사 숙제를 도와줄게.

Lisa 그거 좋은 생각이다. 무슨 문젠데?

Andrew 선생님이 이걸 설명할 때는 이해했는데, 문제 푸는 데에는 적용을 못 시키겠어.

Lisa 그 문제들 어디 한 번 봐봐.

Andrew 이게 내가 풀지 못한 것들이야.

1. 두 사람은 어떤 과목에 대해 말하고 있는가?
   ★a. 역사와 기하학 b. 역사와 지리
   c. 기하학과 지리 d. 위의 것 모두

2. 이 상황에 어울리는 속담은 무엇인가?
   a. 로마는 하루 아침에 이루어지지 않았다.(천 리 길도 한 걸음부터)
   b. 서투른 직공이 자기 연장만 탓한다.
   ★c. 내 등을 긁어주면 나도 네 등을 긁어주겠다.(상부상조)
   d. 반짝인다고 다 금은 아니다.

[3–4] 다음 대화를 듣고 질문에 답하시오.

스크립트

Andy What is an SAT?

Counselor It is a test that many colleges use to evaluate students. So, if you want to go to college, you should take the test.

Andy When can I take it?

Counselor The test is offered several times throughout the year, so you can choose the most convenient time.

Andy	How do I register for it?
Counselor	You can register by mail or online, but why don't you visit the test administrator's website for more information? The URL is www.collegeboard.com.

해석

Andy	SAT가 무엇입니까?
상담원	많은 대학들이 학생(입학생)들을 선정하기 위해 치르는 시험이예요. 그래서 대학에 가길 원한다면 그 시험을 치러야 합니다.
Andy	언제 칠 수 있나요?
상담원	시험은 일 년에 여러 차례 시행됩니다. 그러니 가장 편한 때로 선택할 수 있습니다.
Andy	시험 등록은 어떻게 하죠?
상담원	우편이나 온라인 상으로 등록할 수 있어요. 더 상세히 알고 싶으면 시험 관리 사이트를 방문해 보시겠어요? 웹 사이트 주소는 www.collegeboard.com입니다.

3. SAT에 관해 주어지지 <u>않은</u> 정보는 무엇인가?
   a. 학생들이 SAT를 쳐야 하는 이유
   b. SAT 시험 등록 방법
   ★c. SAT 시험을 대비한 공부 방법
   d. SAT에 대해 더 많은 정보를 얻을 수 있는 곳

4. 시험은 얼마나 자주 출제되는가?
   a. 일 년에 두 번　　　b. 매달
   c. 일 년에 한 번　　★d. 일 년 동안 수차례

[5–6] 다음 대화를 듣고 질문에 답하시오.

스크립트

Sunny	When you go to college, what are you going to major in, Brad?
Brad	I want to be an engineer, but my parents want me to be a lawyer.
Sunny	Why?
Brad	They think lawyers make a lot of money.
Sunny	Why do you want to be an engineer?
Brad	I really love robots. I'll never forget the moment when I first saw talking robots. Since then, I've dreamed of making robots myself.
Sunny	If you like engineering that much, I think you need to convince your parents to support your decision to become an engineer.

해석

Sunny	Brad, 넌 대학에 가면 무엇을 전공하고 싶니?
Brad	난 공학자가 되고 싶은데 우리 부모님은 내가 변호사가 되길 바라서.
Sunny	왜?
Brad	변호사가 돈을 잘 번다고 생각하시거든.
Sunny	넌 왜 공학자가 되고 싶은데?
Brad	난 로봇이 정말 좋아. 말하는 로봇을 처음 봤던 그 순간을 잊을 수가 없어. 그 후부터 내가 직접 로봇을 만드는 꿈을 키워 왔어.
Sunny	그렇게 공학이 좋다면, 공학자가 되기로 한 네 결심을 지원해 주시도록 부모님을 설득해 봐.

5. 여자아이의 마지막 말이 의미하는 것은 무엇인가?
   a. 우리는 부모님 말씀을 들어야 한다.
   ★b. 우리는 정말로 자신이 원하는 것을 해야 한다.
   c. 부모님들은 때로 자기 자식들을 이해하지 못한다.
   d. 공학은 남자에게 좋은 직업이다.

6. Brad는 왜 공학자가 되길 원하는가?
   a. 과학에 꽤 소질이 있어서
   b. 돈을 많이 벌고 싶어서
   c. 그의 부모가 그가 공학자가 되길 원해서
   ★d. 로봇을 만드는 것에 관심이 있어서

[7–8] 다음 이야기를 듣고 질문에 답하시오.

스크립트

Many students worry about failing a class. If you are one of them, here is some advice for you. First, pay close attention to the lectures and take notes during them. If you have questions, do not hesitate to ask your teacher. At home, review all the lecture notes and do all the homework. Most test questions come from the materials covered during lectures and the homework given.

해석

낙제하지 않을까 걱정하는 학생들이 많습니다. 만약 당신이 그 중 한 명이라면, 여기 당신을 위한 몇 가지 조언이 있습니다. 첫째, 강의에 집중하고 강의 동안 필기를 하세요. 질문이 있으면 주저 말고 선생님에게 질문하시고. 집에서는 강의 노트들을 모두 복습하고 숙제를 다 해야 합니다. 시험 문제들은 대부분 강의 중에 다루어진 내용과 내준 숙제에서 나오니까요.

7. 이 단락의 주요 화제는 무엇인가?
   a. 강의하는 방법　　　b. 숙제를 잘하는 방법
   ★c. 낙제하지 않는 방법　　d. 수업을 복습하는 방법

8. 이 단락에서 언급되지 않은 조언은 무엇인가?

★a. 수업 전에 수업을 준비하라.
   b. 선생님에게 강의에 관련된 질문을 하라.
   c. 숙제를 모두 해라.
   d. 강의 노트들을 모두 복습하라.

[9~10] 다음 대화를 듣고 질문에 답하시오.

스크립트

Betty	It seems that Joan is spending quite a lot of time doing volunteer work.
Jonathan	You didn't know? She does it just for school credit, and to get recommendation letters for a university application.
Betty	I wondered a little why she was doing it. She really cares about grades.
Jonathan	One must volunteer with sincere motives, not for grades. Don't you think so?
Betty	That's the best reason, Jonathan. But at least she is doing something to help someone.
Jonathan	That is true in a way, but I still believe she is wrong.

해석

Betty	Joan은 자원봉사 활동에 참 많은 시간을 쓰는 것 같아.
Jonathan	너 몰랐어? Joan은 단지 대학을 가기 위해 학점도 따고 추천장도 얻으려고 그러는 거야.
Betty	그녀가 왜 그러는지 조금 의아했었어. Joan은 정말 학점에 신경을 쓰는구나.
Jonathan	점수 때문이 아니라 진정으로 마음에서 우러나서 봉사해야 하는데 말이야. 그렇게 생각하지 않아?
Betty	그게 제일 좋기는 해, Jonathan. 하지만 적어도 그녀가 누군가를 돕고 있기는 하잖아.
Jonathan	한편으론 그렇지만, 난 여전히 그녀가 옳지 않다고 생각해.

9. Joan의 자원봉사에 대한 Jonathan의 태도는 어떠한가?

★a. 못마땅하다   b. 찬성한다
   c. 만족스럽다   d. 좋다

10. Jonathan이 말하고자 하는 것은 무엇인가?

   a. 자원봉사 운영체제를 바꿔야 한다.
   b. 남을 돕는 것은 누구에게나 중요하다.
   c. 고통 없이 얻을 수 있는 것은 없다.
★d. 자신의 이익이 아니라 남을 돕기 위해 봉사해야 한다.

Dictation (Listening Task)　　p. 26

LISTENING 1

give you a homework, give us a break, in other classes, have the same excuse, When is it due, turn it in the day after tomorrow, one more extra day, There you go again

LISTENING 2

Which after-school class, a woodworking class, I was going to take, the class is full, thinking of taking, If you've not decided yet, this year's class project

LISTENING 3

today's experiment, If you have already finished it, turn in the results, go to the library, who have not yet completed, next week, If there are no questions

LISTENING 4

chemistry lab partners, every moment in the lab, tries to get out of the lab, does not want to be late for, on every step of, in a hurry

Dictation (Practice Test)　　p. 27

PRACTICE TEST [1-2]

Have you done, having difficulties with, help me with, with history, What kind of problem, cannot apply it to, Let me take a look at, ones I couldn't solve

PRACTICE TEST [3-4]

It is a test, to evaluate students, want to go to college, When can I take it, choose the most convenient time, How do I register, register by mail or online

PRACTICE TEST [5-6]

what are you going to major in, I want to be an engineer, make a lot of money, I'll never forget the moment, I've dreamed of making robots, convince, to support your decision

PRACTICE TEST [7-8]

worry about failing a class, pay close attention, during them, do not hesitate to ask, review all the lecture notes, covered, the homework given

PRACTICE TEST [9-10]

It seems, is spending quite a lot of time, for school credit, recommendation letters, One must volunteer, doing something to help someone, true in a way

UNIT 4
What's your plan for mother's day?

Getting Ready   p. 29

A

of course, exchange, a fresh start, celebrate, New Year's resolutions, get rid of, accomplish, lose, gain weight, water

B

- Valentines' Day is February second / the second of February. On that day, I give chocolate to my boyfriend/girlfriend.
- April Fool's Day is April first / the first of April. On that day, I fool people.
- Mother's Day is the second Sunday of May. On that day, I give my mother a nice present.
- Halloween is October thirty-first / the thirty-first of October. On that day, I go trick-or-treating and get candies.
- Thanksgiving Day is the fourth Thursday of November. On that day, I have a big dinner, including turkey.
- Christmas is December twenty-fifth / the twenty-fifth of December. On that day, I decorate my Christmas tree.

A 아래 대화를 읽고 빈칸을 완성하시오.

군침이 돌다, 물론, 기념하다, 새해 다짐, 없애다(버리다), (살을) 빼다, 몸무게가 늘다, 새로운 출발, 교환하다(주고받다), 이루다(달성하다)

Linda 일 년 중 네가 가장 좋아하는 날은 언제야?

James 물론 크리스마스랑 밸런타인데이지. 나는 선물 주고받는 걸 좋아하거든.

Linda 나는 새해 첫날을 좋아하는데. 새롭게 출발을 할 수 있잖아.

James 새해 첫날을 어떻게 기념하니?

Linda 나는 매해 새해 다짐을 해. 하고 싶은 것들과 나쁜 습관같이 버리고 싶은 것들을 적어두지. 그걸 다 이루진 못해도, 그러려고 열심히 노력해.

James 올해 네 다짐은 뭔데?

Linda 다짐 중 하나는 (몸무게를) 10파운드 감량하는 거야. 지금까지 8파운드를 감량하긴 했는데, 다음 주가 추수감사절이라서 다시 몸무게가 늘 것 같아.

James 추수감사절 이야기만 해도 군침이 돈다. 칠면조 먹을 생각을 하니까 말야.

B 특별한 날에 당신은 무엇을 하는가? 친구들과 이야기해 보시오.

[A] 새해 첫날 (1.1)
   밸런타인데이 (2.14)
   만우절 (4.1)
   어머니날 (5월 둘째 일요일)
   핼로윈 (10.31)
   추수감사절 (11월 넷째 목요일)
   크리스마스 (12.25)

[B] 사람들에게 "새해 복 많이 받으세요"라고 말한다
   칠면조를 포함한 푸짐한 저녁을 먹는다
   내 남자친구/여자친구에게 초콜릿을 준다
   내 크리스마스 트리를 장식한다
   사람들을 속인다
   집집마다 돌아다니며 사탕을 받는다
   어머니께 멋진 선물을 드린다

◁))) [A] 새해 첫날은 1월 1일이다.

그날 나는 [B] 사람들에게 "새해 복 많이 받으세요"라고 말한다.

Listening Task   p. 30~31

Listening 1	1. a	2. A. T	B. F
Listening 2	1. c	2. b	3. a
Listening 3	1. a	2. c	
Listening 4	1. b	2. a	3. b

Listening 1   p. 30

다음 대화를 듣고 질문에 답하시오.

스크립트

Alex When are we going to go Christmas shopping, Mom?

Mom I think we will go this Saturday. Why? Can't you wait?

Alex Last year we went to the mall two days before Christmas, and it was packed. Don't you remember?

Mom I know. Lines were too long and parking was terrible.

Alex Let's not wait until the last minute this time. Also, we need to get Christmas cards and a Christmas tree, too.

Mom Don't worry. Your father will take care of those things.

해석

Alex 크리스마스 쇼핑하러 언제 가요, 엄마?

엄마 이번 주 토요일에 가려고 하는데. 왜? 못 기다리겠니?

Alex 작년에는 크리스마스 이틀 전에 쇼핑몰에 가는 바람에 너무 번잡했잖아요. 기억 안 나세요?

엄마	그래. 줄이 너무 길었고 주차하는 것도 끔찍했었지.
Alex	이번에는 마지막까지 기다리지 말자고요. 게다가, 크리스마스 카드와 트리도 사야 하잖아요.
엄마	걱정하지 마. 그건 아빠가 맡으실 거야.

1. 두 사람은 무엇을 의논하고 있는가?
　★a. 언제 크리스마스 쇼핑을 갈 것인가
　b. 어디에서 크리스마스 쇼핑을 할 것인가
　c. 크리스마스 선물로 무엇을 고를 것인가
　d. 크리스마스 저녁식사에 누구를 초대할 것인가

다시 듣고 True(참) 또는 False(거짓)에 표시하시오.

2. A. 소년의 아버지가 크리스마스 트리와 카드를 살 것이다.
　　（T）
　B. 그들은 작년에는 크리스마스 하루 전날 쇼핑을 갔었다.
　　（F）

Listening 2
p. 30

다음 대화를 듣고 질문에 답하시오.

스크립트

Nina	Hi, Kevin.
Kevin	Nina, do you have any plans for Independence Day?
Nina	No, I don't have any plans.
Kevin	We will have a barbecue and see fireworks in the park. Do you want to come?
Nina	Sure, I love fireworks. What time should I be there?
Kevin	Come by 5:00 p.m.
Nina	Do you want me to bring anything?
Kevin	No, we will have everything there.
Nina	OK, then. I'll see you at the park.
Kevin	See you, Nina.

해석

Nina	안녕, Kevin.
Kevin	Nina, 독립기념일에 무슨 계획 있니?
Nina	아니, 아무 계획 없는데.
Kevin	우린 공원에서 바비큐를 먹고 불꽃놀이를 볼 건데. 오지 않을래?
Nina	좋지, 난 불꽃놀이를 아주 좋아해. 몇 시에 가면 돼?
Kevin	오후 5시까지 오면 돼.
Nina	내가 뭐 좀 가져갈까?
Kevin	아니, 우리가 다 준비해 둘 거야.
Nina	그래, 그럼. 공원에서 보자.
Kevin	그때 봐, Nina.

1. Kevin은 무엇을 하고 있는가?
　a. Nina에게 뭔가를 빌려달라고 부탁하고 있음
　b. Nina의 도움에 고마워하고 있음
　★c. Nina를 독립기념일 바비큐 식사에 초대하고 있음
　d. 독립기념일이 무엇인지 설명하고 있음

다시 듣고 질문에 답하시오.

2. 그들은 독립기념일에 무엇을 할 것인가?
　a.　　★b.　　c.　　d.

두 개의 요약을 듣고 올바른 것을 고르시오.

3.

스크립트

a. Nina will come to the park by 5 o'clock to have a barbecue and watch fireworks with Kevin.

b. Nina has an appointment on Independence Day, but she will cancel it because she wants to be with Kevin.

해석

a. ★ Nina는 Kevin과 함께 바비큐를 먹고 불꽃놀이를 보기 위해 5시까지 공원에 올 것이다.

b. □ Nina는 독립기념일에 약속이 있지만, Kevin과 함께 있고 싶어서 그 약속을 취소할 것이다.

Listening 3
p. 31

다음 이야기를 듣고 질문에 답하시오.

스크립트

In America, the New Year's Day celebration starts on the evening of December 31st. On New Year's Eve, close friends and family members get together for a party. They eat, drink, and dance, waiting for midnight. As it gets very close to midnight, everybody starts to count down. And when it is twelve o'clock, everybody shouts "Happy New Year!" then they hug and kiss people around them. The party continues for a few hours, sometimes until dawn.

해석

미국에서 새해 첫날 축하 행사는 12월 31일 저녁에 시작된다. 새해 전날, 가까운 친구들과 가족이 함께 모여 파티를 한다. 사람들은 먹고, 마시고, 춤추면서 자정을 기다린다. 자정이 매우 가까워지면, 사람들은 카운트다운을 시작한다. 12시(자정)가 되면, 모두들 "새해 복 많이 받아!"라고 외치며 주위 사람들과 껴안고 키스를 한다. 파티는 때때로 새벽까지 몇 시간 동안 계속된다.

1. 새해 첫날 축하 행사는 언제 시작되는가?
   ★a. 12월 31일 저녁에   b. 1월 1일 이른 아침에
   c. 새해 첫날 정오에   d. 새해 첫날 저녁에

다시 듣고 질문에 답하시오.

2. 사람들이 새해 첫날 파티에서 하지 않는 것은 무엇인가?
   a. 키스와 포옹   b. 식사와 춤
   ★c. 선물 교환   d. 새해 인사하기

Listening 4 p. 31

다음 이야기를 듣고 질문에 답하시오.

For American people, Thanksgiving Day is a day to visit relatives, so it is one of the busiest travel days of the year. The main food for Thanksgiving dinner is turkey, but there may also be ham, salad, mashed potatoes, apple sauce, and more. Tonight, there will be a big Thanksgiving dinner at our home, and all our relatives living nearby will join us for dinner. I really can't wait for Thanksgiving dinner.

해석
미국인들에게 추수감사절은 친척을 방문하는 날이며, 따라서 추수감사절은 일 년 중 가장 (사람과 차의) 이동이 많은 날이다. 추수감사절 저녁식사의 주요리는 칠면조이지만, 햄, 샐러드, 으깬 감자, 사과소스 및 기타 음식도 있을 것이다. 오늘 밤, 우리 집에서 성대한 추수감사절 저녁식사가 있어서 근처에 사는 모든 친척들이 우리와 함께 저녁을 먹을 것이다. 나는 추수감사절 저녁식사까지 기다릴 수가 없다.

1. 말하는 사람은 추수감사절 저녁식사에 대해 어떻게 느끼는가?
   a. 실망스럽다   ★b. 신난다
   c. 짜증난다   d. 걱정된다

다시 듣고 질문에 답하시오.

2. 이 단락에 관해 사실이 아닌 것은 무엇인가?
   ★a. 말하는 사람은 추수감사절 저녁식사를 하러 친척집에 갈 것이다.
   b. 칠면조는 추수감사절 저녁식사의 주요리이다.
   c. 가족과 친척들은 추수감사절에 함께 모인다.
   d. 추수감사절에 도로는 차들로 매우 혼잡하다.

두 개의 요약을 듣고 올바른 것을 고르시오.

3.

a. The speaker is away from home, and he is on his way back home to see his family.
b. The speaker is explaining what people do and eat on Thanksgiving Day.

해석
a. ☐ 말하는 사람은 집에서 멀리 떨어져 살아서, 그의 가족을 보기 위해 집으로 가는 중이다.
b. ★ 말하는 사람은 추수감사절에 사람들이 무엇을 하며 무엇을 먹는지를 설명하고 있다.

Practice Test p. 32~33

1. a	2. c	3. c	4. d	5. c	6. d
7. d	8. b	9. d	10. b		

[1–2] 다음 대화를 듣고 질문에 답하시오.

Andy   How was your Valentine's Day, Cherry?
Cherry   It was great, Andy. Jake sent me a dozen roses along with a CD I have wanted for a long time. Then, we had a romantic dinner at a French restaurant.
Andy   What did you give to Jake?
Cherry   I gave him a card and some chocolate I made.
Andy   Did you make the chocolate yourself?
Cherry   Yes. I found a recipe in a cookbook. It was quite easy to make. I made one big heart-shaped chocolate with our names written on it.

해석
Andy   밸런타인데이 어땠어, Cherry?
Cherry   근사했어, Andy. Jake가 내가 오랫동안 갖고 싶었던 CD와 함께 장미 열두 송이를 보내줬어. 그리고 나서 우리는 프랑스식 식당에서 낭만적인 저녁식사를 했지.
Andy   넌 Jake에게 뭘 해줬는데?
Cherry   카드와 내가 만든 초콜릿을 줬어.
Andy   초콜릿을 네가 직접 만들었다고?
Cherry   응. 요리책에서 만드는 법을 찾았는데, 만들기 쉽더라고. 하트 모양의 큰 초콜릿을 만들어서 우리 이름을 그 위에 썼지.

1. Cherry가 마지막으로 한 말에 대한 응답으로 올 수 없는 것은 무엇인가?

Andy _____

   ★a. 네가 감히!   b. 사랑스럽기도 하지!
   c. 멋진걸!   d. 낭만적이다!

2. Cherry가 Jake에게 준 선물은 무엇인가?
   a.   b.   ★c.   d.

스크립트

Tanya	Dave, what's your plan for Mother's Day?
Dave	My brothers and I are sending my mother on a cruise with Dad.
Tanya	That is a great idea, but won't it cost a lot of money?
Dave	Yes, it will, but we decided to do it for her anyway because it has always been her dream. What is your plan, Tanya?
Tanya	This year, I am just giving my mother flowers and a pair of shoes, but I should consider something special for next year.

해석

Tanya	Dave, 어머니날에 계획이 어떻게 돼?
Dave	형들과 나는 엄마를 아빠와 함께 유람선 여행을 보내드릴 거야.
Tanya	그거 멋진 생각인걸. 하지만 돈이 많이 들지 않을까?
Dave	응, 많이 들 거야. 하지만 엄마를 위해 보내드리기로 했어. 그게 엄마의 오랜 꿈이었거든. 너는 계획이 어떻게 돼, Tanya?
Tanya	올해는 엄마께 그냥 꽃과 구두 한 켤레를 드리려고. 하지만 내년에는 뭔가 특별한 걸 생각해 봐야겠어.

3. 두 사람은 무엇에 대해 말하고 있는가?
   a. Dave 어머니의 생일을 위한 비밀 계획
   b. Dave의 형을 위한 깜짝 선물
   ★c. 어머니날을 위한 계획
   d. Dave의 오랜 바람

4. Dave의 어머니는 무엇을 받을 것인가?
   a. 아무것도 받지 않는다.   b. 꽃
   c. 꽃과 구두 한 켤레   ★d. 유람선 여행

[5-6] 다음 대화를 듣고 질문에 답하시오.

스크립트

M	Are you coming to the school Halloween party?
W	I'm afraid I can't.
M	Why not?
W	My parents are out of town this week, so I have to put together my younger brother's Halloween costume and then accompany him when he goes trick-or-treating.
M	How nice of you! We will miss you at the party, though.

W	By the way, what are you wearing to the party?
M	I'm wearing a Spider Man costume.
W	I wish I could see that.

해석

남	학교 핼로윈 파티에 올 거야?
여	못 갈 것 같아.
남	왜?
여	부모님이 이번 주에 어디를 좀 가셔서, 내가 남동생에게 핼로윈 복장을 마련해주고 그 후엔 동생이 사탕 얻으러 돌아다니는 데 따라가 줘야 해.
남	좋은 누나네! 하지만 파티에서 모두 널 보고 싶어할 거야.
여	그런데 넌 파티에 뭘 입을 거야?
남	스파이더맨 복장을 입을거야.
여	그걸 볼 수 있으면 좋을텐데.

5. 여자는 왜 학교 핼로윈 파티에 가지 않는가?
   a. 스파이더맨 복장을 입고 싶지 않아서
   b. 부모님이 가지 못하게 해서
   ★c. 동생이 사탕 얻으러 다니는 데에 따라가 줘야 해서
   d. 핼로윈 파티를 무서워 해서

6. 이 대화에 관해 사실인 것은 무엇인가?
   a. 남자는 여자와 함께 사탕을 얻으러 다닐 것이다.
   b. 여자는 파티에서 남자의 댄스 파트너이다.
   c. 여자는 남자에게 스파이더맨 옷을 입으라고 제안한다.
   ★d. 여자의 부모님은 이번 주에 집에 없다.

[7-8] 다음 대화를 듣고 질문에 답하시오.

스크립트

Irene	Do you have plans for tomorrow, Billy? It's April Fool's Day.
Billy	No, Irene. I don't want to fool anybody on April Fool's Day any more.
Irene	Why not?
Billy	On last April Fool's Day, I told my friends that one of our classmates, Tom, had been in a car accident, and everyone took it seriously. But, once they found out it was a lie, everybody became very upset with me. Since then, I promised I would never do anything like that again.
Irene	I see.

해석

Irene	내일 무슨 계획 있어, Billy? 내일 만우절인데.
Billy	없어, Irene. 난 더 이상 만우절에 사람들을 속이고 싶지 않아.
Irene	왜?

Billy	지난 만우절에 내 반 친구 중 한 명인 Tom이 교통사고를 당했다고 친구들에게 말했는데, 모두가 너무 심각하게(=진짜로) 받아들였어. 하지만, 그게 거짓말이라는 것을 알고 나자 모두가 나에게 무척 화를 냈었어. 그때 이후로 그런 짓을 다시는 하지 않겠다고 약속했거든.
Irene	그렇구나.

7. Billy는 작년에 사람들에게 무슨 말을 했는가?
   a. "나 아파서 오늘 학교에 못 가겠어."
   b. "난 다시는 어느 누구에게도 거짓말 하지 않을 거야."
   c. "모두가 네게 화났어, Irene."
   ★d. "Tom이 오늘 아침 차에 치었어!"

8. Billy는 만우절에 왜 다시는 거짓말을 하지 않을 것인가?
   a. 거짓말을 잘 못하기 때문에
   ★b. 사람들을 속인 것과 관련된 나쁜 경험이 있어서
   c. (거짓말을 할) 계획 만드는 것이 귀찮아서
   d. 친구들에게 속고 싶지 않아서

[9~10] 다음 이야기를 듣고 질문에 답하시오.

스크립트

Many countries celebrate Independence Day, the day their country was liberated from another country's rule. For the United States, Independence Day is July 4th. Many people post American flags outside their homes and in the streets. People take the day off from work to have a picnic or a barbecue in the park. In the evening, the sky lights up with fireworks while a band plays the national anthem and other patriotic songs.

해석

많은 나라들이 독립기념일, 즉 그 나라가 다른 나라의 지배로부터 해방된 날을 기념한다. 미국의 독립기념일은 7월 4일이다. 많은 사람들이 집과 거리에 미국 국기를 게양한다. 사람들은 그날 일을 쉬고 공원에서 소풍을 즐기거나 바비큐를 먹는다. 저녁에는 악단이 국가와 다른 애국적인 노래들을 연주하는 가운데 하늘이 불꽃놀이로 환해진다.

9. 미국의 독립기념일은 며칠인가?
   a.   b.   c.   ★d.

10. 사람들이 독립기념일에 하지 <u>않는</u> 것은 무엇인가?
   a. 국기 게양   ★b. 무료 저녁식사
   c. 공원 가기   d. 불꽃놀이 구경

Dictation (Listening Task)   p. 34

LISTENING 1
going to go, Can't you wait, two days before, it was packed, Lines were too long, terrible, until the last minute, we need to get, will take care of

LISTENING 2
any plans for Independence Day, have a barbecue, fireworks in the park, What time should I be there, Come by, want me to bring anything, I'll see you

LISTENING 3
the evening of December 31st, close friends, get together for a party, waiting for midnight, close to midnight, starts to count down, shouts, hug and kiss, for a few hours

LISTENING 4
American people, to visit relatives, one of the busiest, The main food, there may also be, a big Thanksgiving dinner, relatives living nearby, I really can't wait for

Dictation (Practice Test)   p. 35

PRACTICE TEST [1-2]
your Valentine's Day, sent me a dozen roses, I have wanted for a long time, What did you give to, some chocolate I made, yourself, a recipe in a cookbook, heart-shaped

PRACTICE TEST [3-4]
for Mother's Day, sending my mother on a cruise, cost a lot of money, decided to do it, it has always been her dream, This year, I should consider, next year

PRACTICE TEST [5-6]
Are you coming to, I'm afraid I can't, out of town, Halloween costume, accompany, How nice of you, what are you wearing, I wish I could see that

PRACTICE TEST [7-8]
have plans for tomorrow, fool anybody, Why not, in a car accident, took it seriously, found out, became very upset with me, would never do anything like that

PRACTICE TEST [9-10]
Many countries celebrate, was liberated from, July 4th, post American flags, take the day off from work, have a picnic, lights up with, a band plays

UNIT 5
I apologize to you.

A

sorry to tell, can't attend, are supposed to, not coming, can't help it, Sorry to hear that, make it, understanding, my apology, your fault

B

(1)-(d)   (2)-(a)   (3)-(b)   (4)-(c)

A 아래 대화를 읽고 빈칸을 완성하시오.

이해, 참석할 수 없다, 네 잘못, 어쩔 수 없다, 안됐구나(그런 말을 들어 유감이다), 내 사과, 오지 않는, 말하기 미안한, ~하기로 되어 있다, 시간 안에 가다(해내다)

John 여보세요?

Steve John? 나 Steve야. 이런 말 해서 미안한데, 오늘 회의에 참석 못 할 것 같아. 문제가 좀 생겼어.

John 아, 안되는데. 네가 발표를 하기로 되어 있잖아. 네가 안 오면 우린 어떡해?

Steve 정말 미안해. 하지만 어쩔 수가 없어. 동생이 열이 많이 나는데 돌봐줄 사람이 없거든. 동생을 병원에 데리고 가야 해.

John 안됐다. 그러면 넌 언제 올 수 있어? 우리가 시간을 조금 연기할 수도 있는데.

Steve 갈 수 없을 것 같아. 너한테 자료를 넘겨주면 어떨까? 내 대신 네가 발표를 할 수도 있잖아.

John 좋아. 그렇게 해볼게.

Steve 이해해줘서 고마워. 다른 사람에게도 미안하다고 전해줘.

John 그건 걱정 마. 네 잘못이 아니잖아. 아무튼 동생이 빨리 낫길 바란다.

B 아래와 같은 실수를 한다면, 뭐라고 말하겠는가? 친구들과 이야기해 보시오.

[A] (1) 누군가의 발을 밟았다
(2) 누군가의 컴퓨터를 망가뜨렸다
(3) 모임에 늦었다
(4) 누군가의 감정을 상하게 했다

[B] (a) 용서해 주세요. 제가 보상할게요.
(b) 기다리게 해서 미안해요.
(c) 진심이 아니었어요. 죄송해요.
(d) 죄송해요. 괜찮으세요?

◁))) [A]누군가의 발을 밟았을 때, [B]"죄송해요. 괜찮으세요?"라고 말할 수 있다.

Listening 1	**1. b**	**2. A. T**	**B. F**
Listening 2	**1. a**	**2. c**	**3. b**
Listening 3	**1. c**	**2. a**	
Listening 4	**1. b**	**2. d**	**3. b**

Listening 1
p. 38

다음 대화를 듣고 질문에 답하시오.

스크립트

M Hello?

W Where are you, John? I have been waiting for an hour now.

M Oops, we were supposed to have dinner together tonight. I am so sorry. I was so busy, I forgot.

W How can you do that to me again? Stop using the same excuse. I hate you!

M I am really sorry. I will be there in twenty minutes.

W Don't bother. I am going home.

M I'm really sorry. Will you forgive me?

W No, I won't.

해석

남 여보세요?

여 어디야, John? 지금 한 시간째 기다리고 있어.

남 앗 이런, 우리 오늘 밤 저녁 같이 먹기로 했었지. 정말 미안해. 내가 너무 바빠서 깜박했어.

여 어떻게 나한테 또 그럴 수가 있어? 같은 변명은 하지 마. 너 정말 미워!

남 정말 미안해. 20분 안에 도착할게.

여 그럴 필요 없어. 난 집에 갈 거야.

남 진짜 미안해. 용서해 줄래?

여 아니, 용서 안 할 거야.

1. 여자의 심경은 어떠한가?
   a. 걱정한다   ★b. 화가 났다
   c. 창피하다   d. 낙담했다

다시 듣고 True(참) 또는 False(거짓)에 표시하시오.

2. A. 남자는 여자와의 약속을 자주 잊는다. (T)
   B. 여자는 남자와 저녁식사를 하기 위해 좀 더 기다릴 것이다. (F)

22

Listening 2

p. 38

다음 대화를 듣고 질문에 답하시오.

스크립트

W I'm sorry about my dog barking last night.

M It's all right. I used to have a dog, too.

W I don't know what was wrong with him. He just kept barking.

M I think I know what the problem was.

W What was it?

M My cat was walking back and forth near your window last night.

W Oh, that's why. My dog hates cats. Anyway, I apologize for all the barking.

M Don't mention it. It was my fault that my cat was outside near your house.

해석

여 어젯밤에 우리 집 개가 짖어댄 것에 대해 사과드려요.

남 괜찮아요. 저도 한때 개를 키웠는걸요.

여 그 녀석한테 무슨 문제가 있었는지 모르겠어요. 그냥 계속 짖기만 하는 거예요.

남 뭐가 문제였는지 알 것 같은데요.

여 뭐였는데요?

남 우리 고양이가 어젯밤에 댁의 집 창문 근처를 왔다 갔다 했거든요.

여 아, 그래서였군요. 우리 개가 고양이를 싫어하거든요. 아무튼 개가 짖은 거에 대해선 사과드려요.

남 그러지 않으셔도 되요. 우리집 고양이가 댁의 집 주위를 돌아다닌 건 제 잘못인걸요.

1. 두 사람은 무슨 관계인가?

★a. 이웃이다.   b. 동물 조련사이다.

c. 룸메이트이다.   d. 결혼한 부부이다.

다시 듣고 질문에 답하시오.

2. 개가 짖은 이유는 무엇인가?

a. 개는 매일 밤 짖는다.

b. 개가 아팠다.

★c. 고양이가 창문가를 걸어 다녔다.

d. 개는 새 집을 좋아하지 않았다.

두 개의 요약을 듣고 올바른 것을 고르시오.

3.

스크립트

a. The woman is explaining to the man why her dog was barking last night.

b. The woman is apologizing for her dog barking last night.

해석

a. ☐ 여자는 남자에게 그녀의 개가 지난밤에 짖어댄 이유를 설명하고 있다.

b. ★ 여자는 지난밤에 그녀의 개가 짖은 것에 대해 사과하고 있다.

Listening 3

p. 39

다음 이야기를 듣고 질문에 답하시오.

스크립트

Dear Daisy,

This is Kate. I am sorry for what I did last night. I was a bit rude when I told you I couldn't help you. I have been quite sensitive lately since I broke up with Josh last week. Anyway I am really sorry. I did find the information you wanted and I've emailed you and attached the file. I hope it is helpful to you. Please forgive me for my rudeness.
I'll see you at school tomorrow. Bye.

해석

Daisy에게,

나 Kate야. 어젯밤 일에 대해 사과할게. 너를 못 도와주겠다고 한 건 내가 좀 무례했던 것 같아. 지난주에 Josh와 헤어져서 요즘 아주 예민해져 있었거든. 아무튼 정말 미안해. 네가 원하던 정보를 찾아서 이메일로 파일 첨부해서 보냈어. 파일이 너에게 도움이 되었으면 좋겠다. 나의 무례함을 용서해 줬으면 해. 내일 학교에서 봐. 안녕.

1. Kate는 무엇에 대해 사과하고 있는가?

a. 그녀의 지각   b. 거짓말 한 것

★c. 그녀의 무례함   d. 약속을 깬 것

다시 듣고 질문에 답하시오.

2. 이 단락에 대해 사실이 아닌 것은 무엇인가?

★a. Daisy는 그녀의 남자친구와 싸웠다.

b. Kate와 Daisy는 같은 학교에 다닌다.

c. Kate는 Daisy가 자신을 용서하기 바란다.

d. Kate는 이메일에 Daisy가 필요로 하는 파일을 첨부했다.

Listening 4

p. 39

다음 이야기를 듣고 질문에 답하시오.

스크립트

This is a formal letter of apology for the inconvenience you experienced in our store. We're really sorry for the trouble

our employee caused you on your last visit here. We truly regret what happened. That employee is still in training, and he did not understand our store policy completely. We hope you understand. As a token of our regret, we want to present you with the enclosed certificate for a 10% discount on any purchase you make on your next visit to our store.

해석

손님께서 저희 매장에서 겪으신 불편에 대한 공식 사과 편지를 드립니다. 손님께서 지난번 저희 매장을 방문하신 날 저희 직원이 일으킨 물의에 대해 진심으로 사과드립니다. 그런 일이 생겨서 정말 죄송합니다. 그 직원은 아직 교육 중이어서 매장 규정을 아직 완전히 파악하지 못했습니다. 손님께서 이해해 주시기 바랍니다. 사과의 표시로, 다음에 저희 매장을 방문하실 때 손님께서 구매하시는 모든 상품에 대해 10% 할인받을 수 있는 할인권을 동봉하였습니다.

1. 말하는 사람은 무엇에 대해 사과를 하고 있는가?
   a. 잘못된 청구서 ★b. 직원의 실수
   c. 늦은 배송 d. 상품 품절

다시 듣고 질문에 답하시오.

2. 말하는 사람이 손님에게 제시하고 있는 것은 무엇인가?
   a. 10달러짜리 상품권 b. VIP 카드
   c. 세일 중인 상품 목록 ★d. 상품에 대한 10% 할인

두 개의 요약을 듣고 올바른 것을 고르시오.

3.

스크립트

a. The speaker is apologizing for the trouble he caused the customer.

b. The customer will be offered a discount on his or her next purchases as a token of regret.

해석

a. ☐ 말하는 사람은 자신이 고객에게 저지른 문제에 대해 사과하고 있다.

b. ★ 고객은 사과의 표시로 다음 방문 시 구매한 물건에 대해 할인을 받을 것이다.

Practice Test
p. 40~41

1. b	2. a	3. a	4. c	5. d	6. b
7. d	8. b	9. c	10. d		

[1–2] 다음 대화를 듣고 질문에 답하시오.

스크립트

Tom	Mrs. Hopkins?
Mrs. Hopkins	This is she.
Tom	This is Tom from Sam's Appliances. We are supposed to deliver your refrigerator today, but we are out of red refrigerators like the one you ordered. Would you be interested in either white or ivory instead?
Mrs. Hopkins	No, it won't go with my kitchen. When will you have the red one?
Tom	We will have one by next Monday.
Mrs. Hopkins	I will wait until then.
Tom	I apologize, Mrs. Hopkins. Thank you for understanding.

해석

Tom	Hopkins 부인이신가요?
Hopkins 부인	그런데요.
Tom	Sam 전자제품의 Tom이라고 합니다. 오늘 손님의 냉장고를 배달하기로 되어 있는데, 주문하신 빨간색 냉장고의 재고가 없습니다. 대신 흰색이나 아이보리색은 어떠신지요?
Hopkins 부인	아뇨, 그 색은 우리 부엌에 어울리지 않을 거예요. 빨간색이 언제 다시 들어오죠?
Tom	다음 주 월요일에 들어올 겁니다.
Hopkins 부인	그때까지 기다릴게요.
Tom	죄송합니다, Hopkins 부인. 이해해 주셔서 감사합니다.

1. 이 상황으로부터 추론할 수 있는 것은 무엇인가?
   a. Hopkins 부인은 주문을 취소할 것이다.
   ★b. Hopkins 부인은 결국 자신이 원했던 것을 갖게 될 것이다.
   c. Hopkins 부인은 다른 제품을 살 것이다.
   d. Hopkins 부인은 회사에 불만을 제기할 것이다.

2. Hopkins 부인은 어떤 색상의 냉장고를 원하는가?
   ★a. 빨간색 b. 흰색 c. 아이보리색 d. 회색

[3–4] 다음 대화를 듣고 질문에 답하시오.

스크립트

Mr. Lopez	Stella, can I have a minute with you?
Stella	Yes, Mr. Lopez.
Mr. Lopez	I think I was too harsh with you yesterday. I don't think it was your fault that you weren't able to sell the bed.

Stella	Don't worry, Mr. Lopez. It may have been partly my fault. Besides, I had forgotten all about it already.
Mr. Lopez	Will you accept my apology?
Stella	Certainly, Mr. Lopez.

해석

Lopez 씨	Stella, 잠깐 얘기 좀 할 수 있을까요?
Stella	네, Lopez 씨.
Lopez 씨	어제 당신한테 내가 너무 심했던 것 같아서요. 그 침대를 팔지 못했던 게 당신 잘못이 아니라는 생각이 들어요.
Stella	염려마세요, Lopez 씨. 부분적으론 제 잘못이기도 한 것 같아요. 게다가, 이미 그 일에 대해선 벌써 다 잊었어요.
Lopez 씨	내 사과를 받아주는 겁니까?
Stella	그럼요, Lopez 씨.

3. 그들이 대화하는 곳은 어디인가?

★a.　　　　b.　　　　c.　　　　d.

4. Lopez 씨는 왜 Stella에게 사과를 하고 있는가?

　　a. 그가 망가진 물건을 팔았기 때문에
　　b. 그가 손님에게 너무 무례했기 때문에
★c. 그가 Stella에게 너무 심하게 대했기 때문에
　　d. 그가 아무것도 팔지 못했기 때문에

[5-6] 다음 대화를 듣고 질문에 답하시오.

스크립트

Lisa	Tony, I'm sorry about what I said last night.
Tony	You really hurt my feelings when you said I was stupid.
Lisa	I know. I apologize. I was very upset at that moment, so I didn't even realize what I was saying. I didn't mean it. Please forgive me.
Tony	All right, but please don't ever say that again. You really hurt me.
Lisa	I'm so sorry. I promise you that I will never say that again.

해석

Lisa	Tony, 어젯밤에 내가 한 말 사과할게.
Tony	네가 나에게 멍청하다고 해서 정말 상처 받았어.
Lisa	알아. 미안해. 그 순간에 정말 화가 나서 내가 무슨 말을 하고 있는지도 몰랐어. 진심은 아니었어. 부디 용서해 줘.
Tony	그래. 하지만 다시는 그런 말 하지 마. 정말 상처 받았어.
Lisa	정말 미안해. 다시는 그런 말 하지 않겠다고 약속할게.

5. 이 상황에 알맞은 속담은 무엇인가?

　　a. 모험이 없으면 얻는 것이 없다.
　　b. 뿌린 대로 거둔다.
　　c. 오늘 할 일을 내일로 미루지 마라.
★d. 말이 검보다 더 날카롭다.

6. Lisa가 어제 Tony에게 한 말은 무엇인가?

　　a. Tony는 거짓말쟁이다.
★b. Tony는 멍청하다.
　　c. Tony는 절대 약속을 지키지 않는다.
　　d. Tony는 너무 수다스럽다.

[7-8] 다음 대화를 듣고 질문에 답하시오.

스크립트

Boy	Excuse me, sir. Are you the owner of the house?
Man	Yes, why?
Boy	I broke your window glass while playing with my friends.
Man	You are the one who broke it!
Boy	I am really sorry. I will take care of the repair as soon as possible.
Man	Hey, these things happen. I'll have the glass replaced myself. I broke a lot of windows when I was young, too. So I understand.
Boy	Thank you for being so understanding.

해석

소년	실례합니다, 선생님. 이 집 주인이신가요?
남자	그래, 무슨 일이니?
소년	제가 친구들과 놀다가 그만 이 집 창문을 깼어요.
남자	네가 바로 창문을 깬 애구나!
소년	정말 죄송합니다. 가능한 한 빨리 수리하도록 할게요.
남자	얘야, 이런 일은 있기 마련이야. 유리는 내가 갈아 끼우마. 나도 어렸을 때 창문 많이 깼었지. 그래서 다 이해한단다.
소년	이해해 주셔서 감사합니다.

7. 이 집의 주인은 (성품이) 어떠한가?

　　a. 가혹하다　　　　b. 부주의하다
　　c. 이기적이다　　★d. 너그럽다

8. 이 집의 주인에 대해 사실인 것은 무엇인가?

　　a. 그는 경찰을 부를 것이다.
★b. 본인이 창문 유리를 교체할 것이다.
　　c. 그는 소년에게 창문 유리를 사게 할 것이다.
　　d. 그는 소년의 부주의함을 벌할 것이다.

스크립트

People make mistakes and accidents can happen. You can make a mistake and hurt someone knowingly or unknowingly. You don't need to blame yourself too much, but it is very important to know how to resolve the situation. This means that you must learn how to apologize. There are a few useful expressions you can use to apologize: I am sorry, Will you accept my apology?, That was my fault, etc. They are simple, but very useful.

해석

사람은 실수를 하게 마련이고 사고도 일어날 수 있다. 당신도 실수를 할 수 있고 알게 모르게 다른 사람에게 상처를 줄 수도 있다. (그런 경우에) 자신을 너무 탓할 필요는 없지만, 그 상황을 해결하는 방법을 아는 것은 매우 중요하다. 즉, 사과하는 법을 배워야 한다는 뜻이다. 사과할 때 쓸 수 있는 몇 가지 유용한 표현들이 있다: 죄송합니다, 제 사과를 받아주시겠어요?, 그건 제 잘못이었습니다 등등. 이 표현들은 간단하지만 아주 유용하다.

9. 이 단락의 요지는 무엇인가?
   a. 사고는 일어나기 마련이다.
   b. 누구나 실수를 하니까 걱정하지 않아도 된다.
   ★c. 실수를 했을 때는 사과를 하는 것이 중요하다.
   d. 잘못된 사과는 아무 말도 안 하는 것보다 더 나쁘다.

10. 다음 빈 칸에 들어갈 알맞은 말을 고르시오.

> 뭔가 잘못을 했더라도 너무 심하게 자신을[에게]
> _____A_____ 할 필요는 없다. 그 상황을 직시하고
> 진심어린 _____B_____ 을[를] 표하라.

	A		B
a.	사과	--	도움
b.	거짓말	--	동정
c.	표현	--	감사
★d.	탓	--	사과

Dictation (Listening Task) p. 42

LISTENING 1
waiting for an hour, were supposed to, I forgot, Stop using the same excuse, I am really sorry, Don't bother, Will you forgive me

LISTENING 2
I'm sorry about, I used to have, what was wrong, what the problem was, walking back and forth, that's why, I apologize for, Don't mention it, my cat was outside

LISTENING 3
sorry for what I did, a bit rude, sensitive lately, broke up with, attached the file, helpful to you, forgive me for my rudeness

LISTENING 4
a formal letter of apology, our employee caused, regret what happened, in training, As a token of, a 10% discount, on your next visit

Dictation (Practice Test) p. 43

PRACTICE TEST [1-2]
This is she, are supposed to deliver, out of, Would you be interested in, it won't go with, the red one, by next Monday, wait until then, Thank you for understanding

PRACTICE TEST [3-4]
can I have a minute, too harsh with you, weren't able to sell the bed, Don't worry, partly my fault, I had forgotten all about it, Will you accept, Certainly

PRACTICE TEST [5-6]
what I said last night, hurt my feelings, I apologize, didn't mean it, don't ever say that again, hurt me, I promise you

PRACTICE TEST [7-8]
Excuse me, while playing, You are the one, take care of the repair, these things happen, have the glass replaced, when I was young, being so understanding

PRACTICE TEST [9-10]
make mistakes, accidents can happen, don't need to blame yourself, important to know, the situation, how to apologize, a few useful expressions, but very useful

UNIT 6
How was your trip?

Getting Ready

p. 45

A

looking for, travel information, backpacking trip to, travel alone, how long, stay in, planning to, get to, focus on, thoroughly

B

[A] 박스 안의 여행과 [B] 박스 안의 느낌을 골라 자유롭게 응답

A 아래 대화를 읽고 빈칸을 완성하시오.

~에 집중하다, ~하려고 계획 중인, 완전히(철저히), ~을 찾는, 혼자 여행하다, ~로의 배낭여행, ~에 가다, 여행 정보, ~에 머무르다, 얼마나 오래

Gerry 뭘 찾고 있어?

Julio 여행 정보를 좀 찾고 있어. 다음 달에 유럽으로 배낭여행을 갈 계획이거든.

Gerry 오, 정말? 누구랑 갈거니?

Julio 혼자 여행할 거야.

Gerry 와, 혼자? 얼마나 있을 건데?

Julio 유럽에 한 달 머무를 거야.

Gerry 마음에 두고 있는 특별한 나라라도 있어?

Julio 아직 결정은 안했지만 10개국 이상 가볼까 계획 중이야. 이런 기회는 다시 또 없을 테니까, 가능한 한 많은 나라를 가보려고 해.

Gerry 글쎄, 내가 너라면 몇 곳만 중점적으로 돌아보겠어. 그곳들을 완전히 알 수 있도록 말이지.

Julio 그 말도 맞네. 염두에 둘게.

B 어떤 종류의 여행을 해 보았는가? 친구들과 이야기해 보시오.

[A] 배낭여행	[B] 지루한
휴가 여행	끔찍한
단체 관광	멋진
해외여행	훌륭한
자전 여행	외로운
도시 관광	근사한
수학여행	흥미로운
	감동적인
	내 일생에 가장 멋진 여행

◁))) A: [A]배낭여행 어땠어?   B: [B]좋았어.

Listening Task

p. 46~47

Listening 1	1. d	2. A. T	B. F
Listening 2	1. b	2. c	3. b
Listening 3	1. b	2. c	
Listening 4	1. b	2. a	3. b

Listening I

p. 46

다음 대화를 듣고 질문에 답하시오.

스크립트

Dallas What are you reading, Amy?

Amy I am reading these travel packages.

Dallas Are you going on a vacation?

Amy No, just on a weekend trip. Look at this ad. It says, "A weekend ski trip to Mammoth Ski Resort. Lodging and two days of skiing for just $99." What do you think?

Dallas That sounds like a good deal. What time do they leave?

Amy They leave Friday at 7:00 p.m.

Dallas That sounds even better. I think you should go for it.

Amy I agree.

해석

Dallas 읽고 있는 게 뭐야, Amy?

Amy 패키지 여행에 대해 읽고 있어.

Dallas 휴가 갈 생각이야?

Amy 아니, 그냥 주말 여행. 이 광고 좀 봐. "Mammoth 스키 리조트로의 주말 스키 여행. 99달러에 숙박과 이틀 동안의 스키"라네. 어떤 것 같아?

Dallas 괜찮은 조건인데, 몇 시에 출발하는 거야?

Amy 금요일 오후 7시에 출발해.

Dallas 그건 더 괜찮은걸. 가지 그래.

Amy 좋았어.

1. Amy는 어디에 갈 것인가?

a.   b.   c.   ★d.

다시 듣고 True(참) 또는 False(거짓)에 표시하시오.

2. A. 남자는 그 패키지 여행 상품이 좋은 조건이라고 생각한다. (T)

B. 패키지는 두 명의 숙박과 스키를 포함한다. (F)

27

Listening 2

p. 46

다음 대화를 듣고 질문에 답하시오.

스크립트

Judith　How was your trip to Florida, Ted?

Ted　We never got to Florida.

Judith　What happened?

Ted　There was a big hurricane heading for Florida, so we changed our plans. We went to Louisiana instead.

Judith　Was it boring staying in Louisiana?

Ted　No. We went to a great jazz concert, and we had great food, too. We didn't know it before, but Louisiana is a fun place.

해석

Judith　플로리다 여행 어땠어, Ted?

Ted　플로리다엔 가지 못했어.

Judith　무슨 일이 있었는데?

Ted　플로리다에 큰 허리케인이 닥쳤거든. 그래서 계획을 변경했어. 대신 루이지애나로 갔지.

Judith　루이지애나에서는 지루했어?

Ted　아니. 멋진 재즈 공연도 보고 맛있는 음식도 먹었어. 전에는 몰랐는데, 루이지애나는 아주 재미있는 곳이 더라고.

1. Ted의 가족이 플로리다에 가지 <u>않은</u> 이유는 무엇인가?

　a. 플로리다에 가고 싶지 않아서

★b. 플로리다에 큰 허리케인이 와서

　c. 루이지애나를 더 좋아해서

　d. 재즈 콘서트에 가고 싶어서

다시 듣고 질문에 답하시오.

2. Ted의 여행은 어땠는가?

　a. 지루했다　　　　b. 즐겁지 않았다

★c. 대단히 즐거웠다　　d. 실망스러웠다

두 개의 요약을 듣고 올바른 것을 고르시오.

3.

스크립트

a. Because of a big hurricane, Ted did not go to Florida. He stayed home instead.

b. Because of a big hurricane, Ted had to change his plans and go to Louisiana, where he had a great time.

해석

a. □ 큰 허리케인 때문에 Ted는 플로리다에 가지 않았다. 대신 그는 집에 머물렀다.

b. ★ 큰 허리케인 때문에 Ted는 계획을 바꿔 루이지애나에 갔고, 그곳에서 즐거운 시간을 보냈다.

Listening 3

p. 47

다음 이야기를 듣고 질문에 답하시오.

스크립트

I cannot fall asleep because I'm excited and worried about my one-month backpacking trip to Europe with my friends that starts tomorrow. This is my first time to travel abroad, and one month is not a short time. Furthermore, we are planning to go to ten countries, and each country speaks a different language. But my biggest concern is about my friends. Although we are good friends, we may have some disagreements along the way. Even now, we have not quite decided which countries to visit.

해석

내일부터 친구들과 한 달 기간의 유럽 배낭여행을 떠나게 되어 설레고 걱정이 되기도 해서 잠이 오지 않는다. 나는 이번이 내게는 처음 가보는 해외여행인데다 한 달은 짧지 않은 시간이다. 게다가, 우리는 10개국을 가볼 계획인데, 나라마다 제각기 다른 언어를 쓴다. 그러나 가장 큰 걱정은 내 친구들이다. 비록 우리가 친하긴 하지만, 여행하는 동안 불화가 생길지도 모른다. 심지어 지금도 어느 나라를 갈 것인지 완전히 결정하지도 못했다.

1. 말하는 사람이 잠들지 못하는 이유는 무엇인가?

　a. 할 일이 많아서

★b. 유럽 여행이 걱정스러워서

　c. 혼자 여행가고 싶지 않아서

　d. 친한 친구가 없어서

다시 듣고 질문에 답하시오.

2. 말하는 사람은 얼마간 유럽에 머물 것인가?

　a. 일주일　　b. 2~3주　★c. 한 달　　d. 두 달

Listening 4

p. 47

다음 이야기를 듣고 질문에 답하시오.

스크립트

Yesterday, my family went to Santa Monica Beach. Many people were there because it was a long weekend and the weather was warm. Some people were playing volleyball or fishing, but most of the people were just sunbathing, and few people were swimming.

I was wondering why there were so few swimmers. I soon realized why when I went into the water; the water was too cold.

어제 우리 가족은 산타모니카 해변에 갔다. 긴 주말 연휴였고 날씨까지 따뜻해서 사람들이 많았다. 몇몇 사람들은 배구나 낚시를 하는 사람들이 있었지만 대부분은 그저 일광욕을 하고 있었다. 수영하는 사람은 극히 적었다. 수영하는 사람들이 왜 그렇게 적은지 의아했는데, 물에 들어가 보고서 곧 그 이유를 알게 되었다. 물이 너무나 차가웠다.

1. 산타모니카 해변의 날씨는 어땠는가?
   a. 가벼운 소나기가 내렸다   ★b. 따뜻했다
   c. 서늘하고 흐렸다   d. 바람이 불었다

다시 듣고 질문에 답하시오.

2. 이 상황과 관련 없는 그림은 무엇인가?
   ★a.   b.   c.   d.

두 개의 요약을 듣고 올바른 것을 고르시오.

3.

스크립트

a. The speaker had a great time playing volleyball and swimming at Santa Monica beach.
b. Despite the warm weather, not many people at the beach went swimming because the water was too cold.

해석
a. □ 말하는 사람은 산타모니카 해변에서 배구와 수영을 하면서 즐거운 시간을 보냈다.
b. ★ 따뜻한 날씨에도 불구하고 물이 너무 차가워서 해변에 있는 많은 사람들이 수영을 하지 않았다.

Practice Test
p. 48~49

| 1. d | 2. b | 3. a | 4. b | 5. c | 6. c |
| 7. d | 8. c | 9. a | 10. d | | |

[1~2] 다음 대화를 듣고 질문에 답하시오.

스크립트

Jane Sam, I heard that you are planning to travel alone.
Sam   That is right.
Jane Why would you travel alone? You'll be lonely, and you'll have to do everything by yourself.
Sam   You are probably right. But if you travel alone, you can go anywhere you want at anytime you want.

Jane I see your point, but you will have no one to share the experience with.
Sam   You're right about that, too, but that's the way I like to travel.

해석
Jane Sam, 너 혼자서 여행 간다면서?
Sam   맞아.
Jane 왜 혼자 여행 가? 외롭기도 할테고 혼자서 모든 걸 처리해야 할텐데.
Sam   아마 네 말이 맞을지도 몰라. 하지만 혼자서 여행하면 내가 원하는 때에 내가 가고 싶은 아무 곳이나 갈 수 있잖아.
Jane 네 생각은 알겠지만, 너와 여행 경험을 같이 나눌 사람이 아무도 없잖아.
Sam   그것 역시 맞는 말이야. 하지만 난 그렇게 여행하는 게 좋아.

1. 혼자 여행하는 것에 대한 여자의 태도는 어떠한가?
   a. 질투가 난다   b. 관심 있다
   c. 긍정적이다   ★d. 부정적이다

2. Sam의 말에 따르면, 혼자 여행해서 좋은 점은 무엇인가?
   a. 돈을 절약할 수 있다.
   ★b. 자신이 가고 싶은 곳을 고를 수 있다.
   c. 새로운 친구를 사귈 수 있다.
   d. 기억에 남을 시간을 많이 가질 수 있다.

[3~4] 다음 대화를 듣고 질문에 답하시오.

스크립트

Eva   Brad, let's go on a vacation together this summer.
Brad Good idea. We had fun the last time we took a vacation together.
Eva   Do you want to go to Miami Beach again?
Brad Maybe this time around, we should try Key West.
Eva   That sounds even better! I will check hotels. Why don't you check out which airline has the cheapest airfare?
Brad OK. How many days are we staying there?
Eva   I can take a week vacation.
Brad I have no problem with that.

해석
Eva   Brad, 이번 여름에 같이 휴가 가자.
Brad 좋은 생각이야. 지난번에 같이 휴가 갔을 때 정말 재있었어.

Eva	마이애미 해변에 또 갈까?
Brad	이번에는 키웨스트에 가 보자.
Eva	그게 더 낫겠다! 난 호텔을 알아볼게. 넌 어느 항공사가 항공 요금이 가장 싼지 알아볼래?
Brad	그래. 거기서 며칠 정도 보낼까?
Eva	난 일주일간 휴가 낼 수 있어.
Brad	그건 나도 문제 없어.

3. 두 사람은 키웨스트에 어떻게 갈 것인가?
   ★a.   b.   c.   d.

4. 이 대화에서 추론할 수 있는 것은 무엇인가?
   a. 그들은 키웨스트에서 한 달간 지낼 것이다.
   ★b. 그들은 호텔에 묵을 것이다.
   c. 그들은 전에 함께 키웨스트에 간 적이 있다.
   d. 이번이 그들이 함께 가는 첫 여행이다.

[5–6] 다음 이야기를 듣고 질문에 답하시오.

스크립트

If you're going to a new country, keep the following advice in mind. First, learn the country's culture, food, and climate before you go. Secondly, don't try to visit too many places in one journey. Focus on one area and explore the area fully. Meet with the natives. Try their traditional food, and see how they live. A market place would be a good place to start all that. Be sure to rest if you're tired.

해석

만약 새로운 나라를 가게 된다면, 다음 조언을 염두에 두어라. 먼저, 떠나기 전에 그 나라의 문화, 음식, 그리고 기후에 대해 알아두어라. 둘째, 한 번의 여행에 너무 많은 곳을 방문하려고 하지 마라. 한 지역에만 집중해서 그 지역을 완전히 탐방해라. 그곳 사람들과 만나보라. 그들의 전통 음식을 맛보고, 그들이 어떻게 살고 있는지 보라. 시장은 그 모든 것을 시작하기에 좋은 장소가 될 것이다. 그리고 피곤할 때는 반드시 휴식을 취해라.

5. 말하는 사람은 _____.
   a. 새로운 나라를 가는 데 대한 조언을 요청하고 있다
   b. 갈 장소의 목록을 만들고 있다
   ★c. 해외여행에 대해 조언을 주고 있다
   d. 혼자 여행하는 것에 대한 정보를 찾아보고 있다

6. 말하는 사람이 여행에 관해 조언하지 않은 것은 무엇인가?
   a. 떠나기 전에 외국의 문화를 알아보라.
   b. 그 지역 사람들이 어떻게 사는지 보려면 시장에 가라.
   ★c. 가능한 한 많은 장소를 다녀라.
   d. 여행하는 동안 휴식을 취해라.

[7–8] 다음 대화를 듣고 질문에 답하시오.

스크립트

M Honey, let's go on a city tour.
W How long does it take?
M Well, there are two different tours. One will take about two hours, and the other one will take four hours.
W How do they differ?
M The two-hour tour will only cover Westminster Abbey and the London Tower. But the four-hour tour will also cover the Imperial War museum.
W Why don't we go for the first tour?

해석

남 여보, 우리 도시 관광을 갑시다.
여 시간이 얼마나 걸려요?
남 음, 두 개의 다른 관광(코스)이 있는데, 하나는 두 시간 정도 걸리고 다른 하나는 네 시간이 걸린다고 하는군.
여 어떻게 다른데요?
남 두 시간짜리 관광은 웨스트민스터 사원과 런던 탑만 갈 수 있어요. 네 시간짜리 관광은 임페리얼 전쟁 기념관도 돌아보는군.
여 앞의 걸(=두 시간짜리 관광)로 갈까요?

7. 여자의 마지막 말에 남자는 어떻게 대답하겠는가?

   | 남자 _____. |

   a. 그럼, 박물관에 갑시다.
   b. 미안하지만, 난 관광에는 관심이 없소.
   c. 음, 당신은 집에 있는 게 낫겠소.
   ★d. 좋아요. 지금 당장 여행사에 전화하겠소.

8. 두 여행 상품의 차이점은 무엇인가?
   a. 가격   b. 시간과 가격
   ★c. 시간과 가는 장소   d. 가는 장소와 가격

[9–10] 다음 이야기를 듣고 질문에 답하시오.

스크립트

It was not an easy task getting to the world's highest lake, Lake Titicaca. Because it is so high in altitude, I had difficulty breathing. I became sick as I got closer to the lake. I thought I was going to die. But, once I arrived at the lake, I was amazed by its beauty and size. Even though I was sick while I was at the lake, it was the greatest journey of my life.

세상에서 가장 높은 곳에 있는 호수인 티티카카 호수에 가는 것은 쉬운 일이 아니었다. 그곳은 고도가 아주 높아서 숨쉬기가 힘들었다. 호수에 가까이 다가갈수록 몸은 더 힘들었다. 꼭 죽을 것만 같았다. 하지만, 일단 호수에 도착하자 호수의 아름다움과 크기에 감탄하게 되었다. 비록 호수에 있는 동안 컨디션은 좋지 않았지만, 그 여행은 내 평생 가장 멋진 여행이었다.

9. 말하는 사람은 어떤 장소에 대해 이야기하고 있는가?
   ★a. 세상에서 가장 높은 곳에 있는 호수
   b. 세상에서 가장 유명한 산
   c. 세상에서 가장 큰 나라
   d. 세상에서 가장 큰 사막

10. 말하는 사람은 왜 몸이 아프게 되었는가?
    a. 그 장소가 너무 멀어서
    b. 상한 음식을 먹어서
    c. 오랜 시간 비행기를 타서
    ★d. 그 장소가 고도가 높은 곳에 있어서

Dictation (Listening Task) p. 50

LISTENING 1
travel packages, going on a vacation, on a weekend trip, A weekend ski trip to, Lodging and two days of skiing, That sounds like a good deal, sounds even better, go for it

LISTENING 2
How was your trip, got to, What happened, a big hurricane heading for, changed our plans, instead, boring staying in, had great food, We didn't know it before, a fun place

LISTENING 3
cannot fall asleep, one-month backpacking trip to Europe, time to travel abroad, planning to go to, speaks a different language, my biggest concern, disagreements along the way, which countries to visit

LISTENING 4
went to, the weather was warm, playing volleyball or fishing, sunbathing, few people, there were so few swimmers, when I went into the water, too cold

Dictation (Practice Test) p. 51

PRACTICE TEST [1-2]
I heard that, travel alone, everything by yourself, anywhere you want, I see your point, share the experience with, that's the way

PRACTICE TEST [3-4]
go on a vacation together, had fun, this time around, I will check hotels, which airline, cheapest airfare, staying, take a week vacation

PRACTICE TEST [5-6]
going to a new country, country's culture, before you go, Focus on, explore the area fully, how they live, a good place, Be sure to rest if you're tired

PRACTICE TEST [7-8]
go on a city tour, How long does it take, different tours, How do they differ, tour will only cover, Why don't we go for

PRACTICE TEST [9-10]
the world's highest lake, so high in altitude, became sick as I got closer, amazed by its beauty and size, was sick, the greatest journey of my life

UNIT 7
We don't talk to each other.

Getting Ready   p. 53

A

have made, getting along, quarrel, open conversation, closer, in love, asked me out, break up, constant

B

- A: How are you getting along with your roommate?
  B: We are very close. We have a lot in common.
- A: How are you getting along with your boss?
  B: We are not getting along very well. We have difficulties sharing our opinions at work.
- A: How are you getting along with your new friend?
  B: We don't talk to each other any more. We had a big fight last month.

A 아래 대화를 읽고 빈칸을 완성하시오.

나에게 데이트 신청을 했다, 더 친한, 끊임없는, 진솔한 대화, 사랑하는(좋아하는), 지내는(어울리는), 헤어지다, 싸우다, 만들었다

Cathy   Angela, 새로운 학교에서 어떻게 지내?
Angela   아직까진 좋아. 친구들도 몇몇 사귀었고 내 룸메이트와도 잘 지내고 있어.
Cathy   잘됐구나. 너도 알다시피, 내 룸메이트와 난 너무 자주 싸워서 오랫동안 서로 말도 안했잖아.
Angela   맞아, 그 애는 항상 널 짜증나게 했지.
Cathy   그거 알아? 우리 지난주에 진솔한 대화를 나눌 기회가 생겨서 지금은 더 친해지려고 노력하고 있어.
Angela   그거 멋진걸!
Cathy   좋은 소식이 또 있어. 내가 좋아했던 Tom 기억나? 그가 어제 나에게 데이트 신청을 했어.
Angela   그 사람 Lisa랑 사귀고 있지 않았어? 걔네들 헤어졌니?
Cathy   그렇다고 들었어. 끊임없는 문제들이 좀 있었다고 하더라.

B 그들은 어떻게 지내고 있는가? 친구들과 이야기해 보시오.

[A] 서로 사랑한다, 매우 가깝다, 그다지 잘 지내지 못한다, 더 이상 서로 이야기하지 않는다

[B] 지난달에 크게 싸웠다, 올해 여름에 결혼한다, 직장에서 의견을 나누는 데 어려움이 있다, 공통점이 많다

A: 당신의 남자친구(새로운 친구/상사/룸메이트)와 어떻게 지내요?
B: 우리는 [A]서로 사랑해요. 우리는 [B]올해 여름에 결혼할 거예요.

Listening Task   p. 54~55

Listening 1	1. d	2. A. F	B. F
Listening 2	1. b	2. d	3. a
Listening 3	1. c	2. d	
Listening 4	1. a	2. c	3. a

Listening 1   p. 54

다음 대화를 듣고 질문에 답하시오.

스크립트

Judy   Patrick, what's going on? You look upset.
Patrick   It's my roommate again, Judy.
Judy   You guys have too many problems these days. The last time it was the rent money issue. What is it now?
Patrick   We agreed on sharing house cleaning chores, but he did a bad job. For me, he is too messy, but he thinks that I am too neat.
Judy   If you have constant problems, I think you need to look for a new roommate.
Patrick   I think so, too.

해석

Judy   Patrick, 무슨 일 있니? 기분이 안 좋아 보여.
Patrick   또 내 룸메이트 때문이야, Judy.
Judy   너희들 요즘 문제가 너무 많더라. 지난번에는 집세 문제였잖아. 이번엔 무슨 일이야?
Patrick   집 청소를 나눠서 하기로 동의했었는데, 그 애가 너무 형편없이 해서 말야. 내가 보기엔 그가 너무 지저분한데 그는 내가 너무 깔끔을 떤다고 생각해.
Judy   너희 둘 사이에 끝없이 문제가 생긴다면, 네가 새로운 룸메이트를 구해야 될 것 같은데.
Patrick   나도 그렇게 생각해.

1. Patrick과 그의 룸메이트는 이번에는 어떤 문제를 겪고 있는가?
   a. 집세   b. 장보기   c. 지나친 소음   ★d. 집 청소 문제

다시 듣고 True(참) 또는 False(거짓)에 표시하시오.

2. A. Patrick과 그의 룸메이트는 매우 잘 지내왔다. (F)
   B. Judy는 Patrick에게 룸메이트와 화해하라고 제안하고 있다. (F)

Listening 2   p. 54

다음 대화를 듣고 질문에 답하시오.

Toby　How long have you two been going out together, Nancy?

Nancy　We have been dating for three years now.

Toby　That is a long time. How did you guys first meet?

Nancy　He came to the café where I work to have coffee. I fell in love with him the very first time I saw him, so I asked him out first.

Toby　Are you guys going to get married?

Nancy　Yes. Actually, he proposed to me last week. We're getting married at the end of this year.

Toby　Congratulations!

해석

Toby　너희 둘 얼마나 오래 사귀었니, Nancy?

Nancy　이제 3년째 사귀고 있어.

Toby　오래 되었네. 처음에 둘이 어떻게 만났어?

Nancy　내가 일하는 카페에 그가 커피를 마시러 왔었어. 그를 보자마자 첫눈에 사랑에 빠졌지. 그래서 내가 먼저 데이트를 신청했어.

Toby　너희들 결혼할거니?

Nancy　응. 실은 지난주에 그가 내게 청혼했어. 우린 올해 말에 결혼할 거야.

Toby　축하해!

1. Nancy와 그녀의 남자친구는 처음에 어디서 만났는가?
   a.   b.   c.   ★d.

다시 듣고 질문에 답하시오.

2. Nancy가 다음에 할 가장 적절한 말은 무엇인가?
   a. 천만에.   b. 유감이다.   c. 괜찮아.   ★d. 고마워.

두 개의 요약을 듣고 올바른 것을 고르시오.

3.

a. Nancy is telling her friend about how she and her boyfriend first met and when they're getting married.

b. Nancy and her boyfriend have been going out together for two years, and they're planning to get married next year.

해석

a. ★ Nancy는 친구에게 자신과 남자친구가 처음 어떻게 만났는지, 언제 결혼할 건지 말해주고 있다.

b. ☐ Nancy와 남자친구는 2년 동안 사귀었고 내년에 결혼할 계획이다.

Listening 3   p. 55

다음 이야기를 듣고 질문에 답하시오.

If you find it difficult to have a father-and-son talk, I strongly suggest going on a trip together. Even though my father and I love each other, we never had an opportunity to have an open conversation. But, everything changed after a fishing trip with my father last year. The trip was long and we did not have much to do, so we started to talk. Eventually, we began to talk about some things we never discussed before.

해석

당신이 만약 부자 간의 대화에 어려움이 있다면, 나는 함께 여행가는 것을 적극 제안한다. 내 아버지와 나는 서로 사랑하는데도 불구하고 진솔한 대화를 나눌 기회를 한번도 갖지 못했었다. 그러나 작년에 아버지와 낚시 여행을 다녀온 후로 모든 것이 변했다. 여행은 길고 할 것은 그다지 많지 않아서, 우리는 대화를 나누기 시작했다. 결국 우리는 전에는 한번도 이야기해 본 적이 없던 것들에 대해 이야기를 나누게 되었다.

1. 이 단락의 주제는 무엇인가?
   a. 낚시 여행이 지루한 이유
   b. 낚시 여행을 준비하는 법
   ★c. 부자 간의 좋은 대화를 할 수 있는 방법
   d. 여름 동안 낚시를 갈 곳

다시 듣고 질문에 답하시오.

2. 여행에 대해 사실인 것은 무엇인가?
   a. 그들은 물고기를 많이 잡았다.
   b. 짧은 여행이었다.
   c. 끔찍한 여행이었다.
   ★d. 그들은 작년에 낚시를 하러 갔다.

Listening 4

p. 55

다음 이야기를 듣고 질문에 답하시오.

스크립트

Matthew and I were good friends for a long time, but we are not talking these days. It started because he forgot to come to the library to help me with my homework. I waited all day in the library. He asked me for forgiveness several times, but I was too upset to forgive him. Now, he is not calling me any more. I think I should call him and tell him how narrow-minded I was.

해석

Matthew와 나는 오랫동안 친한 친구였지만, 요즘은 서로 말을 하지 않는다. 그가 나의 숙제를 도와주러 도서관에 오기로 한 것을 잊어버려서 시작된 일이다. 나는 하루 종일 도서관에서 그를 기다렸었다. 그는 내게 여러 번 용서를 구했지만, 난 너무 화가 나서 그를 용서할 수 없었다. 지금은 그가 더 이상 내게 전화를 하지 않는다. 아무래도 그에게 전화해서 내가 얼마나 속이 좁았었는지 말해야 할 것 같다.

1. 말하는 사람은 지금 Matthew에 대해 어떻게 느끼고 있는가?
   ★a. 미안해한다   b. 화가 났다
   c. 무관심하다   d. 실망했다

다시 듣고 질문에 답하시오.

2. 말하는 사람은 왜 Matthew에게 화가 났는가?
   a. Matthew가 그에게 말을 걸지 않아서
   b. Matthew가 그의 시험 공부를 도와주지 않아서
   ★c. Matthew가 그의 숙제를 도와주기로 한 것을 잊어서
   d. Matthew가 절대 용서를 빌지 않아서

두 개의 요약을 듣고 올바른 것을 고르시오.

3.

스크립트

a. The speaker was angry about his friend Matthew because Matthew broke a promise to him. Now the speaker is willing to be friends with Matthew again.

b. The speaker has called his friend Matthew several times to ask for forgiveness, but Matthew never called back.

해석

a. ★ 말하는 사람은 그의 친구인 Matthew가 자신과의 약속을 깨서 그에게 화가 났다. 말하는 사람은 지금은 Matthew와 다시 친구로 지내고자 한다.

b. ☐ 말하는 사람은 그의 친구 Matthew에게 여러 번 전화하여 용서를 구했지만 Matthew는 결코 다시 전화를 해주지 않았다.

Practice Test

p. 56~57

1. c   2. a   3. b   4. b   5. d   6. b
7. c   8. a   9. d   10. b

[1~2] 다음 대화를 듣고 질문에 답하시오.

스크립트

Barbara Jane is driving me crazy, Alfred.

Alfred   What does she do, Barbara?

Barbara She is nice in front of me, but she says bad things about me behind my back.

Alfred   Does she do that to you, too? You are not the only victim. She does that to many people, so nobody wants to talk with her any more.

Barbara Do you think I should tell her not to do that any more?

Alfred   That's no use. I did that already, but she hasn't changed.

해석

Barbara Jane 때문에 미치겠어, Alfred.

Alfred   그녀가 뭘 어떻게 하는데, Barbara?

Barbara 그녀는 내 앞에선 친절한데, 내 뒤에선 나에 대한 험담들을 하고 다녀.

Alfred   그녀가 너한테도 그러니? 너만 피해자가 아니야(=너만 당한 게 아니야). 그녀가 많은 사람들한테 그렇게 해서, 아무도 그녀와 더 이상 이야기하고 싶어하지 않아.

Barbara 내가 그녀에게 더 이상 그러지 말라고 이야기해볼까?

Alfred   소용 없어. 내가 이미 (이야기) 해 봤는데, 하나도 변한 게 없어.

1. Barbara는 왜 Jane에게 화가 났는가?
   a. Jane이 항상 늦기 때문에
   b. Jane이 Barbara와의 약속을 어겼기 때문에
   ★c. Jane이 Barbara에 대해 다른 사람들에게 험담을 해서
   d. Jane이 Barbara와 말을 하지 않아서

2. Jane에 대해 사실이 아닌 것은 무엇인가?
   ★a. 그녀는 자신을 바꾸려고 애쓰고 있다.
   b. 그녀는 Barbara가 앞에 있을 때만 친절하다.
   c. 그녀는 다른 사람들과 어울리지 못한다.
   d. 그녀는 계속해서 사람들에 대해서 험담을 한다.

스크립트

Even though everybody has friends, not too many people know how to keep a good relationship with them. Here are a few tips for keeping a good relationship with your friends. First, don't reveal your friends' secrets to others. A relationship without trust doesn't last long. Second, you must understand that your friends may have different ways of thinking than you and they may like different things. Lastly, you should be there for your friends not only during good times but also during bad times.

해석

모두가 친구를 가지고 있지만, 친구와 좋은 관계를 유지하는 방법을 아는 사람은 많지 않다. 여기 당신의 친구와 좋은 관계를 유지하기 위한 몇 가지 조언이 있다. 첫째, 당신 친구의 비밀을 다른 사람들에게 말하지 말아야 한다. 신뢰가 없는 관계는 오래 가지 못한다. 둘째, 당신 친구들이 당신과는 생각하는 방식이나 좋아하는 것이 다를 수 있다는 것을 이해해야 한다. 마지막으로, 좋을 때 뿐만 아니라 나쁠 때(즉, 친구가 힘든 때)에도 친구의 곁에 있어주어야 한다.

3. 이 단락에서는 몇 개의 조언을 주었는가?
   a. 두 개   ★b. 세 개   c. 네 개   d. 다섯 개

4. 좋은 관계를 유지하기 위한 방법으로 언급되지 <u>않은</u> 것은 무엇인가?
   a. 친구들의 비밀을 지켜주어야 한다.
  ★b. 친구들이 당신을 도와줄 때 그들에게 감사해야 한다.
   c. 당신과 친구들이 다르다는 것을 이해해야 한다.
   d. 당신의 친구들이 당신을 필요로 할 때 도와주어야 한다.

스크립트

Differences in personality or in lifestyle preference are among the main reasons why many married couples break up. If two people have very different personalities or lifestyles, being together may not be fun. Often, one person must make sacrifices in order for the other person to be happy. Therefore, finding someone with whom you can be happy over a long period of time is more important than just finding someone to love.

해석

성격이나 선호하는 생활방식에서의 차이는 많은 부부들이 헤어지는 주요 이유이다. 만일 두 사람이 너무 다른 성격이나 생활방식을 갖고 있다면, 함께 있는 것이 즐겁지 않을 것이다. 종종, 다른 사람이 행복하기 위해서는 한 사람이 희생을 해야 한다. 따라서, 오랜 기간 동안 함께 있어서 행복할 수 있는 사람을 찾는 것이, 단지 사랑하는 사람을 찾는 것보다 더 중요하다.

5. 이 단락은 무엇에 관한 내용인가?
   a. 좋은 친구를 찾는 방법
   b. 손상된 인간관계를 개선하는 법
   c. 생활방식을 바꾸는 방법
  ★d. 커플 관계에서 중요한 것

6. 많은 부부들이 헤어지는 주요 원인은 무엇인가?
   a. 그들은 서로 사랑하지 않는다.
  ★b. 그들은 서로 성격이나 생활방식이 다르다
   c. 그들은 그들의 문제를 파악하지 못한다.
   d. 그들은 배우자를 위해 희생을 하지 않는다.

스크립트

Mr. Miller	Ted, do you have some time tonight?
Ted	Yes, Mr. Miller. Is there any problem?
Mr. Miller	No, there is no problem at all. I just want to have dinner with you. Although you have been working for me for more than a year, we've never had a chance to talk together.
Ted	I see, Mr. Miller. Where shall we meet?
Mr. Miller	Come to my office at seven. I'll make a reservation at a restaurant near the office.
Ted	Yes, sir.

해석

Miller 씨	Ted, 오늘 밤에 시간 좀 있나?
Ted	네. Miller 씨. 무슨 문제라도 있나요?
Miller 씨	아니, 아무 문제 없네. 그냥 자네와 저녁 식사라도 같이 하고 싶어서. 자네가 나를 위해 일 년 넘도록 일했는데, 같이 함께 이야기를 나눌 기회도 전혀 없었지 않나.
Ted	알겠습니다, Miller 씨. 어디서 뵐까요?
Miller 씨	7시에 내 사무실로 오게나. 사무실 근처에 있는 식당을 예약해 두겠네.
Ted	네, 알겠습니다.

7. 두 사람은 어떤 관계인가?

	Miller 씨		Ted
a.	아버지	–	아들
b.	운전기사	–	승객
★c.	고용주	–	직원
d.	교장	–	학생

8. Miller 씨는 왜 Ted와 저녁 식사를 하고자 하는가?

　★a. Ted와 개인적으로 이야기를 하고 싶어서

　　b. Miller 씨가 혼자 저녁 식사를 하고 싶지 않아서

　　c. Ted에게 문제가 있어서

　　d. Ted가 7시에 사무실에 왔기 때문에

[9–10] 다음 대화를 듣고 질문에 답하시오.

스크립트

Len	Brenda, you are close to Cathy, right?
Brenda	Well, I know her, but not very well. Why?
Len	I would like to go out with her, and I was hoping you could introduce me to her.
Brenda	In that case, Len, I think you need to ask Lisa. They have been friends since elementary school. You know Lisa well, right?
Len	I didn't know they were close. Then, I will ask Lisa. Thank you for the information, Brenda.
Brenda	You are welcome.

해석

Len	Brenda, 너 Cathy와 친하지, 그렇지?
Brenda	음, 그 애를 알긴 하지만 잘 알지는 못해. 왜?
Len	그녀와 사귀고 싶은데 네가 그녀에게 나를 좀 소개해 주었으면 해서.
Brenda	그런 경우라면, Len, 내 생각에는 Lisa에게 부탁하는 게 좋을 것 같아. 그 애들은 초등학생 때부터 친구거든. 너 Lisa는 잘 알지, 그렇지?
Len	그 둘이 친하다는 건 몰랐어. 그럼 내가 Lisa에게 부탁해 볼게. 알려줘서 고마워, Brenda.
Brenda	천만에.

9. Len은 왜 Brenda에게 자신을 Cathy에게 소개해 달라고 부탁했는가?

　　a. Cathy가 그의 프로젝트를 도와주길 바라기 때문에

　　b. Cathy가 초등학교 교사라서

　　c. Cathy가 Lisa에 대해 많은 것을 알기 때문에

　★d. Cathy와 사귀고 싶어서

10. 누가 Len을 Cathy에게 소개해 줄 것인가?

　　a. Brenda

　★b. Lisa

　　c. 그가 자기 스스로 소개할 것이다.

　　d. 아무도 안 해줄 것이다.

Dictation (Listening Task)   p. 58

LISTENING 1

what's going on, upset, too many problems, the rent money issue, sharing house cleaning, too messy, too neat, constant problems, look for a new roommate

LISTENING 2

How long have you two, have been dating, first meet, fell in love with him, asked him out, get married, proposed to me, at the end of this year

LISTENING 3

find it difficult to have, going on a trip, love each other, open conversation, a fishing trip, last year, did not have much to do, never discussed before

LISTENING 4

good friends, not talking, started, forgot to come to the library, waited all day, asked me for forgiveness, too upset to forgive, calling me any more, narrow-minded I was

Dictation (Practice Test)   p. 59

PRACTICE TEST [1-2]

driving me crazy, What does she do, in front of, behind my back, do that to you, nobody wants to talk, tell her not to do, That's no use, hasn't changed

PRACTICE TEST [3-4]

how to keep a good relationship, a few tips, reveal your friends' secrets, without trust, last long, different ways of thinking, be there, during bad times

PRACTICE TEST [5-6]

in personality, among the main reasons, break up, being together, be fun, to be happy, you can be happy, to love

PRACTICE TEST [7-8]

do you have some time, any problem,
have dinner with you, for more than a year,
a chance to talk, shall we meet, make a
reservation at

PRACTICE TEST [9-10]

close to, not very well, go out with her, could
introduce me to her, In that case, friends
since elementary school, they were close,
You are welcome

UNIT 8
Is there anything wrong?

Getting Ready   p. 61

A

What's wrong, terrible stomachache, Didn't
I tell you, couldn't find, take this, Why don't
you, need to, You should have, worry

B

(a)-(5) (b)-(3) (c)-(2) (d)-(6) (e)-(1) (f)-(4)

A 아래 대화를 읽고 빈칸을 완성하시오.

> 내가 너한테 말하지 않았나, 찾을 수 없었다, 이것을
> 먹어라, ~했어야 했다, 무슨 문제야, 걱정하다, ~하는 게
> 어때, ~할 필요가 있다, 극심한 복통

Tracy 무슨 문제 있어요, 여보? 땀을 흘리잖아요.

Bob 복통이 너무 심해서.

Tracy 탈이 날 줄 알았어요. 내가 너무 많이 먹지 말라고 하지 않
았어요? 약은 먹었어요?

Bob 아니, 비상 약품 상자에서 약을 찾을 수 없던데.

Tracy 그럴 리가요. 여기 무엇인가 있을 텐데요. 아, 찾았어요. 여
기요, 이걸 물 많이 마시고 삼켜요.

Bob 고마워.

Tracy 병원에 데려다 줄까요? 당신 진찰 받아봐야 할 것 같아요.

Bob 아니, 잠을 좀 자면 괜찮아질 것 같아. 간밤에 전혀 잠을 못
잤거든.

Tracy 적어도 나한테는 아프다고 말을 했어야죠.

Bob 걱정 말아요. 벌써 다 나아가는 것 같으니까.

Tracy 그럼 침대에 가서 잠 좀 자요.

B 문제의 종류와 다음의 상황을 연결하시오.

〈문제의 종류〉

(1) 건강	(2) 공부	(3) 도구/연장
(4) 관계	(5) 직장	(6) 쇼핑

〈상황〉

> (a) 이 프로젝트를 처리할 수 없을 것 같아요. 내 능력
> 밖이에요.
>
> (b) 복사기가 고장 났어요.
>
> (c) 시험에 떨어질까봐 걱정이에요.
>
> (d) 이 셔츠에 찢어진 곳이 있네요. 환불받고 싶어요.
>
> (e) 발목을 삔 것 같아요. 정말 아파요.
>
> (f) James와 싸웠어요. 그와 화해하려면 어떻게 해야
> 할까요?

Listening Task p. 62~63

Listening 1   1. b   2. A. F   B. F
Listening 2   1. b   2. c   3. a
Listening 3   1. c   2. a
Listening 4   1. d   2. d   3. a

Listening 1 p. 62

다음 대화를 듣고 질문에 답하시오.

스크립트

Veronica   Wow, the traffic is really bad. Do you think we can make it to the airport on time, Robert?

Robert   You should have known that the traffic on the way to the airport is always bad.

Veronica   I knew it would be bad, but not this bad.

Robert   What time is our flight?

Veronica   It's at 12:30 p.m.

Robert   I think we can make it this time, but next time, let's give ourselves plenty of time.

Veronica   I agree.

해석

Veronica   이런, 차가 엄청 막히는군. 제시간에 공항에 도착할 수 있을까, Robert?

Robert   공항 가는 길이 항상 (교통이) 나쁘다는 걸 염두에 뒀었어야지.

Veronica   나쁠 줄은 알았지만 이렇게까지 심할 줄은 몰랐지.

Robert   우리 비행기가 몇 시지?

Veronica   오후 12시 30분 비행기야.

Robert   이번에는 시간에 맞출 수 있겠지만, 다음에는 여유 있게 출발하자고.

Veronica   그래.

1. 다음 중 이 대화와 관련 있는 그림은 무엇인가?
   a.   ★b.   c.   d.

다시 듣고 True(참) 또는 False(거짓)에 표시하시오.

2. A. 공항으로 가는 교통 흐름은 주말에는 보통 그다지 나쁘지 않다. (F)

   B. 그들은 12시 반에 공항에서 누군가를 데려오기로 되어 있다. (F)

Listening 2 p. 62

다음 대화를 듣고 질문에 답하시오.

스크립트

Chris   Are you OK, James?

James   I broke up with Cindy. She got upset because I have been late for our dates a few times.

Chris   I knew something like that would happen sooner or later. You are never on time.

James   Chris, I am already upset; you don't have to make me feel even worse.

Chris   I am giving you some advice. Everybody says you are always late.

James   Really? Then, I should change.

Chris   You really should. Now, go call Cindy and tell her that you'll never be late again.

James   I think I should.

해석

Chris   너 괜찮은 거야, James?

James   Cindy와 헤어졌어. 내가 데이트에 몇 번 늦었더니 화를 내더라구.

Chris   조만간 그런 일이 생길 줄 알았어. 넌 항상 늦잖아.

James   Chris, 나 화났으니까 너까지 더 보태 줄 필요는 없어.

Chris   너에게 충고해 주는 거야. 다들 네가 항상 늦는다고 한단 말이야.

James   정말? 그러면, 내가 바뀌어야 되겠네.

Chris   정말 그래야 해. 그러니까, Cindy에게 전화해서 다시는 늦지 않겠다고 말해.

James   그래야 할 것 같아.

1. Cindy가 James에게 화난 이유는 무엇인가?
   a. James가 그녀의 시계를 망가뜨려서
  ★b. James가 데이트에 늦어서
   c. James가 거짓말을 해서
   d. James가 그녀에게 다시 전화해 주지 않아서

다시 듣고 질문에 답하시오.

2. Chris는 James에게 무엇을 해주고 있는가?
   a. 허락   b. 칭찬   ★c. 충고   d. 사과

두 개의 요약을 듣고 올바른 것을 고르시오.

3.

스크립트

a. James understood his fault, and he is willing to apologize to his girlfriend.

b. James is very upset because his friends think he is always late for meetings.

해석

a. ⭐ James는 자신의 잘못을 알고 여자 친구에게 사과를 하려고 한다.

b. ☐ James는 친구들이 그가 모임에 항상 늦는다고 생각해서 화가 났다.

Listening 3 p. 63

다음 이야기를 듣고 질문에 답하시오.

스크립트

Dear Abby, I am in an awkward situation. I have two close friends with whom I get along very well, but they seem to be on bad terms with each other these days. After they quarreled several times over a school project, they stopped talking to each other even in class. I have tried to help them make up, but it's been no use. I can't take it any more. If you have any suggestions, please let me know.

해석

Abby 선생님, 저는 난처한 상황에 처해 있어요. 저와 잘 지내는 친한 친구 두 명이 있는데, 요즘 그 둘의 사이가 안 좋아 보여요. 학교 프로젝트를 하면서 몇 번 말다툼을 한 이후로 수업 시간에도 서로 말하지 않아요. 화해시키려고 애써 봤지만, 소용이 없었어요. 더 이상 견딜 수가 없어요. 좋은 방안이 있으면 알려주세요.

1. 말하는 사람의 문제점은 무엇인가?

   a. 친구들과 말다툼을 했다.
   b. 학교 프로젝트를 끝내지 못했다.
   ★c. 친구 두 명이 서로 잘 지내지 못하고 있다.
   d. 학교 프로젝트와 관련하여 파트너와 문제가 있다.

다시 듣고 질문에 답하시오.

2. 말하는 사람은 이 상황에 대해 어떻게 느끼는가?

   ★a. 속수무책이다   b. 만족한다
   c. 전율을 느낀다   d. 무관심하다

Listening 4 p. 63

다음 이야기를 듣고 질문에 답하시오.

스크립트

If your school grades do not improve even though you study hard, then you should check your study habits. First, do not try to memorize everything you read without first understanding it. Secondly, you need to learn how to divide up your time evenly among the subjects you study. Many students tend to spend too much time only on the subjects they like. Thirdly, if studying alone is boring and difficult, forming a study group is an excellent idea.

해석

열심히 공부해도 학교 성적이 오르지 않는다면, 자신의 공부 습관을 점검해 보아야 한다. 첫째, 읽은 내용을 먼저 이해하지 않은 채 모든 것을 외우려고만 하지 마라(즉, 이해하고 나서 외우도록 하라). 둘째, 공부하는 과목별로 시간을 고르게 분배하는 방법을 배워야 한다. 많은 학생들이 자신이 좋아하는 과목에만 지나치게 많은 시간을 투자하는 경향이 있다. 셋째, 혼자 공부하는 것이 지루하거나 어렵다면, 스터디 모임을 만드는 것도 훌륭한 방법이다.

1. 이 단락에 가장 알맞은 제목은 무엇인가?

   a. 영어를 정복하는 방법
   b. 성공적인 삶을 위해 해야 할 것들
   c. 암기를 위한 최선의 방법
   ★d. 학교 성적을 올리는 방법

다시 듣고 질문에 답하시오.

2. 이 단락에서 제시되지 않은 조언은 무엇인가?

   a. 읽은 것을 이해하려고 해라.
   b. 공부 시간을 현명하게 사용해라.
   c. 모임을 짜서 공부해라.
   ★d. 선생님께 가능한 한 질문을 많이 해라.

두 개의 요약을 듣고 올바른 것을 고르시오.

3.

스크립트

a. The speaker is giving several tips for getting better grades to those who study hard but don't seem to improve their grades.

b. The speaker is explaining why he can't get better grades even though he studies so hard.

해석

a. ⭐ 말하는 사람은 열심히 공부해도 성적이 오르지 않는 학생들을 위해 더 나은 성적을 얻을 수 있는 몇 가지 조언을 해주고 있다.

b. ☐ 말하는 사람은 자신이 열심히 공부하고도 좋은 성적을 얻지 못하는 이유를 설명하고 있다.

| 1. a | 2. a | 3. b | 4. d | 5. b | 6. a |
| 7. d | 8. c | 9. c | 10. d | | |

[1-2] 다음 대화를 듣고 질문에 답하시오.

Jessica We are out of paint.

Ben I thought you bought enough paint.

Jessica I didn't want to buy too much. Don't worry. I will go to the paint shop now.

Ben I don't think the paint shop is open now.

Jessica What time is it?

Ben It's 9:30, and they close at 9:00.

Jessica Well, we can continue tomorrow.

Ben Next time, get a sufficient amount. They give a 100% refund on unused paint.

Jessica I will remember that next time.

해석

Jessica 페인트가 다 떨어졌네.

Ben 네가 충분히 샀을 거라고 생각했는데.

Jessica 너무 많이 사고 싶지 않아서. 걱정 마. 지금 페인트 가게에 가 볼게.

Ben 지금 페인트 가게는 영업 안 할 거야.

Jessica 몇 신데?

Ben 9시 반이야. 거기는 9시에 문 닫아.

Jessica 그럼, 내일 계속하지 뭐.

Ben 다음에는 충분한 양을 사. 쓰지 않은 페인트는 백 퍼센트 환불해 주니까.

Jessica 다음 번엔 명심할게.

1. 두 사람에게 생긴 문제는 무엇인가?
  ★a. 페인트가 다 떨어졌다.
  b. (페인트) 색상이 가구와 어울리지 않는다.
  c. 페인트가 너무 비싸다.
  d. 페인트를 환불받을 수 없다.

2. 가게는 언제 문을 닫는가?
  ★a. 9시
  b. 9시 30분
  c. 10시
  d. 주말에는 문을 열지 않는다.

[3-4] 다음 대화를 듣고 질문에 답하시오.

Sarah Jeff, are you sick?

Jeff Yes, I have a toothache. I took a pain reliever, but it is not helping.

Sarah Why don't you see a dentist?

Jeff I am afraid of seeing a dentist.

Sarah If you don't, it will only get worse.

Jeff I can bear it. It may go away after a while.

Sarah I don't think so. If you don't see a doctor now, you may lose your tooth.

Jeff All right. I will.

해석

Sarah Jeff, 어디 아파?

Jeff 응, 이가 아파. 진통제를 먹었는데 도움이 안 되는 것 같아.

Sarah 치과에 가 보지 그래?

Jeff 난 치과 가는 게 무서워.

Sarah 치과에 안 가면 상태가 더 나빠지기만 할 거야.

Jeff 참을 수 있어. 조금 지나면 치통이 없어질 거야.

Sarah 그렇지 않아. 지금 치과에 가지 않으면 이를 뽑아야 할지도 모른다고.

Jeff 알았어. 갈게.

3. Jeff는 다음에 무엇을 할 것인가?
  a. ★b. c. d.

4. 이 상황에 어울리는 속담은 무엇인가?
  a. 건강한 신체에 건전한 마음이 깃든다.
  b. 조금 아는 지식이 위험하다.(=선무당이 사람 잡는다.)
  c. 인내가 미덕이다.
  ★d. 제때의 한 바늘은 후에 아홉 바늘을 덕 본다.(제때 손을 쓰면 큰일을 피할 수 있다.)

[5-6] 다음 대화를 듣고 질문에 답하시오.

Harrison Sally, can I talk with you for a moment?

Sally What is it, Harrison?

Harrison I took my brother's new digital camera out without asking, and I dropped it. What should I do?

Sally "Honesty is the best policy." I think you should tell him what happened and ask for his forgiveness.

Harrison Won't he get angry?

Sally I am sure he will, but you should take the responsibility for it anyway.

Harrison Yes, you're right. Thank you for the suggestion.

Harrison	Sally, 잠깐 얘기 좀 할 수 있어?
Sally	뭔데, Harrison?
Harrison	우리 형의 새 디지털 카메라를 물어보지도 않고 들고 나왔는데 그만 떨어뜨려 버렸어. 어떻게 하지?
Sally	"정직이 최선의 방책"이라잖아. 내 생각에는 형에게 무슨 일이 있었는지 얘기하고 용서를 구하는 게 좋을 것 같은데.
Harrison	화내지 않을까?
Sally	화는 내겠지만, 어쨌든 그 일에 대한 책임은 져야지.
Harrison	그래, 네 말이 맞아. 조언 고마워.

5. Harrison이 문제에 대해서 느끼는 심정은 어떠한가?

   a. 안심된다   ★b. 걱정된다

   c. 불쾌하다   d. 실망스럽다

6. Sally의 조언은 무엇인가?

   ★a. 사실을 말하고 용서를 빌어라.

   b. 형에게 새 디지털 카메라를 사주어라.

   c. 카메라를 수리해라.

   d. 우선 카메라를 제자리에 갖다 놓아라.

[7–8] 다음 이야기를 듣고 질문에 답하시오.

스크립트

Have you tried to lose weight? I've tried several times. I drank only a cup of juice for breakfast, ate a light lunch, and skipped dinner entirely. It seemed to work in the beginning, but soon I felt weak and dizzy. I even had to be hospitalized. It was a terrible experience. So, if you want to lose weight, don't just skip meals. Eat light and exercise. That's the best and the only safe way to lose weight.

해석

체중 감량을 해 보셨나요? 전 여러 번 시도해 봤어요. 아침에는 주스 한 잔만 마시고, 점심은 가볍게 먹고, 저녁은 건너뛰었죠. 초기에는 효과가 있는 것 같았지만, 곧 기력이 없어지고 현기증을 느꼈어요. 심지어 입원까지 하게 되었죠. 끔찍한 경험이었어요. 그러니 여러분도 만약 체중 감량을 하고 싶다면, 무작정 식사를 거르지는 마세요. 적게 먹고 운동을 하세요. 그게 체중을 줄이는 최선이자 안전한 단 한 가지 방법이에요.

7. 이 단락의 요지는 무엇인가?

   a. 건강한 삶을 위해서는 체중을 감량해야 한다.

   b. 체중 감량을 할 때에는 가능한 한 적게 먹도록 해라.

   c. 몸이 약하다고 느끼면 규칙적으로 운동해라.

   ★d. 식사를 거르는 것은 좋은 체중 감량 방법이 아니다.

8. 말하는 사람이 체중 감량을 위해 추천하는 것은 무엇인가?

   a. 물을 많이 마셔라.

   b. 다이어트 전문가와 상의해라.

   ★c. 운동하고 식사를 가볍게 해라.

   d. 정크푸드(=패스트푸드 같은 인스턴트 식품)를 먹지 말고 채식주의자가 되어라.

[9–10] 다음 대화를 듣고 질문에 답하시오.

스크립트

Joan	Hello?
David	Hello, Joan? Why do you sound panicky?
Joan	I smell gas in my apartment.
David	Calm down and shut the main valve off first. Then, open all the doors and windows.
Joan	OK. What else should I do? I am so panicked that I cannot think of anything else.
David	After you do what I have told you, call the gas company and ask for a technician.
Joan	I see.
David	And, do not light up a match or turn on the stove.
Joan	OK. Thanks.

해석

Joan	여보세요?
David	여보세요, Joan이니? 왜 그렇게 목소리가 겁에 질렸어?
Joan	아파트 안에서 가스 냄새가 나.
David	진정하고, 우선 가스 메인 밸브를 잠가. 그러고 나서 문과 창문을 모두 열어.
Joan	그럴게. 그리고 또 뭘 해야 하지? 너무 겁나서 아무것도 생각할 수가 없어.
David	내가 말한 것들을 다 하고 나서, 가스회사에 전화해서 기술자를 한 명 보내달라고 해.
Joan	그래.
David	그리고, 성냥이나 난로를 켜지 마.
Joan	알았어. 고마워.

9. Joan은 왜 당황하고 있는가?

   a. 아파트에 불이 나서

   b. 집에 들어갈 수가 없어서

   ★c. 집에서 가스가 새서

   d. 지난밤 도둑이 아파트에 침입해서

10. 대화에 따르면, Joan은 _____ 말아야 한다.

   a. 기술자를 부르지   b. 난로를 끄지

   c. 창문을 열지   ★d. 성냥을 켜지

Dictation (Listening Task)   p. 66

LISTENING 1
the traffic, make it to the airport on time, You should have known, on the way to, I knew it would, What time is our flight, let's give ourselves plenty of time

LISTENING 2
broke up with, late for our dates, happen sooner or later, never on time, I am already upset, make me feel even worse, giving you some advice, I should change, you'll never be late again

LISTENING 3
in an awkward situation, get along very well, seem to be on bad terms, over a school project, talking to each other, it's been no use, I can't take it, any suggestions

LISTENING 4
school grades do not improve, check your study habits, memorize everything, first understanding it, divide up your time, tend to spend too much time, forming a study group

Dictation (Practice Test)   p. 67

PRACTICE TEST [1-2]
out of paint, you bought enough paint, buy too much, I don't think, they close at, continue tomorrow, give a 100% refund, I will remember that

PRACTICE TEST [3-4]
are you sick, I have a toothache, not helping, see a dentist, I am afraid of, only get worse, go away after a while, lose your tooth

PRACTICE TEST [5-6]
talk with you for a moment, without asking, What should I do, tell him what happened, ask for his forgiveness, should take the responsibility, for the suggestion

PRACTICE TEST [7-8]
lose weight, ate a light lunch, seemed to work, felt weak and dizzy, a terrible experience, want to lose weight, skip meals, the best and the only safe way

PRACTICE TEST [9-10]
sound panicky, I smell gas in, shut the main valve off, What else should I do, I cannot think of anything else, call the gas company, light up a match, turn on the stove

UNIT 9
I enjoyed the musical.

Getting Ready   p. 69

A
how about seeing, rented, what kind of, romantic comedy, recommended, action movies, the plot, a love story, Who's starring, main characters, favorite stars

B, C
박스 안의 엔터테인먼트 종류와 영화 종류를 넣어 자유롭게 응답

A 아래 대화를 읽고 빈칸을 완성하시오.

> 주인공, 추천했다, 줄거리, 사랑 이야기, 어떤 종류의, 가장 좋아하는 배우, 보는 것이 어때, 로맨틱 코미디, 액션 영화, 누가 출연하는지, 빌리다

Jane   Kathy, 오늘 밤에 영화 보지 않을래? 내가 Notting Hill DVD를 빌려 왔어.

Kathy   어떤 종류의 영화야?

Jane   로맨틱 코미디야. 내 친구 한 명이 정말 재밌었다면서 추천해 줬어.

Kathy   글쎄, 난 로맨틱 코미디 영화는 별로 좋아하지 않아서 말야. 난 The Italian Job 같은 액션 영화가 좋아.

Jane   Kathy, 일단 한번 봐 봐. 후회하지 않을 거야.

Kathy   줄거리 알아?

Jane   그냥 사랑 이야기라고 하던데. 내가 아는 건 그게 다야.

Kathy   출연하는 배우는 누구야?

Jane   Hugh Grant와 Julia Roberts가 주인공이래.

Kathy   음… Hugh Grant는 내가 제일 좋아하는 배우 중 하나야. 몇 시에 가면 돼?

Jane   6시쯤 와. 뭐 시켜 먹던가 근처 식당에 가서 밥 먹자. 그러고 나서 영화 보면 될 것 같아.

Kathy   좋아. 이따 봐.

B 어떤 종류의 엔터테인먼트를 좋아하는가? 친구들과 이야기해 보시오.

> 영화, 연극, 팝 콘서트, 클래식 공연, 뮤지컬, 마술 쇼

◁)) 나는 뮤지컬을 보러 가는 것을 좋아한다. 나는 전에 미녀와 야수를 본 적이 있다.

C 어떤 종류의 영화를 좋아하는가? 친구들과 이야기해 보시오.

액션	로맨틱 코미디	공포
스릴러	코미디	공상 과학

◁)) 나는 Die Hard와 같은 액션 (영화)를 좋아한다.

Listening Task   p. 70~71

Listening 1	1. b	2. A. F	B. T
Listening 2	1. d	2. d	3. b
Listening 3	1. a	2. c	
Listening 4	1. c	2. b	3. a

Listening 1   p. 70

다음 대화를 듣고 질문에 답하시오.

스크립트

Jackie What are the tickets for, Maria?

Maria These are tickets for a play.

Jackie A play? Which one?

Maria *Romeo and Juliet* by William Shake-speare.

Jackie Do you know the plot?

Maria Well, I know it is a sad love story where two young lovers from families who hate each other fall in love and die at the end.

Jackie How do they die?

Maria Well, I don't know exactly how. I will let you know more after I see the play.

해석

Jackie 그 표는 무슨 표야, Maria?

Maria 연극표야.

Jackie 연극? 무슨 연극?

Maria 윌리엄 셰익스피어의 "로미오와 줄리엣"이야.

Jackie 줄거리 알아?

Maria 글쎄, 서로 증오하는 가족들 사이의 어린 두 연인이 사랑에 빠지고 결국 죽는 슬픈 사랑 이야기라는 것 정도만 알아.

Jackie 어떻게 죽는데?

Maria 글쎄, 어떻게 죽는지는 정확히 몰라. 내가 연극을 보고 난 후에 더 알려줄게.

1. 두 사람은 무엇에 관해 이야기하고 있는가?
   a. 두 사람이 이전에 본 적이 있는 슬픈 사랑 이야기
   ★b. Maria가 보러 갈 슬픈 사랑 이야기
   c. 두 사람이 이미 본 로맨틱 코미디 영화
   d. 두 사람이 보러 갈 로맨틱 코미디 영화

다시 듣고 True(참) 또는 False(거짓)에 표시하시오.

2. A. 두 사람은 이번 주말에 함께 연극을 보러 갈 것이다. (F)
   B. Maria는 친구에게 "로미오와 줄리엣"의 내용에 관해 얘기하고 있다. (T)

Listening 2   p. 70

다음 대화를 듣고 질문에 답하시오.

스크립트

Jessica Tom, what kind of movies do you like?

Tom I like action movies, and Ken Morris is my favorite movie star.

Jessica Really? I didn't know.

Tom Well, what kind of movies do you like, Jessica?

Jessica I like horror movies.

Tom Oh, really? I can see why boys like them, but I don't understand why girls like that kind of movie.

Jessica Well, I think it's because we love to scream during the movie. It is a great way to release stress.

Tom Really? I would never have guessed.

해석

Jessica Tom, 넌 어떤 종류의 영화를 좋아해?

Tom 액션 영화를 좋아해. 그리고 Ken Morris는 내가 가장 좋아하는 영화배우야.

Jessica 정말? 몰랐네.

Tom 그럼, 넌 어떤 종류의 영화를 좋아하니, Jessica?

Jessica 난 공포 영화를 좋아해.

Tom 오, 그래? 남자들이 그런 영화를 좋아하는 건 알겠는데, 난 왜 여자들이 그런 종류의 영화를 좋아하는지 모르겠더라.

Jessica 글쎄, 아마도 영화 보는 동안 비명 지르는 걸 좋아해서 그런 것 같아. 스트레스를 해소하는 데 좋은 방법이거든.

Tom 그래? 정말 몰랐네.

1. 두 사람은 무엇에 관해 이야기하고 있는가?
   a. 그들이 가장 좋아하는 취미
   b. 그들이 가장 좋아하는 가수
   c. 그들이 가장 좋아하는 영화배우
   ★d. 그들이 가장 좋아하는 영화 장르

다시 듣고 질문에 답하시오.

2. 남자의 마지막 대답이 의미하는 것은 무엇인가?
   a. 그는 공포 영화를 보러 가고 싶어한다.
   b. 그도 영화 보는 동안 비명 지르는 것을 좋아한다.
   c. 그는 스트레스를 해소할 필요가 없다.
   ★d. 그는 비명을 지르는 것이 스트레스 해소의 한 방법이 될 거라고 생각하지 못했다.

두 개의 요약을 듣고 올바른 것을 고르시오.

3.

스크립트

a. A boy and a girl are talking about the kind of movies they like. Both of them like action movies and horror movies.

b. The boy expresses surprise that the girl would like horror films. She says that girls like them because they like to release stress by screaming during the movie.

해석

a. ☐ 한 소년과 소녀가 그들이 좋아하는 영화 종류에 대해 이야기하고 있다. 둘 다 액션 영화와 공포 영화를 좋아한다.

b. ★ 소년은 소녀가 공포 영화를 좋아하는 것에 놀라워 한다. 소녀의 말에 따르면, 여자들은 영화 중에 소리 지르는 것으로 스트레스를 푸는 것을 좋아하기 때문에 공포 영화를 좋아한다.

Listening 3

p. 71

다음 이야기를 듣고 질문에 답하시오.

스크립트

The musical, *Yesterday Once More*, was one of the biggest budgeted and the most successful of recent musicals. Jessica has been in love with this musical ever since she first listened to the soundtrack. But she has not been able to go to the musical since the musical has never been performed in her town. Finally, it will come to her town. It will be playing at the Washington Theater starting next Friday. She is so thrilled.

해석

뮤지컬 "Yesterday Once More"는 최근 뮤지컬 가운데 가장 많은 예산을 들였으며 가장 성공한 뮤지컬 중 하나이다. Jessica는 이 뮤지컬 배경음악을 처음 들은 이후로 계속 이 뮤지컬에 빠져 있었다. 하지만 그녀가 사는 고장에서는 이 뮤지컬 공연을 하지 않았기 때문에 그녀는 이 뮤지컬을 보러 갈 수 없었다. 마침내, 그녀가 사는 곳에서 이 뮤지컬이 공연을 하게 되었다. 다음 주 금요일부터 Washington 극장에서 상연될 것이다. 그녀는 매우 흥분해 있다.

1. Jessica가 흥분해 있는 이유는 무엇인가?
★a. 보고 싶었던 뮤지컬을 보러 갈 수 있어서
  b. 유명한 뮤지컬의 사운드 트랙을 사서
  c. 새 뮤지컬이 제작되고 있어서
  d. 성공적인 뮤지컬에서 공연할 수 있어서

다시 듣고 질문에 답하시오.

2. Jessica가 이 뮤지컬에서 가장 좋아하는 것은 무엇인가?
  a. 줄거리   b. 의상
★c. 사운드 트랙   d. 주연 배우

Listening 4

p. 71

다음 이야기를 듣고 질문에 답하시오.

스크립트

Going to a concert should be both exciting and memorable, but the last concert we went to was neither. It was my worst concert ever. Even though the concert was performed by a famous rock group, it was poorly organized. Tickets were oversold, so we had to stand. Furthermore, we could barely hear the band because the sound system was poorly set up. Even the lighting went out once in the middle of the concert.

해석

콘서트에 가는 것은 아주 신나고도 잊혀지지 않는 일이어야 하지만, 우리가 최근 갔던 콘서트는 그렇지 않았다. 이제까지의 콘서트 중 최악이었다. 유명한 록 그룹의 공연이었음에도 불구하고 행사 준비가 허술했다. 표를 (좌석 수보다) 너무 많이 팔아서 우리는 서서 봐야 했다. 게다가, 음향 장치도 허술해서 밴드의 음악을 거의 들을 수가 없었다. 심지어 공연 도중에 조명이 한 번 꺼지기도 했다.

1. 콘서트에 대한 말하는 사람의 태도는 어떠한가?
  a. 두근거린다   b. 기대된다
★c. 만족스럽지 않다   d. 만족스럽다

다시 듣고 질문에 답하시오.

2. 콘서트에 대해 사실이 아닌 것은 무엇인가?
  a. 록 콘서트였다.
★b. 표가 잘 팔리지 않았다.
  c. 일부 관객은 밴드가 연주하는 것을 들을 수 없었다.
  d. 조명에 문제가 있었다.

두 개의 요약을 듣고 올바른 것을 고르시오.

3.

스크립트

a. The speaker went to a rock concert, but he was very disappointed because of some problems.

b. The speaker went to a rock concert by his favorite rock group. Even though there were some problems, he enjoyed the concert very much because the performance of the group was excellent.

해석

a. ★ 말하는 사람은 록 콘서트를 보러 갔었다. 하지만 몇 가지 문제 때문에 그는 아주 실망했다.

b. □ 말하는 사람은 자신이 가장 좋아하는 록 그룹 콘서트에 갔다. 비록 몇 가지 문제점은 있었지만, 그룹의 공연이 아주 훌륭했기 때문에 그는 즐겁게 콘서트를 보았다.

Practice Test
p. 72~73

1. d	2. b	3. b	4. d	5. a
6. c	7. a	8. c	9. b	10. c

[1–2] 다음 대화를 듣고 질문에 답하시오.

스크립트

Halley Did you see the movie *Friends and Enemies* that started yesterday?

Julio Yes, I did. It is a gangster movie, but it has a great story and lots of special effects.

Halley What is the story about?

Julio It is about childhood friends becoming enemies later on in their lives.

Halley Who are the main characters?

Julio John Anderson and Adam Williams.

Halley They never acted in gangster movies before, did they?

Julio No, you're right. That's why it was different, too.

해석

Halley 어제 개봉한 "Friends and Enemies"라는 영화 봤어?

Julio 응, 봤어. 갱스터 영화인데 스토리가 정말 좋고 특수 효과도 많아.

Halley 줄거리가 어떻게 돼?

Julio 어릴 적 친구들이 나중에 적이 되는 이야기야.

Halley 주인공이 누군데?

Julio John Anderson과 Adam Williams야.

Halley 그 배우들은 지금껏 갱스터 영화에 출연한 적이 없잖아, 그렇지?

Julio 맞아. 그게 또한 그 영화가 뭔가 다른 이유야.

1. 그들은 어떤 종류의 영화에 대해 이야기하고 있는가?
   a. 공상 과학 영화　　b. 로맨틱 코미디 영화
   c. 공포 영화　　★d. 갱스터 영화

2. 영화에 관해 언급되지 않은 것은 무엇인가?
   a. 주인공　★b. 영화 감독　　c. 개봉일　　d. 줄거리

[3–4] 다음 이야기를 듣고 질문에 답하시오.

스크립트

Today, I had a great time as a member of the audience for the sit-com *The Family*. It was so exciting to see the actors in person. They looked just the same as they do on TV. Even though the show was only thirty minutes long, the actual filming took more than two hours. I didn't know it would take that long. After the filming, I had a chance to talk with the actors. I even had my picture taken with them.

해석

오늘 나는 "The Family"라는 시트콤의 방청객이 되어 즐거운 시간을 보냈다. 배우들을 실제로 보게 되어서 정말 흥분되었다. 배우들은 TV에서와 똑같아 보였다. 프로그램은 고작 30분짜리지만, 실제 녹화는 2시간 이상이나 걸렸다. 나는 촬영이 그렇게 오래 걸릴지 몰랐다. 녹화 후에는 배우들과 이야기를 할 수 있는 기회도 생겼다. 심지어 그들과 사진도 같이 찍었다.

3. 이 단락의 주요 화제는 무엇인가?
   a. "The Family"의 제작 팀원 되기
   ★b. 시트콤 관객으로 참여하기
   c. "The Family" 배우와의 데이트
   d. "The Family"에 엑스트라 배우로 출연하기

4. 어떤 그림이 그녀가 오늘 한 일을 가장 잘 나타내는가?
   a.　　　　b.　　　　c.　　　★d.

[5–6] 다음 대화를 듣고 질문에 답하시오.

스크립트

Alex Helen, let's go to a classical music concert this Friday.

Helen I am not a great fan of classical music, Alex. I don't think I would enjoy it.

Alex You should try this one because this is performed outdoors. I am sure you will enjoy it.

Helen A classical music concert outdoors?

Alex Yes. You will see the stars and feel the breeze during the concert.

Helen Mmm, it really sounds different. I will try it, Alex.

Alex Good decision, Helen.

해석

Alex Helen, 이번 주 금요일에 클래식 공연에 같이 가자.

Helen 난 클래식 음악을 그다지 좋아하지 않아, Alex. 별로 재미있을 것 같지 않은데.

Alex	이번 공연은 한번 가 봐. 야외에서 공연하거든. 분명 재미있을 거야.
Helen	클래식 공연을 야외에서 한다고?
Alex	응. 연주가 진행되는 동안 별도 보고 산들바람도 느낄 수 있어.
Helen	음. 뭔가 좀 다른 것 같군. 한번 가 볼게, Alex.
Alex	훌륭한 결정이야, Helen.

5. 이 콘서트는 왜 다른 콘서트와 다른가?
　★a. 야외 콘서트라서
　b. 유명한 지휘자에 의해 공연되어서
　c. 그 고장에서 한번도 공연된 적이 없어서
　d. 둘이 함께 갔던 첫 번째 콘서트여서

6. 대화에 따르면, Helen은 ＿＿＿＿＿＿＿＿＿＿＿.
　a. 클래식 음악에 대해 많이 안다
　b. 클래식 음악을 좋아한다
　★c. 클래식 음악을 그다지 좋아하지 않는다
　d. 음악을 들을 시간이 많지 않다

[7–8] 다음 대화를 듣고 질문에 답하시오.

스크립트

Tracy	How was the magic show last night?
Gerry	It was almost a comedy show.
Tracy	What happened?
Gerry	We laughed a lot because the magician made so many mistakes. One time, the rabbit stuck his head out when it was not supposed to. The audience noticed the rabbit, but the magician didn't. Needless to say, the trick was ruined.
Tracy	It sounds like it was rather fun.
Gerry	Yes, I had a good time. If you love to laugh, go check it out.

해석

Tracy	어젯밤 마술 쇼는 어땠어?
Gerry	거의 코미디 쇼였어.
Tracy	무슨 일이 있었어?
Gerry	마술사가 너무 많은 실수를 하는 바람에 많이 웃었지. 한 번은, 토끼가 그만 나오지 않았어야 할 때 고개를 내밀어버린 거야. 관객들은 토끼를 다 봤는데, 마술사는 눈치를 못 챘어. 두말할 것도 없이 마술은 엉망이 됐지 뭐.
Tracy	재미있었겠는걸.
Gerry	맞아. 정말 재밌었어. 웃고 싶다면 가서 한번 봐.

7. 마술 쇼에 대한 남자의 태도는 어떠한가?
　★a. 만족스럽다　　　b. 화난다
　c. 불만스럽다　　　d. 걱정스럽다

8. 마술 쇼에서 생긴 문제는 무엇이었는가?
　a. 쇼가 너무 늦게 시작했다.
　b. 남자가 표를 잘못 샀다.
　★c. 마술사가 너무 많은 실수를 했다.
　d. 토끼가 사라져버렸다.

[9–10] 다음 대화를 듣고 질문에 답하시오.

스크립트

Kathy	How was *The Stomp*?
John	It was awesome. Even though they didn't use any of the conventional instruments such as drums, they created a great sound using only cooking knives, papers, brooms, and pencils. They worked amazingly well together.
Kathy	Making music with knives and papers? Wow!
John	That wasn't everything. They also had dance moves that were both beautiful and humorous. I think the performers were dancers as well as musicians.
Kathy	No wonder that performance is so popular now.

해석

Kathy	"The Stomp" 공연은 어땠어?
John	굉장했어. 드럼 같은 전통적인 악기는 전혀 사용하지 않았지만, 요리용 칼, 종이, 빗자루, 그리고 연필과 같은 도구들만으로 굉장한 소리를 만들어 내더라고. 그 도구들은 함께 정말 훌륭한 소리를 냈어.
Kathy	칼과 종이로 음악을 만들어? 와!
John	그게 다가 아니야. 아름다우면서도 익살스러운 춤동작도 있었어. 그 공연가들은 음악가 뿐만 아니라 무용수이기도 한 것 같았어.
Kathy	요새 그 공연이 그렇게 인기 있는 것도 당연하네.

9. 여자의 마지막 말이 의미하는 것은 무엇인가?
　a. 그녀는 공연이 너무 현대적이라고 생각한다.
　★b. 그녀는 공연이 굉장하다는 데에 동의한다.
　c. 그녀는 공연에 아무런 관심이 없다.
　d. 그녀는 사람들이 왜 그 공연을 좋아하는지 이해할 수 없다.

10. 공연에서 사용되지 않은 도구는 무엇인가?
　a. 연필　　　b. 빗자루　　★c. 드럼　　　d. 요리용 칼

Dictation (Listening Task) — p. 74

LISTENING 1
the tickets for, tickets for a play, know the plot, sad love story, fall in love and die, let you know, after I see the play

LISTENING 2
what kind of movies, action movies, favorite movie star, horror movies, love to scream, a great way to release stress, I would never have guessed

LISTENING 3
one of the biggest, most successful, has been in love with, listened to the soundtrack, never been performed, will be playing at, starting, so thrilled

LISTENING 4
Going to a concert, exciting and memorable, was performed by, rock group, Tickets were oversold, hear the band, sound system, set up, the lighting went out

Dictation (Practice Test) — p. 75

PRACTICE TEST [1-2]
that started yesterday, gangster movie, has a great story, special effects, childhood friends becoming enemies, main characters, acted in, That's why it was different

PRACTICE TEST [3-4]
as a member of the audience, exciting to, actors in person, just the same as they do, took more than two hours, a chance to talk, had my picture taken

PRACTICE TEST [5-6]
let's go to, a great fan of, enjoy it, should try, performed outdoors, classical music concert, sounds different, Good decision

PRACTICE TEST [7-8]
magic show, comedy show, We laughed a lot, magician made so many mistakes, The audience noticed, the trick was ruined, sounds like, rather fun, go check it out

PRACTICE TEST [9-10]
It was awesome, instruments, created a great sound, worked amazingly well, Making music, dance moves, both beautiful and humorous, performers, performance is so popular

---

UNIT 10
You did a good job!

Getting Ready — p. 77

A
done with, clever, working on, tried hard, with enthusiasm, no problem, capable of, encouraging, make me feel, good lab partner

B
(1)-(c) (2)-(a) (3)-(e) (4)-(b) (5)-(f) (6)-(d)

A 아래 대화를 읽고 빈칸을 완성하시오.

> 힘을 주는, 좋은 실험실 파트너, ~을 끝낸, ~를 하는 중, ~하게 느끼다, 열심히 노력했다, 문제 없는, ~할 수 있는, 열정적으로, 똑똑한

Joan 수학 숙제 다 끝냈다.

Tony 어, 정말? 넌 정말 똑똑하다. 난 아직도 하는 중이야.

Joan 전혀 안 그래. 그냥 열심히 한 거야.

Tony 넌 정말 열정적으로 했다는 걸 내가 알아. 하지만 난 아냐. 어쨌든, 이것 좀 봐줄래? 아무래도 뭔가 실수한 거 같아.

Joan 어디 보자. 음, 문제 없는데. 단지 끝마치는 데 시간이 좀 걸리는 것 뿐이야.

Tony 이건 내 능력 밖이야.

Joan 아냐! 넌 네가 원하는 건 무엇이든 할 수 있는 능력이 있어. 너 자신을 믿어 봐.

Tony 고마워, Joan. 넌 무척 힘이 돼. 넌 내가 무엇이든 할 수 있다고 느끼게 하거든.

Joan 너도 좋은 실험실 파트너야.

B 이런 상황에서 당신은 어떤 칭찬을 할 수 있는가? 친구들과 이야기해 보시오.

> [A] (1) 잘 차려입다
> (2) 노인이 무거운 상자를 옮기는 것을 도왔다
> (3) 노래 대회에서 상을 탔다
> (4) 어려운 수학문제를 풀었다
> (5) 당신을 위해 맛있는 피자를 만들었다
> (6) 컴퓨터 바이러스를 퇴치했다

> [B] (a) 넌 정말 친절하구나!
> (b) 너는 참 똑똑하다.
> (c) 오늘 정말 멋져 보여.
> (d) 고마워, 컴퓨터를 잘 다루는구나.
> (e) 축하해! 네가 자랑스러워.
> (f) 정말 맛있었어. 너무 잘 먹었어.

◁)) 당신의 친구가 [A]잘 차려입었다면, 당신은 [B]"오늘 정말 멋져 보여"라고 말할 수 있다.

Listening Task   p. 78~79

Listening 1   1. c   2. A. T   B. F
Listening 2   1. d   2. b   3. a
Listening 3   1. d   2. a
Listening 4   1. c   2. a   3. b

Listening 1   p. 78

다음 대화를 듣고 질문에 답하시오.

스크립트

Clair Kurt, thank you very much for coming to change the flat tire for me last night, especially since it was raining.

Kurt Don't even mention it. What are friends for? I'm glad you called me.

Clair Well, I do appreciate it. Why don't you come to my house tomorrow? I'd like to take you out to a nice dinner. We can go to a movie after that.

Kurt You don't have to do that. But if you insist, I'd love to.

해석

Clair Kurt, 어젯밤에 펑크 난 타이어를 갈아주러 와 줘서 정말 고마워. 비까지 내렸는데 말야.

Kurt 그런 말 하지 마. 친구 좋다는 게 뭐야? 내게 전화하길 잘했어.

Clair 어쨌든, 정말 고마워. 내일 우리집에 오지 않을래? 내가 맛있는 저녁 식사를 살게. 저녁 먹고 영화 보러 가도 좋고.

Kurt 그렇게까지 하지 않아도 되는데. 하지만 네가 정 고집한다면, 기꺼이 갈게.

1. 어제 여자에게 무슨 일이 있었는가?
   a.   b.   ★c.   d.

다시 듣고 True(참) 또는 False(거짓)에 표시하시오.

2. A. 여자는 남자에게 전화하여 도움을 청했다. (T)
   B. 남자는 여자를 저녁 식사에 초대할 것이다. (F)

Listening 2   p. 78

다음 대화를 듣고 질문에 답하시오.

스크립트

W How is the work going?

M It is done. Why don't you take a look at it?

W Wow, it really came out great. How did you know the room would look better with gray rather than white?

M I once painted a similar room with gray, and it came out really nice, too.

W I think experience matters. I'm glad that I listened to you. You're the expert.

M I am glad you like it.

해석

여 작업은 어떻게 되어가고 있나요?

남 끝났습니다. 한번 보시겠어요?

여 와, 정말 멋지게 되었군요. 방을 흰색보다 회색으로 칠하면 더 좋아 보일 걸 어떻게 아셨어요?

남 전에 비슷한 방을 회색으로 칠한 적이 있었는데 그때도 정말 멋지게 나왔거든요.

여 역시 경험이 중요하군요. 당신 말을 듣기를 잘 했어요. 당신은 역시 전문가예요.

남 맘에 든다니 기쁘군요.

1. 여자가 만족해하는 이유는 무엇인가?
   a. 남자가 매우 열심히 일해서
   b. 남자가 일을 빨리 끝내서
   c. 남자가 그녀가 원했던 색으로 방을 칠해서
   ★d. 남자가 그 방에 어울리는 색을 골라서

다시 듣고 질문에 답하시오.

2. 남자의 직업은 무엇인가?
   a. 목수   ★b. 페인트공   c. 기술자   d. 전기 기사

두 개의 요약을 듣고 올바른 것을 고르시오.

3.

스크립트

a. The woman is satisfied with the color and thanks the man for choosing it.

b. The woman is satisfied with the color but complains about the price.

해석

a. ★ 여자는 색깔이 마음에 들었고 남자가 그 색을 골라주어 고마워하고 있다.

b. □ 여자는 색깔은 마음에 들었지만 가격에는 불만이 있다.

Listening 3   p. 79

다음 이야기를 듣고 질문에 답하시오.

스크립트

Even though we made mistakes, it was a good game. Most of you guys were very enthusiastic, and I know you did your best. First of all, John, you tried really hard out there. And Sam, you made a really smart play in the second inning. If we just cut down on

the mistakes and try a little harder, I think we can win next time. You guys have the ability to win.

해석
비록 실수는 있었지만, 훌륭한 시합이었다. 여러분들 대부분이 매우 열성적이었고 최선을 다했다는 것을 안다. 무엇보다도, John, 자네는 정말로 열심히 했네. 그리고 Sam, 2회에서 정말 재치 있는 플레이를 했어. 우리가 실수만 줄이고 조금만 더 열심히 한다면 다음 번엔 승리할 수 있으리라 생각한다. 여러분 모두 승리할 능력이 있다.

1. 이 단락에 대해 사실인 것은 무엇인가?
   a. 그들의 첫 시합이었다.
   b. 그들은 이번에 실수를 줄였다.
   c. 말하는 사람은 팀워크가 좋지 않은 것을 불평하고 있다.
   ★d. 팀은 시합에 졌다.

다시 듣고 질문에 답하시오.
2. 말하는 사람의 직업은 무엇인가?
   ★a. 코치   b. 영업자   c. 상담자   d. 프로 게이머

Listening 4   p.79

다음 이야기를 듣고 질문에 답하시오.

스크립트
Today, Len was awarded "The Bravest Man of the City" award at City Hall for saving two people from drowning in the Sacramento River. Last Saturday, Len went fishing and saw a boy falling into the water. Then, the boy's father dived into the water to save the boy, but because the water was too cold to swim in, the father almost drowned. Len went into the river with a rope and saved them both.

해석
오늘 Len은 새크라멘토 강에 빠진 두 사람을 구해준 것에 대해 시청에서 수여하는 "가장 용감한 시민 상"을 받았다. Len은 지난주 토요일에 낚시를 갔다가 한 소년이 물에 빠지는 것을 보게 되었다. 그리고 나서 소년의 아버지가 소년을 구하기 위해 물로 뛰어들었다. 하지만 수영하기엔 물이 너무 차가워서, 그 아버지는 거의 익사할 뻔했다. Len은 밧줄을 가지고 강으로 들어가서 둘 다 구해냈다.

1. Len이 "가장 용감한 시민 상"을 받은 이유는 무엇인가?
   a. 차가운 강물에서 수영을 할 수 있어서
   b. 물을 두려워하지 않아서
   ★c. 물에 빠진 사람 두 명을 구해서
   d. 그가 전문 구조원이어서

다시 듣고 질문에 답하시오.
2. Len은 왜 새크라멘토 강에 갔는가?
   ★a. 낚시하러   b. 보트 타러
   c. 수영하러   d. 스케이트 타러

두 개의 요약을 듣고 올바른 것을 고르시오.

3.

스크립트
a. Len almost drowned when he went fishing, but he survived thanks to a brave man.
b. Len was brave for saving two people from drowning by using a rope.

해석
a. ☐ Len은 낚시하러 갔다가 물에 빠져 죽을 뻔 했다. 하지만 한 용감한 사람 덕분에 목숨을 건졌다.
b. ★ Len은 용감하게도 밧줄을 이용해 물에 빠진 두 사람을 구해냈다.

Practice Test   p. 80~81

| 1. c | 2. a | 3. b | 4. d | 5. b |
| 6. c | 7. a | 8. b | 9. a | 10. d |

[1–2] 다음 대화를 듣고 질문에 답하시오.

스크립트
Linda Hi, Steve. Where did you get that shirt?
Steve Why, Linda? Is there anything wrong with it?
Linda No, no. That shirt would not look good on most people, but it looks great on you.
Steve Thanks, Linda. From now on, I will feel great when I wear this shirt. Honestly, I was not confident enough to wear this shirt before today. I thought the color was too bright.
Linda Don't worry, Steve. You look great in it.
Steve That's enough, Linda. I'm turning red from embarrassment.

해석
Linda 안녕, Steve. 그 셔츠 어디서 샀니?
Steve 왜, Linda? 이 셔츠 이상해?
Linda 아니, 그게 아니라. 그런 셔츠는 아무나 어울리지는 않는데 넌 정말 잘 어울려서.
Steve 고마워, Linda. 이제부터 이 셔츠를 입을 때마다 기분이 좋겠는걸. 솔직히 오늘까지도 이 옷을 입는 데 자신이 없었거든. 색깔이 너무 밝은 것 같아서 말이야.
Linda 걱정 마, Steve. 너무 잘 어울려.
Steve 그만해, Linda. 부끄러워서 얼굴 빨개지잖아.

49

1. 여자는 무엇에 대해 말하고 있는가?
   a. 남자의 친절함   b. 남자의 좋은 직업
   ★c. 남자의 옷   d. 남자의 좋은 매너

2. 남자는 셔츠에 대해 처음 어떻게 생각했는가?
   ★a. 너무 밝다.   b. 너무 꼭 낀다.
   c. 너무 낡았다.   d. 너무 비싸다.

[3–4] 다음 대화를 듣고 질문에 답하시오.

스크립트

Ben   Roy, that was a great speech that you made yesterday.

Roy   You really think so? I felt very nervous in front of so many people.

Ben   You didn't sound nervous at all. You sounded fine.

Roy   It's nice to hear that, but I was terrified. They say public speaking is worse than death. I realized exactly what they meant when I stood on stage.

Ben   I've never made a public speech, but I think I can understand what you mean.

해석

Ben   Roy, 어제 네가 한 연설 아주 훌륭했어.

Roy   정말 그렇게 생각해? 많은 사람들 앞에 서니까 너무 긴장됐어.

Ben   전혀 긴장한 것처럼 안 들리던데. 좋았어.

Roy   그렇다니 다행이지만 난 무서웠어. 사람들이 그러잖아, 대중 연설은 죽는 것보다 더 끔찍하다고 말이야. 무대에 서 보니까 그 말이 무슨 말인지 정확히 알겠더라.

Ben   난 연설을 해 본 적은 없지만 네 말이 무슨 뜻인지는 알 것 같아.

3. 이 상황을 가장 잘 묘사한 그림은 무엇인가?
   a.   ★b.   c.   d.

4. 어제 Roy가 느꼈을 심경으로 알맞지 않은 것은 무엇인가?
   a. 불안했다   b. 걱정스러웠다
   c. 긴장이 되었다   ★d. 유쾌했다

[5–6] 다음 대화를 듣고 질문에 답하시오.

스크립트

W   Tony, you did a great job. The sales went up by 200% compared to the same time last year. You are the best salesperson I have ever had. What is your secret?

M   There is no secret. I do my best to help customers. I don't pressure my customers to buy things. The customers know that I try to sell only what they need. Therefore, whenever they need anything, they know who to ask.

W   That is a great secret.

해석

여   Tony, 수고했네. 작년 같은 시기보다 판매율이 200% 신장했어. 자넨 내가 만난 사람들 중 최고의 영업자야. 비결이 뭔가?

남   비결은 없습니다. 고객들을 돕는 데 최선을 다하는 것 뿐이에요. 전 손님들에게 물건을 사라고 강요하지 않아요. 손님들은 내가 그들이 원하는 것만 팔 거라는 것을 알아요. 그래서 손님들은 무언가 필요할 때면, 누구를 찾아야 할지 아는 거죠.

여   그거 훌륭한 비결인걸.

5. 이 대화는 _____A_____ 와(과) _____B_____ 사이의 대화이다.

	A		B
a.	손님	—	점원
★b.	관리자	—	영업자
c.	교수	—	조교
d.	도서관원	—	학생

6. Tony의 성공의 비결은 무엇인가?
   a. 그는 모든 고객들에게 가능한 한 많이 팔았다.
   b. 그는 가능한 한 비싼 품목을 팔았다.
   ★c. 그는 고객이 필요로 하는 것만 팔았다.
   d. 그는 고객에게 많은 질문을 했다.

[7–8] 다음 대화를 듣고 질문에 답하시오.

스크립트

W   Bobby, can I ask you something?

M   Sure. What is it?

W   I don't know how to respond when people give me compliments. What should I say if I hear "You are smart?" If I say "Thank you," it sounds like I agree that I am smart.

M   I think "Thanks" is fine. But if you feel awkward saying that, what about "That's very nice of you?" That'll be better than saying nothing.

해석

여   Bobby, 뭐 좀 물어봐도 돼?

남   그럼. 뭔데?

여 사람들이 나를 칭찬하면 뭐라고 해야 할지 모르겠어. "넌 정말 똑똑해" 같은 말을 들으면 뭐라고 말해야 하지? "고마워"하고 말하면 내가 똑똑하다는 말에 수긍하는 것 같아서 말이야.

남 내 생각엔 "고마워"하고 말하는 것 정도는 괜찮은 것 같은데. 하지만 네가 그렇게 말하는 게 어색하다면 "그렇게 말해 주다니 당신은 참 좋은 사람이에요"라고 하면 어떨까? 아무 말도 안하는 것보단 그게 나을 거야.

7. Bobby의 말에 대한 여자의 응답으로 알맞은 말은 무엇인가?

여자	

★a. 도와줘서 고마워.　　　　b. 행운을 빌어.
c. 다신 그런 말 하지 마.　　d. 네가 부러워.

8. 이 대화의 주요 화제는 무엇인가?
a. 적절한 칭찬하기
★b. 칭찬에 대한 적절한 응답
c. 사람을 기분 좋게 만드는 몇 가지 방법
d. 칭찬의 이점과 단점

[9–10] 다음 이야기를 듣고 질문에 답하시오.

스크립트
Giving compliments to a person is a very good thing. You can compliment a person about many things, and it makes the person feel good and proud. You can, for example, compliment a person about how well he's dressed, how nice he acted, and how well he did at work. So, go ahead and compliment people around you. You'll also feel great seeing them happy.

해석
누군가를 칭찬하는 것은 매우 좋은 일이다. 어떤 사람에게 할 수 있는 칭찬에는 여러 가지가 있고, 그 칭찬은 그 사람을 기분 좋게 하고 자신을 자랑스럽게 느끼도록 해 준다. 예를 들어, 그가 얼마나 멋지게 차려 입었는지, 얼마나 친절하게 행동했는지, 얼마나 일을 잘했는지에 대해 칭찬할 수 있다. 그러니 당장 당신 주변의 사람들을 칭찬해 보자. 행복해하는 그들을 보면서 당신도 역시 기분이 좋을 것이다.

9. 이 단락에 관해 사실인 것은 무엇인가?
★a. 칭찬은 사람을 기분 좋게 한다.
b. 칭찬하는 것은 가치 있는 일이지만 복잡하다.
c. 사람들은 대체로 칭찬을 받으면 수줍어한다.
d. 다른 사람들 앞에서 칭찬해 주는 것이 더 좋다.

10. 칭찬의 예로 언급되지 않은 것은 무엇인가?
a. 사람들의 좋은 행동을 칭찬하라.
b. 사람들이 입은 옷에 대해 칭찬하라.
c. 사람들이 직장에서 이룬 것을 칭찬하라.
★d. 사람들의 머리좋음에 대해 칭찬하라.

Dictation (Listening Task)　　p. 82

LISTENING 1
coming to change the flat tire, it was raining, Don't even mention it, do appreciate it, take you out to, after that, if you insist

LISTENING 2
How is the work going, take a look at it, came out great, look better, experience matters, You're the expert, glad you like it

LISTENING 3
very enthusiastic, did your best, tried really hard, a really smart play, cut down on the mistakes, win next time, ability to win

LISTENING 4
The Bravest Man of the City, two people from drowning, went fishing, falling into the water, dived into the water, the father almost drowned, with a rope, saved them both

Dictation (Practice Test)　　p. 83

PRACTICE TEST [1-2]
Where did you get, anything wrong with it, looks great on you, I will feel great, was not confident, the color was too bright, That's enough, I'm turning red

PRACTICE TEST [3-4]
a great speech, in front of so many people, sound nervous at all, I was terrified, worse than death, on stage, made a public speech

PRACTICE TEST [5-6]
The sales went up, the best salesperson, What is your secret, do my best, pressure my customers to buy, sell only what they need, whenever they need anything

PRACTICE TEST [7-8]
can I ask you something, how to respond, What should I say if I hear, it sounds like I agree, feel awkward saying that, That'll be better

PRACTICE TEST [9-10]
Giving compliments, compliment a person about, feel good and proud, how well he's dressed, did at work, people around you, seeing them happy

UNIT 11
What kind of pet do you have?

Getting Ready   p. 85

A

a pet, a pet shop, raise, imitate, What do you feed, attacked, Speaking of, endangered, habitats, cut down

B

• I'm interested in having hamsters as a pet. They are so little and cute like squirrels.
• I'm interested in having lizards as a pet. I want something unusual for a pet.
• I'm interested in having parrots as a pet. They are the only animal that can say something.

A 아래 대화를 읽고 빈칸을 완성하시오.

공격했다, 따라하다, 멸종 위기의, ~ 이야기가 나와서 말인데, 키우다, 애완동물, 무엇을 먹이니, 애완동물 가게, 서식지, 베어지다

Julie 너 원숭이를 애완동물로 키우네! 놀라워. 어디서 샀어?

Dan 작년에 애완동물 가게에서 샀어. 원숭이는 어린아이 같아서 키우기 정말 재밌어. 내 원숭이는 나를 따라하는 걸 매우 좋아해.

Julie 원숭이 키우는 게 어렵지는 않아? 뭘 먹이는데?

Dan 음, 원숭이는 거의 아무거나 다 먹을 수 있어. 내 원숭이는 자기 것이든 남의 것이든 상관 안 해. 옆집 개 먹이를 빼앗아 먹으려고 그 개를 공격한 적도 있다니까.

Julie 원숭이 이야기가 나와서 말인데, 어떤 야생 원숭이는 서식지를 잃어서 멸종 위기에 처한 종(種)이 되었다고 들었어.

Dan 정말?

Julie 응, 필리핀의 어떤 원숭이가 거의 멸종되다시피 했는데, 서식지의 나무가 너무 많이 베어져서 그렇대.

Dan 마음이 아프네.

B 애완동물로 무엇을 키우고 있는가? 친구들과 이야기해 보시오.

[A] 도마뱀   햄스터   앵무새   물고기

[B] 그것들은 무언가 말을 할 수 있는 유일한 동물이다.
그것들이 헤엄치는 것을 보면 마음이 편안하다.
그것들은 다람쥐처럼 아주 작고 귀엽다.
나는 애완동물로 특이한 것을 원한다.

◁)) 나는 애완동물로 [A]물고기를(을) 키우는 것에 관심이 있다. [B]그것들이 헤엄치는 것을 보면 마음이 편안하다.

Listening Task   p. 86~87

Listening 1	1. c	2. A. F	B. T
Listening 2	1. d	2. a	3. b
Listening 3	1. b	2. d	
Listening 4	1. c	2. b	3. a

Listening 1   p. 86

다음 대화를 듣고 질문에 답하시오.

스크립트

Sally Look at those swans, Don. Aren't they lovely?

Don Wait, Sally, let's not get too close to them.

Sally What? Don't tell me that you're scared of swans.

Don Actually, I am. I was attacked by a goose when I was a child. Since then, I haven't liked big birds.

Sally I have seen people scared of snakes or bugs, but not birds.

Don Well, this might sound funny, but I don't get scared by snakes or bugs.

해석

Sally 저 백조들 좀 봐, Don. 사랑스럽지 않니?

Don 잠깐, Sally, 백조에게 너무 가까이 다가가지 말자.

Sally 뭐? 설마 너 백조를 무서워한다고 말하려는 건 아니겠지.

Don 사실, 무서워 해. 어렸을 때 거위에게 공격을 받은 적이 있는데, 그때부터 큰 새들을 싫어해.

Sally 뱀이나 벌레를 무서워하는 사람들은 봤어도 새를 무서워하는 사람은 못 봤는데.

Don 음, 좀 우습게 들릴지는 모르지만, 난 뱀이나 벌레는 무서워하지 않아.

1. Don이 무서워하는 것은 무엇인가?
   a. 뱀   b. 벌레   ★c. 새   d. 없다

다시 듣고 True(참) 또는 False(거짓)에 표시하시오.

2. A. Don은 어렸을 때 벌레에게 공격당한 일이 있다. (F)
   B. Sally는 백조를 무서워하는 사람을 본 적이 없다. (T)

Listening 2

p. 86

다음 대화를 듣고 질문에 답하시오.

스크립트

Man Did you find anything you like?

Girl I think I like hamsters, but I wonder if they are easy to raise.

Man It is not as difficult as you think.

Girl What do they eat?

Man You can feed them fresh vegetables and nuts.

Girl How about cookies and chocolates?

Man They are too sweet for hamsters, and you shouldn't feed them garlic or onion either.

Girl I think I will take a pair of them and a cage.

Man OK.

해석

남자 마음에 드는 걸 찾았니?

소녀 햄스터가 마음에 들어요. 하지만 햄스터가 키우기 쉬운지 궁금하네요.

남자 네가 생각하는 만큼 힘들지는 않아.

소녀 햄스터는 무얼 먹나요?

남자 신선한 야채와 견과류를 먹이면 된단다.

소녀 쿠키나 초콜릿은요?

남자 그건 햄스터에게는 너무 달아. 그리고 마늘이나 양파를 먹이지 않도록 주의하렴.

소녀 햄스터 한 쌍과 우리 하나를 살게요.

남자 그래.

1. 소녀는 어디에 있는가?
   a.　　　　b.　　　　c.　　　★d.

다시 듣고 질문에 답하시오.

2. 햄스터가 먹을 수 있는 것은 무엇인가?
   ★a. 야채와 견과류　　b. 쿠키와 초콜릿
   c. 마늘과 양파　　　d. 위의 것 모두

두 개의 요약을 듣고 올바른 것을 고르시오.

3.

스크립트

a. The girl is telling the man some interesting stories about raising hamsters at home.

b. The girl is interested in raising hamsters, and she is asking the man questions about what to feed them.

해석

a. ☐ 소녀는 남자에게 집에서 햄스터를 기르는 것에 관한 재미있는 이야기를 해주고 있다.

b. ★ 소녀는 햄스터를 키우는 것에 관심이 있어서 남자에게 햄스터 먹이에 대해 묻고 있다.

Listening 3

p. 87

다음 이야기를 듣고 질문에 답하시오.

스크립트

Pets are animals we keep for fun or for companionship. Traditionally, animals like dogs and cats were considered pets, but nowadays many other animals are also considered pets. Although traditional pets, such as dogs, cats, birds, or fish are still more popular, some people have pet pigs or sheep. Less common pets, such as snakes and lizards, are gaining popularity fast. Even though spiders and ants are rare pets, there are some people who keep them as pets.

해석

애완동물은 재미를 위해 또는 친구를 삼기 위해 키우는 동물이다. 전통적으로는 개나 고양이 같은 동물들이 애완동물로 여겨졌지만, 요즘은 다른 많은 동물들도 애완동물로 여겨진다. 개, 고양이, 새, 또는 물고기 같은 전통적인 애완동물이 여전히 더 인기가 있긴 하지만, 몇몇 사람들은 돼지나 양을 애완동물로 키운다. 뱀이나 도마뱀처럼 덜 흔한 애완동물도 빠르게 인기를 끌고 있다. 거미와 개미는 애완용으로 흔하지 않긴 하지만, 그것들을 애완용으로 키우는 사람들도 있다.

1. 이 단락의 주요 화제는 무엇인가?
   a. 애완동물일 수 없는 동물들
   ★b. 다양한 종류의 애완동물들
   c. 과거와 미래의 애완동물들
   d. 사람들이 애완동물을 키우지 않는 이유

다시 듣고 질문에 답하시오.

2. 이 단락에 따르면, 가장 흔하지 <u>않은</u> 종류의 애완동물은 무엇인가?
   a. 개와 고양이　　　b. 새와 물고기
   c. 뱀과 도마뱀　　★d. 거미와 개미

Listening 4

p. 87

다음 이야기를 듣고 질문에 답하시오.

스크립트

Today, the biggest problem many wild animals face is loss of their habitats. Every day, a large number of trees are cleared from forests for development, and others destroyed for natural resources, such as wood or minerals. Excessive hunting is another big reason for the endangerment of wild animals. Many animals are hunted for their furs or for their body parts.

해석

오늘날, 많은 야생동물들이 직면한 가장 큰 문제는 그들의 서식지가 없어진다는 것이다. 날마다 엄청난 수의 삼림이 개발로 인해 베어지고 목재나 광물 같은 천연자원을 얻기 위해 파괴된다. 지나친 사냥도 야생동물이 멸종 위기에 처하게 된 또 다른 큰 이유이다. 많은 동물들이 그들의 모피나 몸 일부를 얻기 위한 목적으로 사냥된다.

1. 이 단락은 주로 무엇에 관한 것인가?
   a. 우리가 야생동물을 보호해야 하는 이유
   b. 야생동물들이 사는 장소
   ★c. 야생동물들의 멸종 위기
   d. 사냥을 위한 중요한 조언

다시 듣고 질문에 답하시오.

2. 이 단락에 따르면, 사람들은 왜 야생동물을 죽이는가?
   a. 사람들이 야생동물들을 무서워하기 때문에
   ★b. 모피를 얻기 위해
   c. 야생동물들이 사람들의 집을 습격해서
   d. 야생동물들이 숲을 파괴해서

두 개의 요약을 듣고 올바른 것을 고르시오.

3.

스크립트

a. Many wild animals are endangered by destruction of forests and excessive hunting.
b. Even though people continuously hunt wild animals, the population of wild animals has actually increased.

해석

a.★ 많은 야생동물들이 숲의 파괴와 지나친 사냥에 의해 멸종 위기에 처해 있다.
b.□ 인간은 끊임없이 야생동물 사냥을 계속하지만, 야생동물의 수는 실제로는 증가했다

Practice Test

p. 88~89

1. a	2. c	3. d	4. a	5. d	6. b
7. c	8. d	9. d	10. b		

[1~2] 다음 대화를 듣고 질문에 답하시오.

스크립트

Diane Paul, what did you do over the weekend?
Paul I went to the zoo.
Diane You must have had a lot of fun.
Paul No, I felt bad.
Diane Why?
Paul I felt sorry for the animals in the cages. I believe wild animals should live in the wild. It was really sad to see the polar bear suffering from the heat.
Diane I agree. But by going to the zoo, people can realize why we should protect animals.
Paul You have a point there, Diane.

해석

Diane Paul, 주말에 뭐 했어?
Paul 동물원에 갔었어.
Diane 재밌었겠네.
Paul 아니, 기분이 나빴어.
Diane 왜?
Paul 우리 안의 동물들이 안됐더라고. 나는 야생동물들은 야생에서 살아야 한다고 생각해. 북극곰이 더위에 고생하는 걸 보니 정말 마음이 아팠어.
Diane 그래 맞아. 하지만 많은 사람들이 동물원에 가봄으로써 왜 동물들을 보호해야 하는지 깨달을 수 있잖아.
Paul 그건 네 말도 맞다, Diane.

1. Paul의 마지막 대답은 어떤 의미인가?
   ★a. 그는 Diane의 의견에 동의한다.
   b. 그는 Diane의 의견에 동의하지 않는다.
   c. 그는 Diane이 말한 것을 이해하지 못한다.
   d. 그는 화제를 바꾸고 싶어 한다.

2. Paul의 말에 따르면, 야생동물들은 _____.
   a. 더 큰 우리에 넣어져야 한다
   b. 아주 위험하다
   ★c. 야생에서 살아야 한다
   d. 야생에서보다 동물원에 있는 것이 더 안전하다

스크립트

M Nice fish tank you have there! I didn't know you liked fish.

W I love fish because they are so relaxing. Do you have any pets?

M I have a pair of parrots.

W I don't like birds because they are too noisy and create a lot of mess.

M That is true. But parrots are fun because they can talk.

W They don't talk. They just imitate what you say.

M I know. But, I feel good when they say, "Have a nice day" to me every morning.

해석

남 멋진 어항을 가졌네! 네가 물고기를 좋아하는지 몰랐는데.

여 난 물고기가 좋아. 마음을 편안하게 해 주거든. 너는 애완동물이 있니?

남 난 앵무새 한 쌍을 키워.

여 난 새는 안 좋아하는데. 새는 너무 시끄럽고 (주변을) 지저분하게 만들잖아.

남 그건 사실이야. 하지만 앵무새는 말을 할 수 있어서 재밌어.

여 앵무새는 말을 못 해. 그냥 네가 하는 말을 따라하는 것뿐이야.

남 알아. 하지만 앵무새가 매일 아침 나에게 "좋은 하루 보내요"라고 말하면 정말 기분이 좋아.

3. 여자는 애완동물로 새를 어떻게 생각하는가?
   a. 매혹적이다　　　　b. 재미있다
   c. 지루하다　　　★d. 성가시다

4. 남자와 그의 앵무새에 대해 사실이 아닌 것은 무엇인가?
   ★a. 그는 세 마리의 앵무새를 키운다.
   b. 그의 앵무새들은 매일 "좋은 하루 보내요"라고 말한다.
   c. 그는 앵무새는 (주변을) 지저분하게 한다는 것에 동의한다.
   d. 그는 앵무새는 애완동물로 기르기 재미있다고 생각한다.

스크립트

Juan Yesterday, I saw a TV show about guide dogs for the blind. It was amazing.

Sunny I saw it, too. They were very smart.

Juan They do so well because they go through a very intense training.

Sunny Do you know there are dogs for the deaf, too?

Juan Really? How do they help their owners?

Sunny When they hear phone calls, door-bells, or alarm clocks, they let their owners know where the sound is coming from.

Juan That's wonderful.

해석

Juan 어제 시각 장애인 안내견에 대한 TV 프로그램을 봤어. 놀랍더군.

Sunny 나도 봤어. 정말 영리하더라.

Juan 안내견은 아주 혹독한 훈련을 거치기 때문에 그렇게 잘하는 거야.

Sunny 너 청각 장애인을 위한 개도 있다는 거 아니?

Juan 정말? 그 개들이 어떻게 주인을 도와?

Sunny 전화 소리, 초인종, 자명종 시계 같은 소리를 들으면, 개가 자기 주인에게 어디서 그 소리가 나는지 알려준대.

Juan 정말 대단하구나.

5. 대화에서 언급되지 않은 소리는 무엇인가?
   a.　　　　b.　　　　c.　　　　★d.

6. 청각 장애인을 위한 안내견은 주인을 어떻게 돕는가?
   a. 아무런 소리가 나지 않을 때 짖어서
   ★b. 중요한 소리를 주인에게 알려서
   c. 위험한 장소에서 멈춰 서서
   d. 조용한 장소로 주인을 데리고 가서

스크립트

Rich Is that your new dog, Tina? How cute.

Tina Yes, it is.

Rich How much did you pay for it?

Tina I didn't pay anything because I got it from an adoption center.

Rich What is an adoption center?

Tina It's a place where wounded or homeless animals are kept and cared for. All of the animals there can be adopted for free.

Rich So, they didn't charge you any money?

Tina No. All you have to do is pay a small fee for their vaccination.

해석

Rich 저게 네 새 강아지야, Tina? 정말 귀엽네.

Tina 응, 맞아.

Rich 얼마 주고 샀어?

Tina 입양 센터에서 데리고 와서 돈은 전혀 내지 않았어.

Rich 입양 센터가 뭐야?

Tina 다치거나 집이 없는 동물들을 데려다 보살피는 곳이야. 거기에 있는 동물은 모두 무료로 입양할 수 있어.

Rich 그래서 아무 돈도 들지 않았단 말이야?

Tina 응. 단지 예방 접종을 위한 수수료만 조금 내면 돼.

7. Tina는 개를 어떻게 갖게 되었는가?
   a. 이미 개를 가지고 있었다.
   b. 어떤 사람이 그녀에게 주었다.
   ★c. 개를 입양했다.
   d. 애완동물 가게에서 샀다.

8. 동물을 입양하기 위해서는 얼마를 지불해야 하는가?
   a. 전혀 지불하지 않는다.
   b. 동물의 실제 가격
   c. 우리 값 조금
   ★d. 예방 접종을 위한 약간의 돈

[9-10] 다음 이야기를 듣고 질문에 답하시오.

스크립트

Sharks use different senses to find food, depending on the distance of their prey. When the prey is very far away, sharks rely on hearing and smell. They can hear their prey several kilometers away and can smell small traces of blood in the water. Sharks rely on their vision only when they are very close to the prey.

해석

상어는 먹이를 찾기 위해 먹이와의 거리에 따라 다른 감각들을 사용한다. 먹이가 아주 멀리 떨어져 있으면, 상어는 청각과 후각에 의존한다. 상어는 먹이의 소리를 수 킬로미터 떨어진 곳에서도 들을 수 있으며, 물 속의 아주 작은 양의 피 냄새도 맡을 수 있다. 상어는 먹이가 매우 가까이에 있을 때에만 시각에 의존한다.

9. 상어는 먹이가 멀리 있을 때 어떤 감각을 사용하는가?
   a. 청각만   b. 시각만
   c. 후각과 시각   ★d. 청각과 후각

10. 이 단락에 따르면, 상어에 대해 사실인 것은 무엇인가?
    a. 상어는 먹이를 찾기 위해 주로 시각을 사용한다.
    ★b. 상어는 먹이가 보이지 않을 때에도 먹이를 찾을 수 있다.
    c. 상어는 먹이의 크기에 따라 다른 감각들을 사용한다.
    d. 상어는 먹이가 멀리 있으면 (먹이의 소리를) 잘 듣지 못한다.

Dictation (Listening Task)   p. 90

LISTENING 1
Aren't they lovely, get too close to, you're scared of swans, attacked by, when I was a child, I haven't liked big birds, snakes, bugs, this might sound funny, get scared by

LISTENING 2
anything you like, if they are easy to raise, as difficult as you think, feed them, vegetables, They are too sweet, shouldn't feed them, a pair of them, a cage

LISTENING 3
we keep for fun, Traditionally, considered pets, still more popular, pet pigs or sheep, Less common, snakes and lizards, popularity, spiders and ants

LISTENING 4
the biggest problem, loss of their habitats, cleared from forests for development, destroyed, Excessive hunting, for their furs, body parts

Dictation (Practice Test)   p. 91

PRACTICE TEST [1-2]
over the weekend, You must have had a lot of fun, I felt bad, animals in the cages, should live in the wild, suffering from the heat, by going to the zoo, why we should protect animals, You have a point

PRACTICE TEST [3-4]
Nice fish tank, you liked fish, they are so relaxing, a pair of parrots, too noisy, a lot of mess, they can talk, imitate what you say, Have a nice day

PRACTICE TEST [5-6]
guide dogs for the blind, go through, intense training, for the deaf, help their owners, phone calls, alarm clocks, where the sound is coming from

PRACTICE TEST [7-8]
How cute, did you pay for it, from an adoption center, wounded or homeless animals, can be adopted for free, charge you any money, a small fee for

PRACTICE TEST [9-10]
different senses, depending on the distance, rely on, smell, several kilometers away, blood, vision, close to

UNIT 12
What should I wear?

Getting Ready p. 93

A

looking for, How about, out of style, go well with, latest, try it on, what size, tight on, in a bigger size, out of, take

B

• The person in the picture is wearing jeans / a white dress shirt with pink stripes.
• The person in the picture is wearing a black leather jacket / a white skirt.
• The person in the picture is wearing a tan suit / a dark brown dress shirt.

A 아래 대화를 읽고 빈칸을 완성하시오.

더 큰 치수로, ~와 어울리다, 어떤 치수, ~에게 끼는, 사다, 최신의, ~를 찾다, 유행에 뒤떨어진, 그것을 한번 입어 보다, ~는 어때, ~가 다 나간(없는)

점원 무엇을 도와드릴까요?
여자 제 흰색 바지와 어울릴 가죽 재킷을 하나 찾고 있어요.
점원 이것은 어떻습니까?
여자 글쎄요... 그 옷은 조금 유행에 뒤떨어져 보여요. 마치 우리 할머니가 입는 옷 같은데요.
점원 알겠습니다... 아! 아마도 이 옷이 마음에 드실 것 같습니다. 이 베이지색 재킷은 손님의 흰색 바지와 잘 어울릴 겁니다. 최신 패션이거든요.
여자 그 옷이 마음에 드네요. 한번 입어 봐도 될까요?
점원 물론이죠. 어떤 치수를 입으세요?
여자 치수 6이요.
점원 이 옷이 치수 6입니다. 여기 있습니다.
여자 음... 이 옷은 저에게는 조금 끼는 것 같아요. 이 재킷이 더 큰 치수로도 있나요?
점원 죄송합니다만, 하나 더 위의 사이즈는 다 나갔네요(없네요).
여자 네, 그럼 그냥 치수 6으로 살게요.

B 그들은 어떤 옷을 입고 있는가? 친구들과 이야기해 보시오.

회색 폴로 셔츠, 흰색 치마, 진한 갈색 와이셔츠, 청바지, 황갈색 양복, 분홍색 줄무늬가 있는 흰색 와이셔츠, 검정색 가죽 재킷

◁)) 사진 속의 사람은 회색 폴로 셔츠를 입고 있다.

Listening Task p. 94~95

Listening 1	1. b	2. A. F	B. T
Listening 2	1. a	2. d	3. b
Listening 3	1. c	2. a	
Listening 4	1. c	2. d	3. b

Listening 1 p. 94

다음 대화를 듣고 질문에 답하시오.

스크립트

M Can I help you?
W Yes. I saw a pair of shoes I liked last week. Let me find them. Umm... Oh, these are the ones.
M Would you like to try them on? What size do you wear?
W My size is six-and-a-half, but let me try both the six-and-a-half and the seven, just in case the six-and-a-half feels small.
M Why don't you try the pair on display? That pair is size seven.
W Let me try them... Well, these fit perfectly. I will take them.
M These are beautiful shoes. You have great taste.

해석

남 무엇을 도와드릴까요?
여 네. 지난주에 마음에 드는 신발을 봤었는데요. 제가 한번 찾아볼게요. 음... 아! 이 신발이에요.
남 한번 신어 보시겠습니까? 치수가 어떻게 되십니까?
여 치수 6.5를 신는데요. 치수 6.5와 치수 7 둘 다 신어 볼게요. 혹시 치수 6.5가 작을 수도 있으니까요.
남 전시되어 있는 신발을 신어 보시죠. 그 신발이 치수 7입니다.
여 신어 볼게요. 음, 이 신발이 딱 맞네요. 이걸로 할게요.
남 예쁜 신발입니다. 센스가 있으시네요.

1. 여자는 어디에 있는가?
   a. 남성복 매장   ★b. 신발 가게
   c. 아기옷 가게   d. 신발 수선점

다시 듣고 True(참) 또는 False(거짓)에 표시하시오.

2. A. 그녀는 치수 7을 신지만, 지금은 치수 6.5를 신어보고 있다. (F)
   B. 그녀가 보통 신는 치수는 6.5이지만, 이번에는 치수 7(인 신발)을 살 것이다. (T)

다음 대화를 듣고 질문에 답하시오.

> 스크립트
>
> **Jay** Mom, what should I wear for today's job interview? I am considering either my black suit or this blue shirt.
>
> **Mom** I don't think you should wear a suit to an interview for a part-time job at an ice cream shop. Why don't you wear the green shirt with white stripes that I bought you last month?
>
> **Jay** OK. What about the pants?
>
> **Mom** I think jeans are fine, and try that brown belt with them.
>
> **Jay** Thanks, Mom.

> 해석
>
> **Jay** 엄마, 오늘 취업 면접에 뭘 입고 가야 하죠? 제 검정색 정장이나 이 파란색 셔츠 중 하나로 고려 중인데요.
>
> **엄마** 아이스크림 가게에서 하는 아르바이트 면접에 정장을 입을 필요는 없을 것 같은데. 내가 지난달에 사준 흰색 줄무늬가 있는 녹색 셔츠를 입는 것이 어떠니?
>
> **Jay** 좋아요. 그럼 바지는 어떤 걸로 하죠?
>
> **엄마** 청바지가 좋을 것 같구나. 그리고 바지에 저 갈색 벨트를 해보렴.
>
> **Jay** 고마워요, 엄마.

1. 이 대화는 무엇에 관한 것인가?
   ★a. 취업 면접에 입을 옷 고르기
   b. 데이트에 입을 옷 사기
   c. 입을 옷이 아무 것도 없다는 불평
   d. TV 인터뷰에 나온 옷에 대한 대화

다시 듣고 질문에 답하시오.

2. 소년은 면접에 어떤 옷을 입을 것인가?
   a.　　　　b.　　　　c.　　　　★d.

두 개의 요약을 듣고 올바른 것을 고르시오.

3.

> 스크립트
>
> a. The boy's mother is helping the boy prepare for the job interview questions.
> b. The boy's mother is suggesting to the boy that he dress casually for his job interview.

> 해석
>
> a. ☐ 소년의 엄마는 소년이 면접 질문에 대해 준비하는 것을 돕고 있다.
> b. ★ 소년의 엄마는 소년에게 면접에 캐주얼한 옷을 입고 가라고 조언하고 있다.

다음 이야기를 듣고 질문에 답하시오.

> 스크립트
>
> This is the dress code of our school. Boys should wear a white dress shirt or a polo shirt, and black or dark blue pants. The belt can be any dark color, such as black, brown, or dark blue, but the shoes must be black. Girls must follow the same dress code as the boys, with the only difference being that girls can wear either pants or a skirt. A tie is optional for both the boys and the girls.

> 해석
>
> 이것이 우리 학교의 복장 규정이다. 남학생들은 흰색 와이셔츠나 폴로 셔츠를 입고 검정색 또는 진한 남색 바지를 입어야 한다. 벨트는 검정색, 갈색, 또는 진한 남색 같은 어두운 색상이면 아무 것이나 되지만, 신발은 반드시 검정색이어야 한다. 여학생들은 남학생들과 같은 복장 규정을 따라야 하지만, 한 가지 다른 점은 여학생은 바지나 치마 중에서 하나를 입을 수 있다는 것이다. 넥타이는 남학생과 여학생 모두 (매든지 안 매든지) 선택 가능하다.

1. 이 단락은 무엇에 관한 것인가?
   a. 한 상점에서 파는 교복
   b. 십대들의 옷에 관한 TV 프로그램에서의 조언
   ★c. 학생들의 옷차림에 대한 교칙
   d. 학생들이 선호하는 패션

다시 듣고 질문에 답하시오.

2. 다음 중 여학생들에게 허용되지 않는 옷은 무엇인가?
   ★a. 갈색 바지　　　　b. 검정색 치마
   c. 흰색 폴로 셔츠　　d. 진한 남색 바지

다음 이야기를 듣고 질문에 답하시오.

> 스크립트
>
> Even though new fashions seem to appear every day, many of them may not be new at all. They might have been popular before. For example, wide ties were in style during the 70s, and narrow ties during the 90s. Today, more people are going back to wide ties again. Similarly, the popularity of jeans has gone up and down. But fortunately for the jeans makers, jeans have never been completely out of fashion.

해석

날마다 새로운 패션이 등장하는 것 같지만, 그 중 많은 것은 전혀 새로운 패션이 아닐 수도 있다. 많은 패션이 이전에 유행하였던 것일 수 있다. 예를 들어, 폭이 넓은 넥타이는 70년대에 유행하였고 폭이 좁은 넥타이는 90년대에 유행하였다. 요즘은 많은 사람들이 다시 폭이 넓은 타이로 돌아가고 있다 (=폭이 넓은 넥타이를 선호하고 있다). 마찬가지로, 청바지의 인기도 오르락내리락해 왔다. 그러나 청바지 제조업자들에게는 다행하게도, 청바지는 한번도 완전히 유행에서 벗어난 적은 없었다.

1. 이 단락의 주제로 가장 좋은 것은 무엇인가?
   a. 청바지의 세계적 유행
   b. 넥타이를 고르는 법
   ★c. 유행 추세의 변화
   d. 70년대의 패션

다시 듣고 질문에 답하시오.

2. 이 단락에 따르면, 청바지는 언제 유행하였나?
   a. 70년대   b. 90년대   c. 오늘날   ★d. 항상

두 개의 요약을 듣고 올바른 것을 고르시오.

3.

스크립트

a. The fashion trends of ties and jeans have always been very different.
b. Some new fashions might have been popular before; ties and jeans are good examples.

해석

a. □ 넥타이와 청바지의 유행 추세는 항상 매우 달랐다.
b. ★ 몇몇 새로운 패션은 예전에 유행했던 것일 수도 있는데, 넥타이와 청바지가 그 좋은 예이다.

Practice Test   p. 96~97

| 1. b | 2. c | 3. b | 4. a | 5. c | 6. b |
| 7. d | 8. c | 9. d | 10. a |

[1–2] 다음 대화를 듣고 질문에 답하시오.

스크립트

Mary   How do I look in these pants, Sabrina? This is the new fall fashion.
Sabrina I like them, Mary. They look kind of funky. Look at all those pockets and zippers.
Mary   I think they will go well with my T-shirts.
Sabrina Do they have them in different colors?

Mary   Yes, they do, but they may be out of sizes in certain colors because this style is hot.
Sabrina Maybe they are out of my size because it's a very popular size.
Mary   You never know. Why don't you find out?
Sabrina I think I will.

해석

Mary   이 바지 나한테 어때 보여, Sabrina? 올해 새 가을 패션인데.
Sabrina 마음에 들어, Mary. 그 옷 발랄해 보인다. 그 많은 주머니와 지퍼 좀 봐.
Mary   이 바지는 내 티셔츠와도 잘 어울릴 것 같아.
Sabrina 그 바지 다른 색상도 있니?
Mary   응. 있는데, 어떤 색상의 바지는 아마 치수가 다 나가고 없을 거야. 이 스타일이 인기가 많거든.
Sabrina 내가 입는 치수는 사람들이 많이 입는 치수라서 아마 다 팔렸을 것 같은데.
Mary   그건 모르지. 한번 알아보지 그래?
Sabrina 그래야겠어.

1. Sabrina가 염려하는 이유는 무엇인가?
   a. 바지가 마음에 드는지 확신할 수 없어서
   ★b. 그 바지가 그녀 치수는 다 팔리고 없을 것 같아서
   c. 바지에 주머니와 지퍼가 너무 많아서
   d. Mary가 입은 것과 같은 옷을 입고 싶지 않아서

2. 대화에서 언급되지 않은 것은 무엇인가?
   a. 치수   b. 색상   ★c. 가격   d. 스타일

[3–4] 다음 대화를 듣고 질문에 답하시오.

스크립트

W Is that your new shirt?
M Yes, I bought this shirt two days ago, but I think it is a little too small for me. What do you think?
W I am sorry to say this, but it is small. I noticed that from the other side of the street. Why did you get one so small?
M I don't know. This is my regular size, fifty-two. But I think I've gained some weight lately.
W Maybe you should either exchange the shirt or do some exercises.
M I cannot exchange this because they don't have it in a different size.
W Then, you have only one choice, right?

여 그거 새로 산 셔츠야?

남 응. 이 셔츠 이틀 전에 샀는데, 나한테 좀 너무 작은 것 같아. 어떻게 생각해?

여 이렇게 말해서 미안하지만, 그 옷은 너한테 작아. 길 건너편에서 봤을 때부터 (작다는 걸) 알겠던걸. 왜 그렇게 작은 옷을 샀어?

남 모르겠어. 이게 내 평상시 치수 52야. 하지만 최근에 살이 좀 찐 것 같아.

여 아무래도 셔츠를 교환하거나 운동을 하거나 해야 할 것 같네.

남 교환은 할 수가 없어. 이 셔츠는 다른 치수로는 나오지 않거든.

여 그렇다면 한 가지 선택 밖에 없네, 그렇지?

3. 셔츠의 어떤 점이 문제인가?

   a. 너무 길다.   ★b. 너무 작다.

   c. 너무 비싸다.   d. 너무 크다.

4. 남자는 무엇을 할 것인가?

  ★a. 운동을 시작할 것이다.

   b. 셔츠를 교환할 것이다.

   c. 또 다른 셔츠를 살 것이다.

   d. 환불을 받을 것이다.

[5–6] 다음 대화를 듣고 질문에 답하시오.

스크립트

W Hi, do you need alterations?

M Yes. I need to have these two pairs of pants cut off a little at the bottom. Can you do it by this afternoon?

W I don't think so. We have a lot of work today. I can have them ready by tomorrow, though.

M I have a date tonight, and I have nothing to wear. Could you do just one pair, then?

W Well, then. I'll do just one pair. Why don't you go change so that I can measure the length?

M Thanks, where is the dressing room?

W Go all the way to the back.

해석

여 어서 오세요. 수선이 필요하세요?

남 네, 이 바지 두 벌의 밑단을 좀 줄여야 하는데요. 오늘 오후까지 해 주실 수 있나요?

여 안 되겠는데요. 오늘은 일이 많아서요. 내일까지는 해드릴 수 있습니다만.

남 오늘 밤에 데이트가 있는데 입을 옷이 없어요. 그러면 바지 한 벌만 수선해 주실 수 있으세요?

여 음, 그렇다면 한 벌만 수선해 드릴게요. 제가 길이를 잴 수 있게 옷을 갈아입어 주시겠어요?

남 감사합니다. 탈의실이 어디에 있나요?

여 뒤편으로 쭉 가세요.

5. 이 대화에 이어질 가장 좋은 응답은 무엇인가?

남자	

   a. 제가 길을 안내해 드리겠습니다.

   b. 제가 직접 하겠습니다.

  ★c. 곧 돌아오겠습니다.

   d. 그러면 내일 다시 오겠습니다.

6. 이 대화에 관해 사실인 것은 무엇인가?

   a. 남자는 바지가 수선될 때까지 이틀을 기다려야 한다.

  ★b. 남자의 바지 중 한 벌은 오후까지 수선될 것이다.

   c. 남자의 바지 두 벌 모두 오후까지 수선될 것이다.

   d. 남자는 바지 수선을 받을 수 없을 것이다.

[7–8] 다음 대화를 듣고 질문에 답하시오.

스크립트

Kim What do you think of her bag?

Sally Ugh, that is totally out of style. When was the last time I saw one of those?

Kim The leather is all worn out. I think she's had that bag for a long time.

Sally And, look at the buckle. It is so huge. I think it is time for her to get a new one.

Kim Speaking of bags, I need a new purse.

Sally Ok, let's shop around. But why don't we eat first?

Kim Sounds good.

해석

Kim 저 여자 가방 어떻게 생각해?

Sally 이런, 완전 구식 가방이네. 저런 가방을 마지막으로 본 게 언제였더라?

Kim 가죽이 완전히 해졌어. 가방을 꽤 오래 쓴 것 같아.

Sally 그리고 저 버클 좀 봐. 너무 크잖아. 저 여자 아무래도 새 가방을 살 때가 된 것 같다.

Kim 가방 이야기가 나왔으니 말인데, 나도 새 지갑이 필요해.

Sally 좋아. 쇼핑하러 가자. 그런데 먼저 뭔가 좀 먹는 게 어때?

Kim 좋은 생각이야.

7. 여자들이 그 가방을 싫어하는 이유는 무엇인가?

   a. 유행이 지나서   b. 낡아서

   c. 버클이 너무 커서   ★d. 위의 것 모두

8. 여자들은 다음에 어디로 갈 것인가?

   a. 쇼핑센터   b. 도서관   ★c. 식당   d. 미장원

스크립트

Even when it comes to buying bags, the difference between men and women shows. Even though men consider bags as something you carry your personal belongings in, women consider them as an important fashion item just like necklaces, sunglasses, or shoes. That is why women sometimes buy bags that are too small or too expensive just because of their look.

해석

가방을 살 때조차, 남자와 여자의 차이점은 드러난다. 남자들은 가방을 개인 소지품을 넣어 다니는 것으로만 여기지만, 여자들은 가방을 목걸이, 선글라스, 또는 신발과 같이 중요한 패션 품목으로 생각한다. 여자들이 가끔 가방의 디자인 하나만 보고 너무 작거나 너무 비싼 가방들을 사는 이유도 그 때문이다.

9. 이 단락의 주제는 무엇인가?
   a. 좋은 가방을 찾는 법
   b. 가방의 유래
   c. 새로운 남성용 가방
   ★d. 여자와 남자의 패션 차이

10. 들은 내용을 바탕으로, 가장 잘 맞는 보기는 무엇인가?

가방을 살 때, 여자들은 ____A____ 에 대해 더 많이 고려하는 반면 남자들은 ____B____ 을(를) 먼저 고려한다.

	A		B
★a.	어떻게 보이는가	-	가방의 기능
b.	얼마인가	-	어디서 만들어졌는가
c.	무엇으로 만들어졌는가	-	얼마나 잘 팔리는가
d.	언제 만들어졌는가	-	어떻게 보이는가

Dictation (Listening Task)   p. 98

LISTENING 1
a pair of shoes, Let me find, try them on, six-and-a-half, six-and-a-half, seven, feels small, the pair on display, these fit perfectly

LISTENING 2
what should I wear, job interview, wear a suit, a part-time job, the green shirt, white stripes, What about, jeans are fine, with them

LISTENING 3
white dress shirt, a polo shirt, black or dark blue, any dark color, must be black, the same dress code, only difference, either pants or a skirt, tie

LISTENING 4
seem to appear, may not be new, might have been popular, were in style, during the 90s, going back to wide ties, jeans, up and down, completely out of fashion

Dictation (Practice Test)   p. 99

PRACTICE TEST [1-2]
How do I look in, fall fashion, pockets and zippers, go well with, in different colors, may be out of sizes, this style is hot, out of my size, You never know

PRACTICE TEST [3-4]
a little too small, What do you think, the other side, my regular size, gained some weight, exchange the shirt, do some exercises, in a different size, only one choice

PRACTICE TEST [5-6]
two pairs of pants cut off a little, I don't think so, have them ready, I have nothing to wear, just one pair, Why don't you go change, measure the length, dressing room, all the way to the back

PRACTICE TEST [7-8]
What do you think of, out of style, When was the last time, worn out, for a long time, it is time for her to get, shop around, eat first, Sounds good

PRACTICE TEST [9-10]
when it comes to, men and women, your personal belongings, important fashion item, necklaces, sunglasses, that are too small, because of their look

UNIT 13
You're always on the Internet!

Listening Task			p. 102~103
Listening 1	1. c	2. A. F	A. T
Listening 2	1. b	2. b	3. a
Listening 3	1. d	2. c	
Listening 4	1. c	2. a	3. a

Getting Ready   p. 101

A

usually, searches, email, surf the net, chat, homepage, post, email you, address, Internet addiction

B

(1)-(d)   (2)-(e)   (3)-(b)   (4)-(c)   (5)-(a)

A 아래 대화를 읽고 빈칸을 완성하시오.

> 너에게 이메일을 보내다, 보통, 인터넷 중독, 홈페이지, 인터넷으로 여기저기 둘러보다, (자료를) 올리다, 주소, 검색, 이메일, 채팅하다

Sam 넌 항상 인터넷을 쓰고 있는 것 같아.

Amy 인터넷이 재미있고 유용해서 많이 써.

Sam 인터넷으로 보통 뭘 하는데? 난 검색을 하거나 이메일 확인할 때에만 사용하는데.

Amy 음, 난 인터넷으로 여기저기 둘러보고, 최신 뉴스도 읽고, 인터넷 쇼핑도 해. 하지만 친구들하고 채팅하는 것도 좋아하지.

Sam 블로그는? 네 홈페이지가 있니?

Amy 응. 멋진 블로그를 갖고 있지. 거의 매일 내가 좋아하는 시를 올려. 내 홈페이지 주소를 이메일로 보내 줄테니까 나중에 와 보렴.

Sam Amy, 이렇게 말하긴 좀 그렇지만, 난 네가 인터넷에 너무 많은 시간을 보내는 것 같아.

Amy 음... 네 말이 맞을지도 몰라. 인터넷에 접속해서 인터넷 중독 증상이 어떤 건지 정보를 좀 알아봐야겠다.

Sam 오, 이런! 너 또 시작이다!

B 왼쪽의 단어와 오른쪽의 정의를 연결하시오.

(1) 즐겨찾기 – (d) 나중에 인터넷 페이지 주소를 클릭해서 해당 페이지를 더 쉽게 찾게 해 주는 인터넷 페이지 주소 목록

(2) 서버 – (e) 네트워크상의 다른 컴퓨터들을 통제하는 주(主) 컴퓨터

(3) 대화방 – (b) 글자 메시지를 통해 온라인상에서 대화를 할 수 있는 장소

(4) 인터넷 뱅킹 – (c) 인터넷으로 청구 요금을 지불할 수 있게 해 주는 서비스

(5) 스팸 메일 – (a) 많은 사람들에게 보내지는 원치 않는 광고성 편지

Listening 1   p. 102

다음 대화를 듣고 질문에 답하시오.

스크립트

Ted Do you have a problem, Cindy?

Cindy Yes, Ted. Whenever I do an Internet search, I get too many results.

Ted I think you need to learn how to narrow down your search with proper keywords.

Cindy How do you do that?

Ted For example, if you want to know how the Internet started, instead of typing in just "Internet," try "Internet history." In that way, you will get the information that is related to the history of the Internet only.

Cindy Now I get it.

해석

Ted 무슨 문제라도 있어, Cindy?

Cindy 응, Ted. 인터넷 검색을 할 때마다 검색 결과가 너무 많이 나와.

Ted 너는 적절한 핵심 단어를 사용해서 검색 범위를 좁히는 방법을 배워야 할 것 같은데.

Cindy 어떻게 그렇게 하는데?

Ted 예를 들어, 만일 인터넷이 어떻게 시작되었는지 알고 싶다면, 그냥 "인터넷"이라고만 입력하지 말고 "인터넷 역사"라고 쳐 봐. 그렇게 하면 인터넷의 역사와 관련된 정보만 보게 될 거야.

Cindy 이제 알겠어.

1. 이 대화는 무엇에 관한 것인가?
   a. 인터넷 연결과 관련된 문제점들
   b. 인터넷의 역사
   ★c. 효과적인 인터넷 검색을 위한 조언
   d. 친구에게서 정보를 얻는 방법

다시 듣고 True(참) 또는 False(거짓)에 표시하시오.

2. A. Cindy는 인터넷 사용법을 전혀 모른다. (F)
   B. Ted는 Cindy에게 더 구체적인 핵심 단어를 입력하도록 제안하고 있다. (T)

Listening 2

p. 102

다음 대화를 듣고 질문에 답하시오.

스크립트

M I wonder why it's taking so long.

W What are you talking about?

M I ordered Star Wars Series DVDs through the Internet the day before yesterday, but they're not here yet.

W Why didn't you get them from local stores?

M Because they're only 45 dollars from an online store. But they're 60 dollars at local stores.

W That is a big difference, but I wouldn't trust online stores.

M That's why you should go to well-known sites.

W I see.

해석

남 왜 이렇게 오래 걸리는지 모르겠네.

여 뭐가 말이야?

남 스타워즈 시리즈 DVD를 그저께 인터넷으로 주문했는데, 아직 도착하지 않아서 말야.

여 왜 근처 상점에서 사지 않고?

남 온라인 상점에서는 45달러거든. 하지만 근처 가게에서는 60달러야.

여 차이가 크네. 하지만 나는 온라인 상점은 못 믿겠어.

남 그게 바로 네가 잘 알려진 사이트를 이용해야 하는 이유야.

여 그렇군.

1. 인터넷으로 물건을 사는 이점은 무엇인가?
   a. 간편함   ★b. 더 싼 가격
   c. 빠른 배송   d. 더 좋은 물건

다시 듣고 질문에 답하시오.

2. 남자는 언제 스타워즈 DVD를 주문했는가?
   a. 어제   ★b. 이틀 전
   c. 사흘 전   d. 일주일 전

두 개의 요약을 듣고 올바른 것을 고르시오.

3.

스크립트

a. The man likes to shop on the Internet because things are cheaper on the Internet, but he is having a problem with delivery this time.

b. The man likes to shop on the Internet because he likes to buy things that are hard to find locally.

해석

a. ★ 남자는 물건값이 싸기 때문에 인터넷으로 쇼핑하는 것 좋아하지만, 이번에는 배달과 관련된 문제를 겪고 있다.

b. ☐ 남자는 (자신이 사는) 지역에서 찾기 어려운 물건을 사는 것을 좋아하기 때문에 인터넷 쇼핑을 좋아한다.

Listening 3

p. 103

다음 이야기를 듣고 질문에 답하시오.

스크립트

Of all the things the Internet can provide, email service may be the most important feature of all. It saves a lot of time and money for many people. But, email service can give you problems like junk mail or a virus. If you get too much junk mail, it is very difficult to find your important mail. If you get a virus, your computer system or the contents in it may be destroyed. So enjoy using email, but be cautious at the same time.

해석

인터넷이 제공할 수 있는 모든 것 중에서 이메일 서비스는 가장 중요한 특징이라 할 수 있다. 이메일 서비스는 많은 사람들의 시간과 돈을 절약해 준다. 하지만 이메일 서비스는 스팸 메일이나 바이러스와 같은 문제를 주기도 한다. 너무 많은 스팸 메일을 받게 되면 중요한 메일을 찾는 것이 매우 어렵게 된다. 만일 바이러스를 받게 되면 컴퓨터 시스템이나 그 안의 내용들이 파괴될 수도 있다. 따라서 이메일 이용을 즐기되, 동시에 (이메일을) 조심해서 이용해야 한다.

1. 말하는 사람은 이메일을 사용하는 것에 관해 어떤 권유를 하고 있는가?
   a. 많은 돈을 쓰지 말아라.
   b. 이메일 서비스를 더욱 자주 이용해라.
   c. 이메일 서비스를 이용하지 말아라.
   ★d. 이메일을 사용할 때 주의해라.

다시 듣고 질문에 답하시오.

2. 단락에 따르면 이메일 서비스의 단점은 무엇인가?
   a. 매우 비싸다.
   b. 메시지를 즉시 보낼 수 없다.
   ★c. 스팸 메일이나 바이러스를 받을 수도 있다.
   d. 파일 첨부가 쉽지 않다.

Listening 4 p. 103

다음 이야기를 듣고 질문에 답하시오.

스크립트

These are the symptoms of Internet addiction. First, you must use the Internet every day, otherwise you feel very insecure. Second, you lose all sense of time when you use the Internet. Third, you don't spend much time outdoors. Fourth, you check your email too many times a day. Lastly, you frequently eat in front of the computer monitor. The more symptoms you have, the more addicted you might be.

해석

이것들이 인터넷 중독 증세이다. 첫째, 당신은 인터넷을 매일 사용해야 하며, 그렇지 않으면(=인터넷을 매일 하지 않으면) 매우 불안해진다. 둘째, 인터넷을 사용하면 시간 감각을 완전히 잃어버린다. 셋째, 바깥에서 많은 시간을 보내지 않는다. 넷째, 하루에도 수없이 이메일을 확인한다. 마지막으로, 컴퓨터 모니터 앞에서 뭔가를 먹는 일이 잦다. 이 같은 증세가 많으면 많을수록, 당신은 (인터넷에) 더 많이 중독되어 있는 것일 수 있다.

1. 이 단락에서 얼마나 많은 인터넷 중독 증세가 논의되었는가?
   a. 세 개　　b. 네 개　　★c. 다섯 개　　d. 여섯 개

다시 듣고 질문에 답하시오.

2. 인터넷 중독 증세가 <u>아닌</u> 것은 무엇인가?
   ★a. 컴퓨터에 너무 많은 돈을 쓴다.
   b. 컴퓨터 모니터 앞에서 자주 뭔가를 먹는다.
   c. 밖에서 시간을 덜 보낸다.
   d. 인터넷을 너무 많이 이용한다.

두 개의 요약을 듣고 올바른 것을 고르시오.

3.

스크립트

a. Internet addiction has many symptoms. The more symptoms you have, the more likely it is that you're addicted to the Internet.

b. Even though many people are spending too many hours a day on the Internet, it is never easy to tell if they're suffering from Internet addiction.

해석

a. ★ 인터넷 중독에는 많은 증상이 있다. 당신이 더 많은 증상을 보일수록 당신은 인터넷에 중독되었을 가능성이 높다.

b. □ 비록 많은 사람들이 인터넷에 너무 많은 시간을 보내고는 있지만, 그들이 인터넷 중독을 겪고 있다고 판단하기는 쉽지 않다.

Practice Test p. 104~105

1. c	2. b	3. a	4. d	5. c	6. d
7. a	8. b	9. a	10. c		

[1~2] 다음 대화를 듣고 질문에 답하시오.

스크립트

Morris　What are you doing, Lindsey?

Lindsey　I am chatting with a friend in Australia. She came to the United States three years ago as an exchange student and she lived with us for about six months.

Morris　How often do you guys chat?

Lindsey　Almost every day. I think I chat more with her than many of my other friends here.

Morris　I chat with my brother in New York, but we only chat once a week or so.

해석

Morris　뭐하고 있어, Lindsey?

Lindsey　호주(=오스트레일리아)에 있는 친구와 채팅하고 있어. 그녀는 삼 년 전에 교환학생으로 미국에 와서 육 개월 정도 우리와 살았었어.

Morris　너희 둘은 얼마나 자주 채팅해?

Lindsey　거의 매일. 나는 여기에 있는 다른 많은 내 친구들보다 그녀와 더 많이 채팅을 하는 것 같아.

Morris　난 New York에 있는 형과 채팅을 해. 우린 일주일에 한 번 정도만 채팅을 하긴 하지만.

1. 그들은 무엇에 관해 이야기하고 있는가?
   a. 이메일 교환
   b. 인터넷을 통한 미팅
   ★c. 인터넷 채팅
   d. 가장 친한 친구의 홈페이지

2. Lindsey의 친구에 대해 사실인 것은 무엇인가?
   a. 그녀는 Lindsey와 일주일에 한 번 채팅한다.
   ★b. 그녀는 육 개월 정도 미국에서 머물렀었다.
   c. 그녀는 미국에 있을 때 혼자 살았다.
   d. 그녀는 지금 오스트리아에 살고 있다.

스크립트

John Gina, did you hear about the movie actress, Sandy Hilton? She is married and has two kids.

Gina I know. I even saw her kids' pictures on the Internet.

John Really? How could anyone put up such personal information on the Internet?

Gina I know! The Internet is great, but so many people are using it wrongly.

John You're right. Exchanging copyrighted materials illegally is another big problem with the Internet.

Gina You mean, things like songs or pictures?

해석

John Gina, 영화배우 Sandy Hilton에 대한 소식 들었어? 그녀가 결혼했고 애도 둘이나 있대.

Gina 그러게. 난 인터넷에서 그녀의 애들 사진도 봤어.

John 정말? 어떻게 인터넷에 그런 개인 정보를 올려 놓을 수 있지?

Gina 그러게 말이야! 인터넷은 대단하지만 너무 많은 사람들이 인터넷을 잘못 사용하고 있어.

John 맞아. 저작권이 있는 자료를 불법으로 주고받는 것도 인터넷과 관련된 또 하나의 큰 문제야.

Gina 노래나 사진 같은 것들 말이지?

3. 이 대화의 주요 화제는 무엇인가?
  ★a. 인터넷의 오용
  b. 노래와 사진을 내려받는 새로운 방법
  c. Sandy Hilton의 비밀 결혼
  d. 인터넷에서 사진을 보는 방법

4. Gina가 인터넷에서 발견한 것은 무엇인가?
  a. Sandy Hilton의 결혼 사진들
  b. Sandy Hilton이 작곡한 노래들
  c. Sandy Hilton의 옛날 영화들
  ★d. Sandy Hilton의 자녀 사진들

[5–6] 다음 대화를 듣고 질문에 답하시오.

스크립트

Michael Ugh, it is happening again.

Kate What is the problem, Michael?

Michael I cannot log onto the Internet. I think it's because too many people have logged in already. Wait, I can log in now.

Kate Good for you.

Michael Ugh! What is it now? I can't get to our school site.

Kate It looks like the server must be down.

Michael Yeah. The school server is too small, so it has been going down too often these days.

Kate I think you need to try later.

해석

Michael 이런, 또 이러네.

Kate 뭐가 문젠데, Michael?

Michael 인터넷에 접속이 안 돼. 너무 많은 사람들이 이미 접속해 있어서 그런가 봐. 잠깐, 이제 접속된다.

Kate 잘됐네.

Michael 이런! 이번엔 또 뭐야? 우리 학교 사이트에 들어갈 수가 없잖아.

Kate 서버가 다운된 것 같은데.

Michael 그러게. 학교 서버는 너무 작아서 요즘 계속 자주 다운돼.

Kate 나중에 다시 해 봐.

5. Michael은 왜 처음에 인터넷에 접속할 수 없었는가?
  a. 그의 컴퓨터가 너무 낡아서
  b. 서버가 다운되어서
  ★c. 너무 많은 사람들이 인터넷에 접속해 있어서
  d. 학교가 서버를 폐쇄해서

6. Michael이 다음에 할 일은 무엇인가?
  a. Kate에게 문제를 찾아내도록 부탁할 것이다.
  b. 다른 사이트에 접속해볼 것이다.
  c. 그의 컴퓨터를 Kate와 함께 수리할 것이다.
  ★d. 학교 서버가 복구될 때까지 기다릴 것이다.

[7–8] 다음 대화를 듣고 질문에 답하시오.

스크립트

M Do you remember the web address of the online dictionary?

W Yes, it is www.nexdictionary.com.

M That's right. I forget it every time.

W Why don't you bookmark the page?

M Because I have so many things in my bookmarks already, it's really hard to find anything from the list. It is faster just to type it in.

W That is why you need to learn how to organize your bookmarks. Let me show you how to do it.

M Thanks.

해석

남 온라인 사전 주소 기억나니?

여 응, www.nexdictionary.com이야.

남 맞아. 난 매번 잊어버리네.

여 그 페이지를 즐겨찾기 해두지 그래?

남 내 즐겨찾기엔 이미 너무 많은 것들이 들어있어서 그 목록에서 무언가를 찾는 건 정말 어려워. 그냥 입력하는 게 더 빨라.

여 그게 바로 네가 즐겨찾기 목록을 정리하는 법을 배워야 하는 이유야. 내가 어떻게 하는지 보여줄게.

남 고마워.

7. 남자의 마지막 말에 적절한 대답이 <u>아닌</u> 것은 무엇인가?

여자	

★a. 절대 안돼!　　　　　　b. 별 것도 아닌걸 뭐.

c. 내가 좋아서 하는 걸.　　d. 천만에.

8. 남자의 문제는 무엇인가?

a. 그가 좋아하는 웹사이트를 어떻게 즐겨찾기해 두는지 모른다.

★b. 그의 즐겨찾기 목록에서 그가 원하는 것을 빨리 찾지 못한다.

c. 어떤 사전을 사용해야 할지 모른다.

d. 자판으로 타자를 치는 것에 능숙하지 못하다.

[9-10] 다음 이야기를 듣고 질문에 답하시오.

스크립트

These are a few examples of how the Internet has changed our way of life. People can easily exchange files and mail from their computers. You can get your bank account information, the latest news, and the weather forecast from anywhere at anytime. Any hard-to-find merchandise can be ordered from any store in seconds. Almost any information you can think of is available over the Internet.

해석

다음은 인터넷이 어떻게 우리 삶의 방식을 바꿨는지에 대한 몇 가지 예다. 사람들은 컴퓨터로 쉽게 파일과 메일을 주고받을 수 있다. 은행 계좌 정보, 최신 뉴스, 그리고 일기 예보도 언제 어디서든지 접할 수 있다. 찾기 어려운 어떠한 상품도 몇 초 안에 어느 상점에서든 주문할 수 있다. 당신이 생각해낼 수 있는 거의 어떤 정보라도 인터넷에서는 입수할 수 있다.

9. 말하는 사람의 인터넷에 대한 태도는 어떠한가?

★a. 긍정적이다　　　　b. 무관심하다

c. 부정적이다　　　　d. 실망스럽다

10. 인터넷의 장점 중 하나가 <u>아닌</u> 것은 무엇인가?

a. 파일 교환이 쉽다.

b. 집에서 은행 계좌를 확인할 수 있다.

★c. 상품을 보지 않고 주문할 수 있다.

d. 정보 획득이 쉽다.

Dictation (Listening Task)　　　p. 106

LISTENING 1
have a problem, do an Internet search, too many results, how to narrow down, proper keywords, how the Internet started, typing in, that is related to, Now I get it

LISTENING 2
why it's taking so long, ordered, the day before yesterday, not here yet, from local stores, only 45 dollars, online store, trust online stores, go to well-known sites

LISTENING 3
Of all the things, the most important feature of all, a lot of time and money, problems like junk mail, virus, too much junk mail, computer system, be destroyed, be cautious

LISTENING 4
Internet addiction, feel very insecure, lose all sense of time, spend much time outdoors, check your email, Lastly, in front of the computer monitor, the more addicted

Dictation (Practice Test)　　　p. 107

PRACTICE TEST [1-2]
chatting with, Australia, an exchange student, for about six months, How often, more with her, many of my other friends, once a week or so

PRACTICE TEST [3-4]
did you hear about, is married, her kids' pictures, put up, personal information, using it wrongly, Exchanging, another big problem, things like

PRACTICE TEST [5-6]
it is happening again, log onto the Internet, have logged in already, Good for you, get to our school site, the server must be down, has been going down, need to try later

PRACTICE TEST [7-8]
the web address of, I forget it every time, bookmark the page, it's really hard to find, from the list, just to type it in, why you need to learn, organize, how to do it

PRACTICE TEST [9-10]
a few examples, our way of life, exchange files and mail, get your bank account, weather forecast, can be ordered, in seconds, available over the Internet

UNIT 14
Don't throw it away!

Getting Ready
p. 109

A

the environment, other products, recycling, turn off, pull out, Energy saving, mass transportation, gas consumption, reusing, garage sale

B

(1)-(c) (2)-(c) (3)-(a) (4)-(a) (5)-(b)
(6)-(c) (7)-(c)

A 아래 대화를 읽고 빈칸을 완성하시오.

> 대중교통, 끄다(잠그다), 재사용, 차고 세일, 재활용, 다른 제품들, 빼다, 에너지 절약, 환경, 연료 소비

교사 오늘은 환경에 관해 얘기해 보도록 하죠. 환경 보호를 위해 여러분이 할 수 있는 일이 있나요?

Julia 깡통이나, 종이, 병 같은 것들은 따로 분리할 수 있어요.

교사 좋아요. 그것들은 또 다른 제품들로 바뀌어 나오겠지요. 그런 걸 재활용이라고 합니다. 또 누구 없나요?

Tony 우리 엄마는 항상 "사용하지 않을 때는 불을 끄고, 물을 잠그고, 콘센트를 빼 놓아라"라고 말씀하세요.

교사 에너지 절약도 환경을 보호하는 좋은 방법이에요. 환경을 보호하는 또 다른 방법으로 대중교통을 이용할 수도 있지요. 대중교통을 이용하면 연료 소비가 줄고 대기오염도 줄어드니까요. 그밖에 다른 것은요?

John 재사용은 어떤가요, 선생님?

교사 예를 들면 어떤 거죠?

John 차고 세일 같은 것이요. 제 동생과 저는 어렸을 때 입던 옷과 장난감, 책 같은 것들을 팔았어요.

교사 훌륭해요. 다른 아이들한테는 아주 좋은 물건들이 될 수 있을 테니까요.

B 환경 보호를 위해 여러분은 어떤 일을 하고 있는가? 친구들과 이야기해 보시오.

[A]
(1) 사용하지 않을 때는 전기 제품의 플러그를 뺀다
(2) 에어컨을 사용하는 대신 선풍기를 켠다
(3) 음식물 쓰레기를 화단에 뿌린다
(4) 신문이나, 알루미늄 캔, 병 같은 것들을 재활용한다
(5) 헤어스프레이를 사용하지 않는다
(6) 운전하는 대신 걷거나 자전거를 타고 학교에 간다
(7) 양치질을 하는 동안 물을 잠가 둔다

[B]
(a) 쓰레기를 너무 많이 배출하지 않기 위해
(b) 환경오염을 줄이기 위해
(c) 에너지 절약을 위해

Listening Task
p. 110~111

Listening 1	1. b	2. A. T	B. F
Listening 2	1. d	2. d	3. b
Listening 3	1. c	2. a	
Listening 4	1. c	2. b	3. a

Listening 1
p. 110

다음 대화를 듣고 질문에 답하시오.

스크립트

Victor Look, Fiona. The smog is really bad.

Fiona That's ugly. I don't think I want to jog today.

Victor Good thinking. Staying outside on a day like this is not good for your health.

Fiona There should be fewer cars, and cars should be smaller in size. Smaller cars cause less smog.

Victor I believe that using mass transportation is an even better way to reduce smog.

Fiona I think you're right. It will also help solve some of the parking and traffic problems.

해석

Victor 봐, Fiona. 스모그가 정말 심각해.

Fiona 끔찍하군. 오늘은 조깅을 안 해야 할 것 같아.

Victor 생각 잘 했어. 오늘 같은 날 밖에 있는 건 건강에도 안 좋으니까.

Fiona 차가 좀 줄어야 해. 차 크기도 작아져야 하고 말이야. 작은 차는 스모그를 덜 배출하거든.

Victor 대중교통을 이용하는 편이 스모그를 줄이는 데 훨씬 더 좋은 방법 같아.

Fiona 네 말이 맞아. 그게 주차 문제나 교통 정체 같은 문제를 해결하는 데에도 도움이 될 거야.

1. 이 대화의 주요 화제는 무엇인가?
   a. 교통 정체   ★b. 대기오염
   c. 소음 공해   d. 에너지 부족

다시 듣고 True(참) 또는 False(거짓)에 표시하시오.

2. A. 스모그 때문에 Fiona는 오늘 조깅을 하지 않을 것이다.
   (T)
   B. 대중교통을 이용하면 스모그 같은 대기 오염이 증가한다.
   (F)

Listening 2
p.110

다음 대화를 듣고 질문에 답하시오.

스크립트

Daisy　I brought some aluminum cans and plastic bottles.

Man　You have four pounds of aluminum cans and two pounds of plastic bottles. I owe you five dollars.

Daisy　Thanks. By the way, what do you do with them?

Man　We sort and send them to other companies. they will turn these into new cans and bottles.

Daisy　Great.

Man　Recycling is protecting the environment. So tell your friends to bring me empty cans and bottles. They can make extra money at the same time, right?

해석

Daisy　알루미늄 캔이랑 플라스틱 병을 좀 가지고 왔어요.

남자　알루미늄 캔 4파운드와 플라스틱 병 2파운드를 가져왔구나. 5달러를 주마.

Daisy　감사합니다. 그런데, 그것들을 가지고 뭐하시는 거예요?

남자　이것들을 분류해서 다른 회사로 보내지. 거기서 새 캔이랑 병으로 탈바꿈 시킨단다.

Daisy　멋지네요.

남자　재활용은 곧 환경 보호야. 그러니까 친구들한테 빈 캔이나 병이 있으면 내게 가져오라고 해라. (환경 보호도 하고) 여분의 돈도 벌 수 있잖니, 그렇지?

1. 이 대화가 이루어지고 있는 장소는?
   a. 교실　　　　　　b. 시장
   c. 철물점　　　　★d. 재활용 센터

다시 듣고 질문에 답하시오.

2. 소녀가 가지고 온 깡통과 병의 총량은 얼마인가?
   a. 2파운드　　　　b. 4파운드
   c. 5파운드　　　★d. 6파운드

두 개의 요약을 듣고 올바른 것을 고르시오.

3.

스크립트

a. The man is explaining to the girl about the environmental problems we face today.

b. The man says recycling is one way to protect the environment.

해석

a.□ 남자는 소녀에게 오늘날 우리가 직면하고 있는 환경 문제에 관해 설명하고 있다.

b.★ 남자는 재활용이 환경을 보호하는 한 가지 방법이라고 말한다.

Listening 3
p.111

다음 이야기를 듣고 질문에 답하시오.

스크립트

Our school will be forming an environmen-tal club. The purpose of our club is to promote recycling and save the environment. We will collect recyclable materials and campaign for environmental protection. We will also create a homepage for the club and discuss environmental issues. the club will meet every Monday after school in the auditorium. Anyone who is interested in the issue is welcome.

해석

우리 학교에서는 환경 클럽을 만들 것입니다. 우리 클럽의 목적은 재활용을 활성화시키고 환경을 보호하는 것입니다. 우리는 재활용이 가능한 물건들을 모으고 환경 보호 캠페인도 벌일 것입니다. 우리는 또한 클럽의 홈페이지를 구축해서 환경 문제에 관한 토론도 할 것입니다. 클럽 회원들은 매주 월요일 방과 후에 강당에서 모임을 가집니다. 이에 대해 관심을 갖고 계신 분은 누구라도 환영합니다.

1. 이 단락의 주목적은 무엇인가?
   a. 스터디 그룹 회원을 모집하는 것
   b. 환경 기금을 모금하는 것
   ★c. 환경 클럽을 광고하는 것
   d. 물건 수집을 홍보하는 것

다시 듣고 질문에 답하시오.

2. 이들은 얼마나 자주 모이는가?
   ★a. 일주일에 한 번　　b. 한 달에 한 번
   c. 매일 방과 후에　　d. 알 수 없음

Listening 4

p.111

다음 이야기를 듣고 질문에 답하시오.

스크립트

There are many simple things you can do to help the environment. One thing you can do is conserve energy by turning off lights and unplugging electrical products when they're not in use. You can save water by taking shorter showers or turning the water off while brushing your teeth. You can try to reduce pollution by using mass transporta-tion such as buses or subways. Finally, recycle as much as you can. Newspaper, cans and bottles are good recyclable items.

해석

환경 보호를 위해 할 수 있는 간단한 일들이 많이 있습니다. 여러분이 할 수 있는 (방법 중) 한 가지는 사용하지 않을 때는 불을 _끄고_ 전기제품의 코드를 뽑아서 에 지를 절약하는 것이지요. 샤워를 간단히 하거나, 양치질을 하는 중에는 물을 잠가둠으로써 물을 절약할 수도 있습니다. 버스나 지하철 같은 대중교통을 이용해서 공해를 줄이도록 하고요. 마지막으로, 가능한 한 많이 재활용을 하도록 하세요. 신문, 캔, 병 같은 것들은 재활용하기 좋은 것들입니다.

1. 이 단락은 무엇에 관한 내용인가?
   a. 에너지의 중요성
   b. 쓰레기에 대한 우려
   ★c. 환경 보호를 위한 조언
   d. 세계적인 환경 문제들

다시 듣고 질문에 답하시오.

2. 환경 보호를 위한 방법으로 제시되지 <u>않은</u> 것은 무엇인가?
   a.   ★b.   c.   d.

두 개의 요약을 듣고 올바른 것을 고르시오.

3.

스크립트

a. You can help protect the environment by doing simple things, such as turning off lights or running water.
b. There are many people who are interested in protecting the environment, but who don't do anything about it.

해석

a. ★ 불을 _끄거나_ 흐르는 물을 잠그는 것 같은 간단한 일을 통해 환경을 보호할 수 있다.
b. □ 환경 보호에 관심은 많으나 환경 보호를 위해 어떤 일도 하지 않는 사람들이 많다.

Practice Test

p.112~113

1. d.	2. c	3. d	4. b	5. c	6. a
7. b	8. c	9. a	10. d		

[1–2] 다음 대화를 듣고 질문에 답하시오.

스크립트

Jack Stop! Are you throwing away that piece of paper?
Ken Yes. It has a little bit of writing on the front.
Jack You can use the back of the paper.
Ken Well, I don't like to use the back of paper.
Jack You are saving many trees and conserving energy by writing on the back of paper, and you are protecting the environment, too.
Ken One sheet of paper will not make a difference.
Jack Yes, it will. It all adds up.

해석

Jack 잠깐! 너 그 종이 버리는 거야?
Ken 응, 앞면에 뭐가 좀 써 있어서.
Jack 종이 뒷면을 쓰면 되잖아.
Ken 음, 종이 뒷면을 쓰는 건 별로 내키지 않는데.
Jack 종이 뒷면을 쓰면 얼마나 많은 나무와 에너지를 절약하게 되는데. 또, 환경도 보호하게 되는 거야.
Ken 겨우 종이 한 장이 무슨 큰 차이가 있겠어.
Jack 차이가 있지. 그게 쌓여봐.

1. 이 대화의 요지는 무엇인가?
   a. 우리는 종이를 제대로 버리는 방법을 배워야 한다.
   b. 어떤 에너지는 나무로부터 생성된다.
   c. 종이의 양면 모두를 사용하는 것은 법으로 정한 것이다.
   ★d. 종이를 적게 사용하는 것은 에너지를 절약하고 환경을 보호하는 한 가지 방법이다.

2. 이 상황에 알맞은 속담은 무엇인가?
   a. 경험이 최고의 선생이다.
   b. 뿌린 대로 거둔다.
   ★c. 티끌 모아 태산이다.
   d. 뜻이 있는 곳에 길이 있다.

스크립트

Doing something for the environment is more important than just knowing the importance of doing something. Everyone wants the streets to be clean, but the streets are littered with cigarette butts, food packages, and chewing gum. Even though people know that mass transportation creates less pollution, most people still insist on driving their own cars. Furthermore, who doesn't know the importance of recycling? Nonetheless, how many people actually recycle? So, if you really care about the environment, take action.

해석

(환경을 위해) 무언가를 해야 한다는 사실의 중요성을 그냥 알고만 있는 것보다, 환경을 위해 무언가를 실제로 하는 것이 더 중요하다. 누구나 깨끗한 거리를 원하지만 길에는 담배 꽁 나 음식물 포장, 껌 같은 것들이 버려져 있다. 대중교통이 공해를 덜 유발한다는 것을 알면서도 대부분의 사람들은 자기 차를 타고 다니길 고집한다. 게다가 재활용의 중요성을 모르는 사람이 어디 있을까? 그러나 실제 재활용을 하는 사람은 얼마나 되는가? 그러니, 당신이 정말 환경을 염려한다면 행동으로 옮겨야 한다.

3. 이 단락의 요지는 무엇인가?
   a. 환경 보호는 정부에서부터 시작되어야 한다.
   b. 환경 보호는 쉬운 일이다.
   c. 우리는 미래를 위해 환경을 오염시켜서는 안 된다.
   ★d. 우리는 환경 보호를 위한 행동에 나서야 한다.

4. 빈칸에는 다음 중 어떤 단어가 들어가야 하는가?

   > 말하는 사람은 환경에 대한 사람들의 태도에
   > _____.

   a. 만족해한다   ★b. 비판적이다
   c. 무관심하다   d. 긍정적이다

[5–6] 다음 대화를 듣고 질문에 답하시오.

스크립트

Teacher   One of these days, we will run out of oil. Then, we will no longer be able to use cars or gas burning heaters. Therefore, let's talk about some other ways to produce energy.

John   I think we should consider solar power. We can change the sun's energy into electricity and save it in a battery for later use.

Teacher   That is very good, John. We can also consider wind and sea waves as other sources of energy in the future.

해석
교사   조만간 석유가 고갈될 겁니다. 그러면 우리는 더 이상 자동차를 타거나 휘발유를 연료로 쓰는 히터를 사용할 수 없게 되겠지요. 그러니까 에너지를 생산할 수 있는 다른 방법들에 대해 얘기해 보도록 합시다.
John   제 생각엔 태양 에너지를 고려해 봐야 할 것 같아요. 태양 에너지를 전기로 변환해서 나중에 사용할 수 있도록 전지에 저장할 수 있을 거예요.
교사   아주 좋아요, John. 미래의 다른 에너지 자원으로 바람이나 파도 같은 것도 생각해 볼 수 있을 거예요.

5. 이 대화의 요지는 무엇인가?
   a. 우리는 전기를 절약해야 한다.
   b. 우리는 대기 오염을 줄여야 한다.
   ★c. 우리는 새로운 형태의 에너지를 생산할 필요가 있다.
   d. 석유는 환경 오염을 일으키므로 사용해서는 안 된다.

6. 미래의 에너지원으로 고려할 수 없는 것은 무엇인가?
   ★a. 석유   b. 태양 에너지   c. 바람   d. 파도

[7–8] 다음 대화를 듣고 질문에 답하시오.

스크립트

Andrea   Did you see the news about the wildfire?
Bryan   Yes. I heard that it was caused by a careless camper. The fire burned 30,000 acres of the forest.
Andrea   One big fire like this will destroy the ecosystem of an area for a long time. Imagine how long it will take for the trees to grow back and the animals to return. It will take many decades.
Bryan   I think one of the ways to conserve the environment is to protect it from disasters.

해석
Andrea   너 산불 뉴스 봤어?
Bryan   응. 캠핑하던 어떤 사람의 부주의 때문에 발생했다고 하더라. 그 불로 삼만 에이커의 숲이 타버렸대.
Andrea   이런 큰 불 하나가 오랫동안 한 지역의 생태계를 파괴하게 되지. 나무들이 다시 자라고 동물들이 다시 돌아오기까지 얼마나 많은 시간이 걸릴지 상상해 봐. 수십 년은 걸릴 거라고.
Bryan   환경 재난 피해를 막는 것도 환경 보존의 한 방법인 것 같아.

7. 이 상황을 가장 잘 묘사한 그림은 무엇인가?

   a.   ★b.   c.   d.

8. 환경 폐해를 회복하는 데 얼마의 기간이 걸리는가?

   a. 수 년   b. 3,000년

 ★c. 수십 년   d. 30,000년

[9–10] 다음 이야기를 듣고 질문에 답하시오.

스크립트

More than 70% of the earth is covered with water. But, more than 97% of the water on the earth is saltwater and another 2% is frozen ice. Of all the water on earth, less than 1% is usable freshwater. However, even this little amount is getting polluted rapidly. Therefore, we must learn to take care of it properly. Otherwise, we will have a big problem in the future.

해석

지구의 70% 이상은 물로 덮여 있다. 그러나 지구상의 물의 97% 이상은 해수이고, 다른 2%는 빙하이다. 지구상의 물 가운데 먹을 수 있는 담수의 양은 1%가 채 되지 않는다. 그러나 이 얼마 안 되는 마실 물까지 급속히 오염되어 가고 있다. 따라서 우리는 물을 제대로 보호하는 방법을 배워야 한다. 그렇지 않으면 앞으로 큰 문제에 봉착할 것이다.

9. 이 단락의 주제는 무엇인가?

 ★a. 물 보존의 중요성

  b. 홍수 통제의 중요성

  c. 물을 절약하는 방법

  d. 해양 오염의 심각성

10. 지구상의 물 중 몇 퍼센트가 우리가 마실 수 있는 담수인가?

  a. 70%   b. 97%   c. 2%   ★d. 1% 미만

Dictation (Listening Task)   p. 114

LISTENING 1

The smog is really bad, That's ugly, Staying outside, not good for your health, fewer cars, cause less smog, using mass transportation, the parking and traffic problems

LISTENING 2

I brought, and plastic bottles, owe you five dollars, what do you do with them, We sort and send them, turn these into, Recycling is protecting, to bring me, make extra money

LISTENING 3

forming an environmental club, promote recycling, save the environment, campaign for, create a homepage, discuss, issues, after school, interested in the issue

LISTENING 4

many simple things you can do, conserve energy, electrical products, they're not in use, by taking shorter showers, turning the water off, reduce pollution, recycle as much as you can, recyclable items

Dictation (Practice Test)   p. 115

PRACTICE TEST [1-2]

throwing away, a little bit of writing, the back of the paper, don't like to use, saving many trees and conserving energy, make a difference, It all adds up

PRACTICE TEST [3-4]

Doing something, knowing the importance of, the streets to be clean, food packages, chewing gum, creates less pollution, still insist on driving, who doesn't know, take action

PRACTICE TEST [5-6]

run out of oil, no longer be able to, some other ways to produce energy, consider solar power, change the sun's energy, save it in a battery, wind and sea waves

PRACTICE TEST [7-8]

the news about the wildfire, by a careless camper, fire burned 30,000 acres, destroy the ecosystem, trees to grow back, to return, take many decades, protect it from disasters

PRACTICE TEST [9-10]

More than 70%, is covered with water, the water on the earth, another 2%, less than 1%, is getting polluted rapidly, take care of, a big problem in the future

UNIT 15
I'm checking ads for used cars.

Listening Task   p. 118~119

Listening 1	1. a	2. A. F	B. T
Listening 2	1. b	2. d	3. b
Listening 3	1. d	2. c	
Listening 4	1. a	2. d	3. a

Getting Ready   p. 117

A

house-for-rent, next semester, can't afford, part-time, bulletin board, apply, contact number, check out, a clearance sale, big help

B

• The woman is looking at a flyer. It is advertising a flea market.
• The woman is looking at an advertising poster. It is advertising a new movie.
• The woman is looking at a newspaper advertisement. It is advertising a new shopping center.

A 아래 대화를 읽고 빈칸을 완성하시오.

> 지원하다, 확인하다, 재고 정리 세일, 아르바이트, 큰 도움, 임대주택, 게시판, (금전적으로) ~할 여유가 되지 않다, 다음 학기, 연락 번호

John 이봐, Meg. 뭘 읽고 있어?

Meg 실은, 신문에 난 임대주택 광고를 확인하고 있는 중이야.

John 괜찮은 곳을 찾았어?

Meg 응, 하지만 (집세를 낼) 여유가 되질 않아.

John 여름 동안 학교 식당에서 아르바이트를 하는 건 어때? 게시판에서 아르바이트 종업원을 구하는 광고를 봤는데.

Meg 아, 정말? 괜찮네! 어떻게 지원하면 돼?

John 여기 연락 번호가 있어. 직접 물어보지 그래? 아, 그리고 혹시 가구 필요한 게 있으면 이 전단지를 한번 봐. 우리 학교 근처의 가구점에서 재고 정리 세일을 하고 있대.

Meg 고마워, John. 큰 도움이 되었어.

B 여자는 무엇을 하고 있는가? 친구와 이야기해 보시오.

[A] TV 광고	전단지	광고 포스터	신문 광고
[B] 새 차	새 영화	벼룩시장	새 쇼핑센터

◁)) 그녀는 [A]TV 광고를(을) 보고 있다. 그것은 [B]새 차를(을) 광고하고 있다.

Listening 1   p. 118

다음 대화를 듣고 질문에 답하시오.

스크립트

Daisy Peter, I need to sell my old bicycle. Do you have any ideas on how to sell it?

Peter Why don't you post an ad on the school's bulletin board?

Daisy Why didn't I think of that? But what kind of information should I put on it?

Peter You should tell the make of the bike, how old it is, and the price.

Daisy OK. Anything else?

Peter Oh, Daisy, don't forget to put your contact number.

Daisy Right. Should I include a photo?

Peter That's a good idea.

해석

Daisy Peter, 내 오래된 자전거를 팔아야겠는데, 어떻게 팔면 될지 좋은 생각 있어?

Peter 학교 게시판에 광고를 붙이는 건 어때?

Daisy 왜 내가 그 생각을 못했지? 그런데 어떤 종류의 정보를 광고에 실어야 해?

Peter 자전거 제조회사명, (자전거가) 몇 년 된 건지, 그리고 가격을 언급해야지.

Daisy 그래. 다른 건?

Peter 아, Daisy, 연락 번호를 적는 것도 잊지 마.

Daisy 맞아. (자전거) 사진도 넣어야 할까?

Peter 그거 좋은 생각이야.

1. 두 사람은 무엇을 하고 있는가?

★a. 중고 자전거 판매 광고를 어떻게 만들지 상의하고 있다.
  b. 중고 자전거를 사려고 하고 있다.
  c. 자전거 가게에서 새 자전거를 사고 있다.
  d. 게시판에 있는 중고 자전거 광고를 읽고 있다.

다시 듣고 True(참) 또는 False(거짓)에 표시하시오.

2. A. Daisy는 Peter에게 새 자전거를 사 주려고 한다. (F)
  B. Daisy는 자전거 사진을 포함한 광고를 게시할 것이다. (T)

Listening 2

p. 118

다음 대화를 듣고 질문에 답하시오.

스크립트

Jessica	What are you reading, Calvin?
Calvin	Look at this flyer. The new bookstore is holding a grand opening sale.
Jessica	Is there anything special?
Calvin	All the magazines are 10% off, and books are 20% off. if you have a membership card, you can always get a 5% discount.
Jessica	That's great. Anything else?
Calvin	Oh, CDs are 30% off, too.
Jessica	When does the sale end?
Calvin	It ends this Sunday.
Jessica	Why don't we go to the sale this Saturday?
Calvin	That's a good idea.

해석

Jessica	뭘 읽고 있어, Calvin?
Calvin	이 전단지 좀 봐. 새로 생긴 서점이 대대적인 오픈 행사 세일을 한대.
Jessica	뭐 특별한 거라도 있어?
Calvin	잡지는 모두 10% 할인이고 책은 20% 할인이네. 그리고 회원 카드가 있으면 항상 5% 할인을 받을 수 있대.
Jessica	그거 좋은걸. 다른 내용은?
Calvin	아, CD도 30% 할인이야.
Jessica	세일이 언제 끝나는데?
Calvin	이번 주 일요일에 끝나.
Jessica	토요일에 세일하는 데 같이 가보지 않을래?
Calvin	좋아.

1. 그들은 세일에 대해 어디서 알게 되었는가?
   a.　　★b.　　c.　　d.

다시 듣고 질문에 답하시오.

2. 세일에 대한 사실인 것은 무엇인가?
   a. 책 - 10% 할인
   b. CD - 5% 할인
   c. 잡지 - 15% 할인
   ★d. 회원 카드 소지 - 항상 5% 할인

두 개의 요약을 듣고 올바른 것을 고르시오.

3.

스크립트

a. A bookstore is holding a clearance sale, and discounts will be given on used books.

b. A sale will be held at a new bookstore, and the speakers plan to go there this Saturday.

해석

a. ☐ 한 서점이 재고 정리 세일을 여는데, 중고책에 대해 할인을 할 것이다.

b. ★ 새 서점에서 세일이 있을 것이고, 두 사람은 이번 주 토요일에 서점에 갈 것이다.

Listening 3

p. 119

다음 이야기를 듣고 질문에 답하시오.

스크립트

The Chicago Hospital is offering summer internship positions to students who are interested in the medical field. The applicants must be over sixteen years old. Although no experience is needed, applicants must have achieved a school grade point average of B or better. Pay is six dollars to eight dollars an hour. Several different positions are available. Anyone who is interested must email an application form by June 7th.

해석

시카고 병원은 의료 분야에 관심이 있는 학생들에게 여름 인턴 자리를 제공합니다. 지원자는 16세 이상이어야 합니다. (의료 분야에) 경험이 있을 필요는 없지만, 지원자들은 B 혹은 그 이상의 학교 성적(GPA)을 받았어야 합니다. 급여는 시간 당 6달러에서 8달러입니다. 다른 많은 자리들도 열려 있습니다. 관심 있는 분은 6월 7일까지 지원서를 이메일로 보내주세요.

1. 광고는 무엇에 관한 것인가?
   a. 한 여름 캠프에서 참가자를 구하고 있다.
   b. 한 병원에서 경험 많은 의사를 구하고 있다.
   c. Chicago에 있는 한 대학에서 의과생들을 구하고 있다.
   ★d. 한 병원에서 여름 동안 인턴직 지원자를 구하고 있다.

다시 듣고 질문에 답하시오.

2. 지원자에게 요구되는 것은 무엇인가?
   a. 의료 분야에서의 경험
   b. 최소 18세 이상의 지원자 연령
   ★c. B 이상의 학점
   d. 추천서

Listening 4

p. 119

다음 이야기를 듣고 질문에 답하시오.

스크립트

Summer is just around the corner. Do you want to make this summer the most memorable summer of your life? If so, join our annual California Coast Bike Tour. This 500-mile bike trip will last 2 weeks. It will start in San Diego and end in San Francisco. During the trip, you will be biking about forty miles a day, and viewing the coastal cities along the beautiful coast line of California. For more information, call us.

해석

여름이 가까웠습니다. 이번 여름을 당신 인생에 가장 기억에 남을 여름으로 만들길 원하십니까? 그렇다면, 일 년에 한 번 있는 우리의 캘리포니아 해변 자전거 여행에 참가하세요. 총 500마일을 달리게 될 이 자전거 여행은 2주간 계속됩니다. 여정은 샌디에이고에서 출발하여 샌프란시스코에서 끝납니다. 이 여행 동안, 당신은 하루에 40마일 정도를 달리면서 캘리포니아의 아름다운 해안선을 따라 있는 해안 도시들을 보게 될 것입니다. 더 많은 정보를 원하시면 저희에게 전화하세요.

1. 그들은 얼마나 자주 이 자전거 여행을 제공하는가?
   ★a. 일 년에 한 번   b. 일 년에 두 번
   c. 두 달마다 한 번씩   d. 한 달에 한 번

다시 듣고 질문에 답하시오.

2. 여행에 대해 사실이 <u>아닌</u> 것은 무엇인가?
   a. 자전거 여행이다.
   b. 전체 여행은 500 마일 정도를 주행할 것이다.
   c. 여행은 샌디에이고에서 출발할 것이다.
   ★d. 여행은 하루에 50마일을 주행할 것이다.

두 개의 요약을 듣고 올바른 것을 고르시오.

3.

스크립트

a. The bike tour is held every year. The tour covers 500 miles from San Diego to San Francisco.
b. A strong bike can last for more than 500 miles, which is the distance from San Diego to San Francisco.

해석

a. ★ 자전거 여행은 해마다 열린다. 여행은 샌디에이고에서 샌프란시스코까지 500마일을 주행한다.
b. □ 튼튼한 자전거는 500마일 이상을 지속할 수(=계속 달릴 수) 있는데, 이 거리는 샌디에이고에서 샌프란시스코까지의 거리이다.

---

1. c	2. a	3. d	4. b	5. c	6. a
7. d	8. b	9. a	10. b		

[1~2] 다음 대화를 듣고 질문에 답하시오.

스크립트

Edward   Dorothy, you have a lot of exercise machines. I didn't know you were into exercising.

Dorothy   Actually, Edward, I haven't touched any of the machines for a long time.

Edward   Then, why did you buy them?

Dorothy   Because whenever I see a new exercise machine on TV commercials, I feel that the new machine will help me to exercise more than I do now. But, once I do get it, I don't use it.

Edward   You should think twice before you buy things.

Dorothy   I think you're right.

해석

Edward   Dorothy, 너 운동기구를 참 많이 갖고 있구나. 네가 운동에 빠져 있는 줄은 몰랐는데.

Dorothy   실은, Edward, 나 오랫동안 이 운동기구들 중 어느 하나도 손댄 적이 없어.

Edward   그럼 왜 그것들을 샀어?

Dorothy   TV 광고에서 새 운동기구를 볼 때마다, 새 기구가 있으면 운동을 지금보다 더 많이 할 것 같았어. 하지만 일단 그걸 사고 나면 쓰지 않게 되더라구.

Edward   넌 물건을 사기 전에 한번 더 생각해야 해.

Dorothy   네 말이 맞는 것 같아.

1. Dorothy는 왜 운동기구를 샀는가?
   a. 운동기구를 수집해서
   b. 운동기구가 할인 중이어서
   ★c. 새로운 운동기구가 운동을 열심히 하도록 해줄 것이라 생각해서
   d. 운동을 많이 해서

2. Edward는 Dorothy에게 물건을 살 때 어떻게 하라고 충고하였는가?
   ★a. Dorothy는 물건을 사기 전에 신중히 고려해야 한다.
   b. Dorothy는 Edward에게 먼저 물어보아야 한다.
   c. Dorothy는 운동기구들을 인터넷에서 주문해야 한다.
   d. Dorothy는 TV에서 물건을 주문하는 것을 그만두어야 한다.

스크립트

Leslie	Rachel, did you find a room yet?
Rachel	I found this room in the newspaper, and on the Internet, I found two places near the school. How about you?
Leslie	I found a rental agency which has hundreds of apartments-for-rent ads.
Rachel	Did you check any of their ads?
Leslie	No, there was a fee to use their service. Let's check what we have first, and if we don't like them, then we can use the agency.
Rachel	Good.

해석

Leslie	Rachel, 방 구했어?
Rachel	신문에서 이 방을 찾았고 인터넷에서도 학교 근처에 있는 방 두 개를 찾았어. 너는?
Leslie	난 수백 개의 임대 아파트 광고를 갖고 있는 임대 중개소를 발견했어.
Rachel	거기 있는 광고 중 뭐라도 봤어?
Leslie	아니, 그 서비스를 이용하는 데에 수수료가 들더라고. 우리가 갖고 있는 광고부터 먼저 확인해 보자. 그것들이 마음에 들지 않으면 그때 중개소에 가 보자고.
Rachel	좋아.

3. 그들은 먼저 무엇을 할 것인가?
   a. 더 많은 광고를 보기 위해 다른 신문을 살 것이다.
   b. 임대 중개소를 이용할 것이다.
   c. 임대 중개소에 광고를 낼 것이다.
   ★d. 신문과 인터넷에서 찾은 광고를 확인할 것이다.

4. 대화에서 언급되지 않은 광고 수단은 무엇인가?
   a. 신문   ★b. 전단지
   c. 인터넷   d. 임대 중개소

[5–6] 다음 이야기를 듣고 질문에 답하시오.

스크립트

Advertisements provide useful information about products, but they also can create false images of products. A good example may be advertisements with famous stars in them. When people buy a product because they liked the celebrities in the advertisements, they are just buying the image of the celebrity, not the product itself. Also, the cost of the advertisements increases the final cost of any product.

해석

광고는 상품에 대한 유용한 정보를 제공해 주지만, 또한 상품에 대한 잘못된 이미지를 만들 수도 있다. 그 좋은 예로는 유명한 스타가 나오는 광고를 들 수 있다. 사람들이 광고 속의 유명인이 좋아서 어떤 상품을 산다면, 그들은 단지 그 유명인의 이미지를 사는 것이지 제품 자체를 사는 것은 아니다. 또한 그런 광고에 드는 비용은 제품의 최종 가격을 상승시킬 뿐이다.

5. 이 단락의 주요 화제는 무엇인가?
   a. 광고하기에 가장 효과적인 방법
   b. 광고에 유명인을 사용하는 것에 대한 다른 의견들
   ★c. 광고의 이점과 단점들
   d. 여러 가지 종류의 광고들

6. 이 단락에 따르면, 유명인에 의한 광고는 _____.
   ★a. 상품의 가격을 더욱 비싸게 만들 것이다.
   b. 사람들이 올바른 상품을 사도록 도울 것이다.
   c. 사람들이 유명인들을 좋아하기 때문에 히트 상품이 될 것이다.
   d. 제품에 관한 정보를 전혀 지니고 있지 않을 것이다.

[7–8] 다음 대화를 듣고 질문에 답하시오.

스크립트

Henry	Sunny, did you see the anti-smoking commercials on TV?
Sunny	Yes, I saw them. Smoking is really a big social problem.
Henry	That is why people are campaigning on TV and through other means, such as on cigarette boxes.
Sunny	Does it work?
Henry	Yes. According to some research, anti-smoking advertisements are very effective in preventing non-smokers from starting to smoke.
Sunny	Then, there should be more advertisements about not smoking.
Henry	Indeed.

해석

Henry	Sunny, TV에서 흡연 반대 광고 봤어?
Sunny	응, 봤어. 흡연은 정말 큰 사회 문제야.
Henry	그게 바로 사람들이 TV나 담뱃갑 같은 다른 수단으로 홍보를 하는 이유지.
Sunny	그게 효과는 있나?
Henry	응. 연구 조사에 의하면, 흡연 반대 광고는 비흡연자들이 흡연을 시작하는 것을 막는 데 아주 효과적이래.
Sunny	그럼 금연 광고를 더 많이 해야겠네.
Henry	정말 그래.

7. 남자는 왜 "정말 그래"라고 했는가?
    a. Sunny와는 다른 의견을 가지고 있어서
    b. Sunny가 한 말을 이해하지 못해서
    c. 그의 의견을 말하고 싶지 않아서
    ★d. Sunny가 한 말에 동의해서

8. 두 사람은 무엇에 관해 이야기하고 있는가?
    a. 왜 흡연이 해로운지
    ★b. 흡연 반대 홍보의 효과
    c. 비흡연자가 어떻게 흡연을 시작하는지
    d. 공공장소에서의 흡연 구역

[9–10] 다음 이야기를 듣고 질문에 답하시오.

스크립트

Even though TV and newspaper ads are the most effective way to advertise, they are very costly. That is why many people believe advertisement through word-of-mouth is the best way to advertise. This cost-free advertisement relies on what people say to others about their products or services. Therefore, for a successful word-of-mouth advertisement, it is important to give good quality products and services to customers. Otherwise, people will advertise how bad the product or the service is.

해석

TV와 신문 광고는 가장 효과적이긴 하지만 매우 비용이 많이 든다. 그것이 바로 많은 사람들이 입소문을 통한 광고가 가장 좋은 광고 방법이라고 믿는 이유이다. 비용이 전혀 들지 않는 이 방법은, 사람들이 다른 사람들에게 그들의 제품이나 서비스에 대해 어떻게 말하느냐에 의존한다. 따라서, 성공적인 입소문 광고를 위해서는 고객들에게 좋은 제품의 품질과 서비스를 제공하는 것이 중요하다. 그렇지 않으면, 사람들은 그 제품이나 서비스가 얼마나 나쁜지에 대해 광고하고 다닐 것이다.

9. 이 단락에 따르면, 가장 좋은 광고 방법은 무엇인가?
    ★a. TV 광고   b. 신문 광고
    c. 입소문   d. 광고판

10. 좋은 입소문 광고를 위해 필요하지 <u>않은</u> 것은 무엇인가?
    a. 좋은 품질의 제품   ★b. 돈
    c. 만족한 고객   d. 좋은 서비스

Dictation (Listening Task)   p. 122

LISTENING 1
I need to sell, on how to sell it, post an ad, bulletin board, should I put on it, the make of the bike, how old it is, put your contact number, include a photo

LISTENING 2
What are you reading, a grand opening sale, anything special, books are 20% off, membership card, get a 5% discount, When does the sale end, Why don't we

LISTENING 3
summer internship positions, medical field, over sixteen years old, no experience is needed, a school grade point average, available, application form, June 7th

LISTENING 4
just around the corner, the most memorable summer, join our annual, 500-mile bike trip, It will start in, end in, forty miles a day, the beautiful coast line, For more information

Dictation (Practice Test)   p. 123

PRACTICE TEST [1-2]
you were into exercising, haven't touched, did you buy them, on TV commercials, help me to exercise more, once I do get it, think twice

PRACTICE TEST [3-4]
did you find a room, near the school, How about you, apartments-for-rent ads, to use their service, what we have, the agency

PRACTICE TEST [5-6]
useful information about, create false images, with famous stars in them, they liked the celebrities, the product itself, the final cost of any product

PRACTICE TEST [7-8]
anti-smoking commercials, big social problem, That is why, on TV and through other means, Does it work, some research, preventing non-smokers, there should be, Indeed

PRACTICE TEST [9-10]
the most effective, costly, advertisement through word-of-mouth, what people say to others, services, word-of-mouth, good quality products, customers, how bad

UNIT 16
I've bought an MP3 player!

Getting Ready   p. 125

A

medical field, Equipment, has been invented, interested in, impossible, for example, without, MP3 players, replacing, will change

B

- I got a new LCD monitor as a gift. I like it because it doesn't take much space on my desk.
- I got a new digital camera as a gift. I like it because I can check the photos I took right away.
- I got a new laser printer as a gift. I like it because it takes less time printing out.

A 아래 대화를 읽고 빈칸을 완성하시오.

대체하는, 의료 분야, MP3 플레이어, 변화시킬 것이다, ~ 없이, 예를 들면, 불가능한, 발명되었다, ~에 관심이 있는, 장비

Julia 뭐하고 있어, Matthew?

Matthew 의학 분야의 새로운 기술에 관한 기사를 읽고 있어. 어려운 수술 동안 의사들을 도와줄 장비가 발명되었대.

Julia 네가 과학 잡지를 읽고 있는 걸 항상 보는데, 너 과학에 관심이 있나 보구나.

Matthew 응, 난 새 기술에 관련된 건 무엇이든 좋아해. 기술은 과거에는 불가능해 보였던 것들을 가능하게 만들어 주고 있어. 예를 들어 전자레인지를 봐. 불을 사용하지 않고 요리를 할 수 있다는 게 놀랍지 않아?

Julia 디지털 카메라와 MP3 플레이어는 어떻고? 필름이나 CD 같은 게 전혀 필요하지 않잖아! 그것들은 아날로그 카메라와 CD 플레이어를 빨리 대체해 가고 있어.

Matthew 새 기술이 나오는 속도로 봤을 때, 30년 후의 우리의 삶이 어떻게 변할지는 상상도 못하겠어.

B 당신이 가지고 있는 것은 무엇인가? 친구와 이야기해 보시오.

[A] LCD 모니터   MP3 플레이어
    레이저 프린터   디지털 카메라

[B] 출력하는 데 시간이 덜 걸린다.
    찍은 사진을 바로 확인할 수 있다.
    책상에 많은 공간을 차지하지 않는다.
    CD를 가지고 다닐 필요가 없다.

나는 선물로 [A]MP3 플레이어를 받았다.
[B]CD를 가지고 다닐 필요가 없기 때문에 그것이 마음에 든다.

Listening Task   p. 126~127

Listening 1	1. c	2. A. T	B. F
Listening 2	1. d	2. a	3. a
Listening 3	1. c	2. b	
Listening 4	1. b	2. a	3. a

Listening 1   p. 126

다음 대화를 듣고 질문에 답하시오.

스크립트

Teacher Today let's talk about things that were not commonly used twenty years ago.

Student Back then, I don't think we had MP3 players and cellular phones.

Teacher That is right. What else?

Student How about LCD monitors and microwave ovens?

Teacher Well, we did not have LCD monitors twenty years ago, but microwave ovens have been around for more than half a century.

Student Really? I didn't know that.

해석

교사 오늘은 20년 전에는 흔히 사용되지 않았던 물건들에 대해 이야기해 봅시다.

학생 그때는 MP3 플레이어나 휴대전화기는 없었던 것 같아요.

교사 맞아요. 그 밖에는요?

학생 LCD 모니터와 전자레인지는요?

교사 음, 20년 전에 LCD 모니터는 없었지만, 전자레인지는 반세기(=50년) 동안이나 있어 왔어요.

학생 정말요? 그건 몰랐네요.

1. 어떤 제품이 20년 전에 사용되었는가?
   a.   b.   ★c.   d.

다시 듣고 True(참) 또는 False(거짓)에 표시하시오.

2. A. 전자레인지는 30년 이상 사용되어져 왔다. (F)
   B. 그들은 20년 후에 이용 가능하게 될 물건들에 관해 이야기하고 있다. (F)

77

Listening 2

p. 126

다음 대화를 듣고 질문에 답하시오.

스크립트

Bob　Wendy, take a look at my new digital camera.

Wendy　It seems like everyone has one these days. What is the big deal about digital cameras, Bob?

Bob　Well, they provide functions that analog cameras don't. They don't need film, and you can see the picture right away.

Wendy　Oh yeah, I always have to wait until the film is developed and printed.

Bob　Furthermore, you can upload pictures to your computer and edit them or send them to others by email easily.

Wendy　No wonder everybody wants one.

해석

Bob　Wendy, 내 새 디지털 카메라 좀 봐.

Wendy　요즘 모두가 다 하나씩은 갖고 있는 것 같더라. 디지털 카메라는 뭐가 그렇게 대단해, Bob?

Bob　음, 디지털 카메라는 아날로그 카메라가 할 수 없는 기능을 제공해 줘. 필름도 필요 없고, (찍은) 사진을 바로 볼 수도 있어.

Wendy　아 그래, 난 항상 필름이 현상되고 인화될 때까지 기다려야 해.

Bob　게다가, 컴퓨터에 사진을 올려서 그 사진을 편집하거나 다른 이들에게 메일로 쉽게 보낼 수도 있어.

Wendy　모두가 디지털 카메라를 갖고 싶어하는 것도 당연하네.

1. Wendy의 마지막 대답은 무슨 의미인가?

　a. 그녀는 여전히 디지털 카메라가 왜 좋은지 이해할 수 없다.

　b. 그녀는 아날로그 카메라를 더 선호한다.

　c. 그녀는 Bob이 무슨 이야기를 하는지 이해하지 못한다.

★d. 그녀는 왜 사람들이 디지털 카메라를 좋아하는지 이해한다.

다시 듣고 질문에 답하시오.

2. 이 대화에 관해 사실인 것은 무엇인가?

★a. Bob은 디지털 카메라를 가지고 있다.

　b. Bob은 디지털 카메라를 살 것이다.

　c. Wendy는 Bob에게 디지털 카메라를 추천하고 있다.

　d. Wendy는 Bob에게 그녀의 디지털 카메라를 보여주고 있다.

두 개의 요약을 듣고 올바른 것을 고르시오.

3.

스크립트

a. Bob and Wendy are talking about the advantages of digital cameras over analog cameras.

b. Bob and Wendy are shopping for a digital camera, and they are discussing which digital camera is good for them.

해석

a.★ Bob과 Wendy는 아날로그 카메라와 비교해서 디지털 카메라가 가지는 장점에 대해 이야기하고 있다.

b.☐ Bob과 Wendy는 디지털 카메라를 사기 위해 쇼핑을 하고 있고 어떤 디지털 카메라가 그들에게 더 좋은지 논의하고 있다.

Listening 3

p. 127

다음 이야기를 듣고 질문에 답하시오.

스크립트

In 1887, Edison invented a way to store sound on a cylinder. Since then, better ways of storing sound have been invented, such as LPs, cassette tapes, CDs, and MP3 files. The CD, which stands for compact disc, is an important milestone in sound storing methods because it was the first popular way to store sound digitally. Now, with MP3 players, thousands of songs can be stored and played with a device that is smaller than a cigarette box.

해석

1887년, Edison은 처음으로 실린더에 소리를 저장하는 방법을 발명했다. 그때 이후로, LP(레코드판), 카세트 테이프, CD, 그리고 MP3 파일 같이 소리를 저장하는 더 나은 방법들이 발명되었다. 소형 디스크(compact disc)를 의미하는 CD는 소리 저장 방법에 있어 획기적인 사건인데, 소리를 디지털로 저장하는 최초의 대중적인 방법이었기 때문이다. 지금은 MP3 플레이어로 수천 곡의 노래가 담뱃갑보다도 작은 장치(즉, MP3 플레이어)에 저장되고 연주될 수 있다.

1. 이 단락의 주요 화제는 무엇인가?

　a. Edison이 발명한 것들

　b. MP3 플레이어의 이점들

★c. 소리 저장 기술의 발전

　d. CD와 MP3 플레이어의 비교

다시 듣고 질문에 답하시오.

2. Edison은 소리를 저장하기 위해 처음 무엇을 사용하였는가?

　a. LP　　　　★b. 실린더

　c. 카세트 테이프　　d. CD

다음 이야기를 듣고 질문에 답하시오.

스크립트

Because machines have rapidly been replacing people in the work place, some people worry that there will be fewer jobs for people in the future. However, others believe that technology will provide us with more and even safer jobs. Although nobody knows how the future will affect us, people's standard of living has gone up as a result of advancing technology. Therefore, it seems unnecessary to worry too much about the effects of the changes in technology.

해석

기계가 급속히 업무 현장에서 사람을 대체해 왔기 때문에 몇몇 사람들은 미래에는 사람을 위한 일자리가 적어질 것이라 걱정한다. 하지만 또 다른 사람들은 기술이 우리에게 더 많고 훨씬 안전한 일자리를 제공해 줄 것이라 믿는다. 비록 미래가 우리에게 어떠한 영향을 미칠지는 아무도 모르지만, 진보하는 기술의 결과로 사람들의 생활수준은 향상되어 왔다. 따라서 기술 변화의 결과에 대해 지나치게 걱정할 필요는 없을 것 같다.

1. 말하는 사람은 무엇에 관해 이야기하고 있는가?
   a. 미래에 등장할 기계들
   ★b. 기술 진보가 사람의 일자리에 어떻게 영향을 미치는가
   c. 기술로 인한 일자리 증가
   d. 사람의 일을 돕는 기계들

다시 듣고 질문에 답하시오.

2. 기술 진보에 대한 말하는 사람의 태도는 어떠한가?
   ★a. 긍정적이다   b. 부정적이다
   c. 무관심하다   d. 염려스럽다

두 개의 요약을 듣고 올바른 것을 고르시오.

3.

스크립트

a. Even though there is a lot of concern about how technology will affect people at work, improvements in technology have only helped improve human life.

b. Even though we have been trying hard to develop new technologies to improve human life, the results have been very disappointing.

해석

a. ★ 기술이 사람들의 일자리에 어떤 영향을 미칠지에 대한 많은 염려가 있음에도 불구하고, 기술 진보는 인간의 삶을 향상시키는 데 도움을 주었다.

b. □ 우리는 인간의 삶을 향상시키기 위해 새로운 기술을 개발하려고 노력해 왔지만, 그 결과는 매우 실망스러웠다.

Practice Test   p. 128~129

1. c	2. a	3. d	4. b	5. d	6. b
7. c	8. a	9. d	10. d		

[1–2] 다음 대화를 듣고 질문에 답하시오.

스크립트

Jake: The traffic is very bad. Wouldn't it be nice if we had cars that could fly? Then, we wouldn't have to complain about traffic.

Celina: That would be nice, but I wish I had a machine that could translate any language. Then, I wouldn't have to worry about my French homework.

Jake: Do you know what would be really nice – a robot that could cook any kind of food.

Celina: That is another great idea. Do you really think we will ever have all these things?

Jake: Someday, I hope.

해석

Jake: 교통이 너무 안 좋네(차가 너무 막히네). 날 수 있는 자동차가 있다면 좋지 않을까? 그러면 교통 정체로 불평할 일도 없을텐데 말야.

Celina: 그것도 좋겠지만 난 무슨 언어든 통역할 수 있는 기계가 있으면 좋겠어. 그러면 내 불어 숙제를 걱정할 필요가 없잖아.

Jake: 뭐가 정말 좋을지 알아? 어떤 종류의 음식이라도 요리해 주는 로봇이라구.

Celina: 그것도 좋은 생각이네. 하지만 우리가 정말 언젠가는 그것들을 갖게 될까?

Jake: 언젠가는 그렇게 되겠지.

1. 대화는 무엇에 대한 것인가?
   a. 그들이 곧 살 것들
   b. 그들이 뉴스 기사에서 읽은 것들
   ★c. 그들이 갖기를 바라는 것들
   d. 위의 사항 모두 해당 없음

2. 두 사람은 어디에 있는가?
   ★a. 차 안   b. 교실   c. 식당   d. 은행

[3-4] 다음 대화를 듣고 질문에 답하시오.

스크립트

Bessie What are you reading, Frank?

Frank Hey, Bessie. I am reading an article about the history of airplanes. According to the article, people flew in hot air balloons and gliders more than a hundred years before the first airplane was invented.

Bessie When was the first airplane invented?

Frank In 1903, but it could only fly for a very short distance. Yet, by 1947, people could fly faster than the speed of sound, and today's space shuttles can fly twenty times faster than the speed of sound.

Bessie That is amazing!

해석

Bessie 뭘 읽고 있는 거야, Frank?

Frank 안녕, Bessie. 비행기의 역사에 관한 기사를 읽고 있어. 기사에 따르면, 사람들은 최초의 비행기가 발명되기 백 년도 더 전에 열기구와 글라이더로 하늘을 날았대.

Bessie 최초의 비행기는 언제 발명된 거야?

Frank 1903년에. 그런데 아주 짧은 거리 밖에 날지 못했대. 하지만 1947년에 와서는 사람들은 음속(=소리의 속도)보다도 빨리 날 수 있게 되었고, 오늘날의 우주비행선은 음속보다 20배나 더 빠르게 날 수 있대.

Bessie 정말 놀랍다!

3. Frank는 어디에서 비행기의 역사를 알게 되었는가?
   a. 비행기에 관한 책에서
   b. 지난밤에 보았던 TV 프로그램에서
   c. 역사 수업 시간에
   ★d. 그가 읽은 기사에서

4. 이 대화에서 언급되지 않은 것은 무엇인가?
   a.   ★b.   c.   d.

[5-6] 다음 대화를 듣고 질문에 답하시오.

스크립트

W Did you see the movie *Troy*?

M Yes, I did. It was a great movie.

W But, did you know that most of the extras in the movie were computer graphics?

M They can't be! They looked so real.

W And most of the boats and the battle scenes were computer-generated, too.

M Wow, that is amazing. That means, one of these days, entire movies can be made without any humans in it.

W I am sure those days are not too far away.

해석

여 영화 Troy 봤니?

남 응, 봤어. 정말 굉장한 영화더라.

여 그런데, 그 영화 속 대부분의 엑스트라가 컴퓨터 그래픽이란 걸 알고 있었어?

남 그럴 리가! 정말 진짜처럼 보였는 걸.

여 대부분의 배와 전쟁 장면도 컴퓨터로 만들어진 거래.

남 와아, 정말 놀라운걸. 그럼 가까운 시일 내에 사람이 출연하지 않아도 영화 전체를 만들 수 있단 얘기잖아.

여 그런 날이 아주 멀지 않은 것은 분명해.

5. 영화 속의 많은 컴퓨터 그래픽에 대한 남자의 태도는 어떠한가?
   a. 만족스럽지 않다   b. 화가 난다
   c. 실망스럽다   ★d. 놀랍다

6. 영화의 어느 부분이 컴퓨터 그래픽이 아니었는가?
   a. 전쟁 장면   ★b. 성   c. 배우   d. 배

[7-8] 다음 대화를 듣고 질문에 답하시오.

스크립트

Teacher Class, do you know who first theorized the laser?

Student No idea, sir.

Teacher It was Albert Einstein in 1917, but the first laser was made possible in the 60s.

Student What happened?

Teacher Well, technology that is worth having takes time to be developed into something useful. Now, you see the laser being used everywhere. Can you name a few products that use the laser?

Student I heard that CD players, laser printers, and some hospital equipment use laser technology.

해석

교사 여러분, 누가 최초로 레이저를 이론화했는지 아나요?

학생 전혀 모르겠어요, 선생님.

교사 1917년에 Albert Einstein이었어요. 하지만 최초의 레이저는 60년대에나 만들어질 수 있었지요.

학생 어째서요?

교사 가질 만한 가치가 있는 기술이 (실제 사용할 수 있는) 유용한 것으로 발전되는 데는 시간이 걸려요. 이제는 레이저가 어디서든 사용되는 걸 볼 수 있지요. 레이저를 사용하는 제품을 몇 가지 댈 수 있겠어요?

학생 CD 플레이어, 레이저 프린터, 그리고 몇몇 병원 장비들이 레이저 기술을 사용한대요.

7. 두 사람은 어떤 관계인가?
   a. 판매원과 손님　　b. 아버지와 딸
   ★c. 교사와 학생　　　d. 기술자와 그의 동료

8. 이 대화에 대해 사실이 <u>아닌</u> 것은 무엇인가?
   ★a. 50년대까지 레이저는 많은 곳에서 사용되었다.
   b. Albert Einstein은 최초로 레이저를 이론화했다.
   c. 몇몇 병원 장비들은 레이저 기술을 사용한다.
   d. 레이저는 오늘날 많은 분야에서 사용된다.

[9~10] 다음 이야기를 듣고 질문에 답하시오.

스크립트

Of all the different fields, the medical field has been affected the most by advancing technology and science. Newly invented medical equipment has made difficult surgeries less difficult, while new drugs cure more diseases. In the near future, small robots will go into our bodies and fix medical problems just like they do in science fiction movies. People will also replace their body parts with mechanical parts, so that they can live a longer and healthier life.

해석

다른 모든 분야들 중, 의학 분야는 기술과 과학 진보에 가장 많은 영향을 받아 왔다. 새롭게 발명된 의료 기구들은 어려운 수술을 덜 어렵게 해주었고, 새 약품은 더 많은 질병을 치료한다. 가까운 미래에는 작은 로봇이 공상 과학 영화에서 하듯이 우리 몸속으로 들어가서 의학적 문제들을 치료할 것이다. 사람들은 또한 신체 일부분을 기계 부품으로 대체하여 더 길고 더 건강한 삶을 살 수 있게 될 것이다.

9. 말하는 사람은 무엇에 대해 이야기 하고 있는가?
   a. 공상 과학 영화 속의 로봇
   b. 어려운 수술이 필요한 환자들
   c. 병원에서 사용되는 기계들
   ★d. 의학 분야에서의 새로운 기술

10. 이 단락에 의하면, 미래에 가능한 것이 <u>아닌</u> 것은 무엇인가?
   a. 환자들은 기계로 된 신체 일부분을 가질 수 있게 될 것이다.
   b. 로봇이 수술에 사용될 것이다.
   c. 더 많은 질병이 새 약품에 의해 치료될 것이다.
   ★d. 사람들은 전혀 약품을 사용하지 않아도 될 것이다.

Dictation (Listening Task)　　　p. 130

LISTENING 1

that were not commonly, twenty years ago, MP3 players, cellular phones, What else, microwave ovens, have been around, half a century

LISTENING 2

new digital camera, It seems like everyone has one, provide functions, see the picture right away, developed and printed, upload pictures, edit them or send them, No wonder, wants

LISTENING 3

In 1887, a way to store sound, better ways of storing sound, such as, compact disc, it was the first popular way, digitally, thousands of songs, that is smaller than

LISTENING 4

machines, people in the work place, fewer jobs, with more and even safer jobs, affect us, standard of living, advancing technology, the effects of the changes in technology

Dictation (Practice Test)　　　p. 131

PRACTICE TEST [1-2]

Wouldn't it be nice, complain about traffic, I wish I had, translate any language, robot, any kind of food, we will ever have

PRACTICE TEST [3-4]

reading an article about, flew in hot air balloons, first airplane, invented, 1903, short distance, the speed of sound, twenty times faster, amazing

PRACTICE TEST [5-6]

most of the extras, computer graphics, They can't be, battle scenes, computer-generated, entire movies, any humans in it, far away

PRACTICE TEST [7-8]

No idea, made possible in the 60s, to be developed into, the laser being used, name a few products, laser printers, hospital equipment

PRACTICE TEST [9-10]

medical field, advancing technology and science, difficult surgeries, cure more diseases, go into our bodies, they do in science fiction movies, replace their body parts, a longer and healthier life

Memo

Memo